Marketing Shares, Sharing Markets

Also by Jesper Blomberg

FINANSMARKNADENS AKTÖRER: Ett Organizational Finance Perspektiv

PROJEKTORGANISATIONEN: Kritiska Analyser Av Projektprat Och Praktik

MYTER OM PROJEKT

ORDNING OCH KAOS I PROJEKTSAMARBETE: En Socialfenomenologisk Upplösning Av En Organisationsteoretisk Pradox

Also by Hans Kjellberg

RECONNECTING MARKETING TO MARKETS (*edited with L. Araujo & J. Finch*)

ORGANISING DISTRIBUTION

Also by Karin Winroth

NÄR MANAGEMENT KOM TILL ADVOKATBYRÅN: Om Professioner, Identitet Och Organisering

Marketing Shares, Sharing Markets

Experts in Investment Banking

Jesper Blomberg and Hans Kjellberg
Stockholm School of Economics, Stockholm, Sweden

Karin Winroth
School of Business Studies, Södertörn University, Stockholm, Sweden

palgrave
macmillan

First published 2012 by
PALGRAVE MACMILLAN

Palgrave Macmillan in the UK is an imprint of Macmillan Publishers Limited, registered in England, company number 785998, of Houndmills, Basingstoke, Hampshire RG21 6XS.

Palgrave Macmillan in the US is a division of St Martin's Press LLC, 175 Fifth Avenue, New York, NY 10010.

Palgrave Macmillan is the global academic imprint of the above companies and has companies and representatives throughout the world.

Palgrave® and Macmillan® are registered trademarks in the United States, the United Kingdom, Europe and other countries.

ISBN 978–0–230–28067–0

This book is printed on paper suitable for recycling and made from fully managed and sustained forest sources. Logging, pulping and manufacturing processes are expected to conform to the environmental regulations of the country of origin.

A catalogue record for this book is available from the British Library.

A catalog record for this book is available from the Library of Congress.

10 9 8 7 6 5 4 3 2 1
21 20 19 18 17 16 15 14 13 12

Printed and bound in Great Britain by
CPI Antony Rowe, Chippenham and Eastbourne

Contents

Figures

Tables

Preface and Acknowledgements

Some ten years ago we started to take an interest in research on the financial markets and their organization quite independently of one another. From three somewhat different perspectives (competence and micro-interaction, professional organizations and market organization), we approached what can be conceived as very central activities in the financial world: issuing and trading shares. Back then we were truly surprised that there were few organizational analyses of financial practices we could find. After crossing paths some five years ago, we started to coordinate our research efforts in what is known today as social studies of finance, by then a rapidly growing field of research. By focusing on one of the more mundane exchange objects within global finance, the old and well-known share, and by accounting for how four distinct groups of experts working within the same organizations (investment banks) coordinate their practices, we hope to make a contribution to this collective endeavour of developing a social science understanding of global finance.

A number of people aside from the authors have collectively contributed to this endeavour. We wish to thank our friend and colleague Peter Hägglund, who took part in formulating the original research project but was unable to participate in its realization. We also wish to thank colleagues who have read different versions of the chapters. In particular, thanks go to the participants of the PMO seminar at Stockholm School of Economics in August 2010, where we presented draft versions of the first five. They provided many useful comments, which helped us improve the book. We are especially grateful to our reviewers, Andreas Werr and Karin Svedberg Helgesson, who helped us bring the individual chapters towards completion. They engaged constructively with earlier drafts of them all and provided extensive comments on how to improve them. We owe thanks also to the Bank of Sweden Tercentenary Fund, which provided funding for the research project P2006:0797, headed by Karin Winroth, which this book reports on. Finally, we acknowledge the help and support of Lisa von Fircks and Gemma d'Arcy Hughes at Palgrave Macmillan.

Jesper Blomberg, Hans Kjellberg
and Karin Winroth
Stockholm

1
Understanding Investment Banking Practices

This book is about stock markets and the professionals that engage with them. Not long ago, financial markets were epitomized by the stock exchange, a physical floor where traders communicated about, and engaged in market transactions on behalf of, buyers and sellers. Developments during the past 25 years or so, however, have fundamentally reshaped the financial markets; these include the liberalization of national regulatory frameworks and the transformations caused by digitization (Sassen, 2005). The result has been a tremendous growth in the number of transactions, the number of products, the number of markets and, not least, in the value of financial assets worldwide.

These changes have also affected the character of stock market work. While stock traders still transmit orders in contemporary stock markets, digitization and growth have led to increased specialization and professionalization. Today, at least four distinct occupational groups – traders, brokers, analysts and corporate bankers – regularly contribute to the machinery of the stock markets, acting both as producers of these financial products and as intermediaries between buyers and sellers. In the financial centres around the world, these experts can all be found working within investment banking organizations that offer investment advice and transaction services to investors. This places the expert groups at the centre of the financial world, and provides them with resources to actively influence its workings.

These simple observations form the starting point for this book and also contain the motives for the two basic issues we seek to address:

(1) *How are investment banking practices organized?* The increasing specialization and division of labour among distinct expert groups working within the same organizations raises questions about how such organizations are coordinated. While the different investment banking experts engage in complementary practices, these practices also lead them to assume different perspectives on their task

environments, such as on the products and markets with which they work (Winroth et al., 2010). To some extent then, they can be said to inhabit distinct social worlds. Hence, the organizing of investment banking must to some extent cope with, and coordinate activities across, these different worlds.

(2) *How do these practices contribute to shape the stock markets?* Given that the experts working in investment banking are in a position to potentially influence the workings of the stock markets, it is interesting that these markets have not become more predictable, despite seemingly increased sophistication; the cycles of bust and boom continue. This raises questions about the experts' role as stabilizers or destabilizers of stock markets and, more generally, about the ways in which investment banking practices contribute to configure the stock markets. As a way of exploring these questions further, let us return to the stock markets and the role of investment banking experts therein.

At the centre of the volatile stock markets

The stock markets are often attributed a central role in the wider financial system, on account of their channelling of capital between corporations and investors, and between different industrial sectors. The centrality of the stock markets is also reflected in their role as a general barometer for the economy as a whole; for instance, in the media coverage of global stock markets and the use of stock market indices such as the Dow Jones and the S&P 500 as shorthand for the current economic situation in the world. This was apparent in the autumn of 2008 when excerpts like the one below appeared in media around the world:

> **Shock waves: Stocks plunge after crisis in investment firms.** Stocks suffered their worst losses in seven years as the failure of investment firm Lehman Brothers Holdings Inc. and the sudden sale of Merrill Lynch & Co stoked investor fears of even deeper problems in the nation's financial system. The Dow Jones industrial average plunged more than 500 points, the biggest one-day drop since September 11, 2001.
>
> (*The Boston Globe*, 16 September 2008. © 2008 The Boston Globe. All Rights Reserved. Used by permission and protected by the Copyright Laws of the United States. The printing, copying, redistribution, or retransmission of this Content without express written permission is prohibited.)

Not only was the financial crisis of 2008 sudden and significant for the global economy, it also emphasized the central role of investment banks. At the heart of the crisis, often described as the worst since the 1930s (Noord, 2009), were a group of highly regarded and influential investment banks that were failing, and pulling others along as they fell.

The crisis in 2008 also served to emphasize that the stock markets are a concern not only for investors, corporations and financial professionals. In addition to familiar consequences such as reduced overall economic activity and mass unemployment, the crisis made clear that pension funds nowadays constitute a very direct link between the financial markets and the man in the street throughout the western world:

> **Collapsing stock market makes poor pension-deal worse.** The new premium pension has been a poor deal for the Swedish pension savers. For the average Swede, the yield has not been better than the bank interest rate, 2.7 percent/year. The collapse on the stock exchange the last few weeks has made the situation even worse. The 5.8 million pension savers in Sweden are not getting value for their money. Only this week, €120 million have disappeared from the Premium Savings Fund, the most popular fund with 2 million savers.
> (*TT Nyhetsbanken*, 20 September 2008, trans.)

Crises such as the one in 2008 underscore the fact that stock markets are highly volatile. While the value of corporate stocks have gradually increased during the past two decades, many stock markets fell by as much as 50 per cent during 2008. Figure 1.1 illustrates the changes in market capitalization (the value of the listed corporations) at the New York Stock Exchange (NYSE) and the London Stock Exchange (LSE) since 1990. For all the efforts made by investment banking experts to domesticate the stocks of corporations, such as by offering rigorous analyses, stock values in these markets dropped 41 and 51 per cent respectively.

The history of the financial markets is full of more or less well-known crises – the tulip mania in Amsterdam in 1637, the South Sea bubble in 1720, the black Mondays on Wall Street in 1929 and 1987, the IT bubble in 2000 and so on. In this connection, it is important to stress that the volatility of stock markets creates opportunities for large gains by buying or selling at the right time. Stock markets are places of speculation where considerable short-term profits can be gained and large losses incurred. Investment banking experts who are explicitly employed to engage in speculative trade undertake much of this activity.

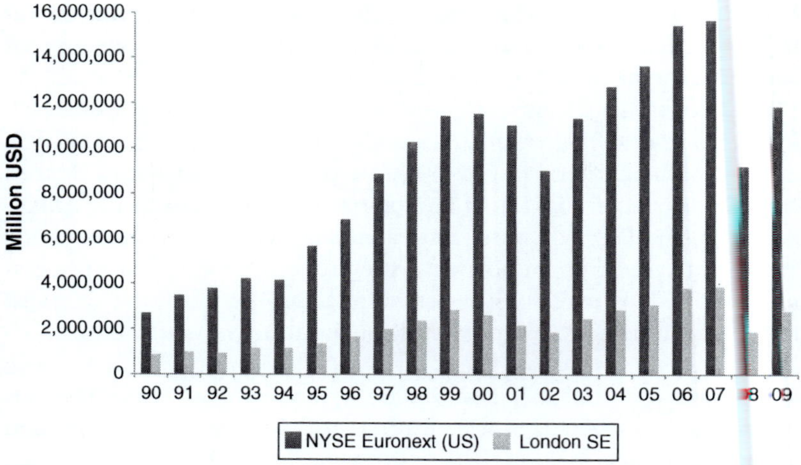

Figure 1.1 Market capitalization at the New York Stock Exchange and the London Stock Exchange, 1990–2009 (based on statistics from the World Federation of Exchanges)

The year 2008 became another year of financial bust. Due to the increasingly globalized financial system, it was difficult to contain the effects, and the negative consequences spread quickly around the world. International committees were formed to discuss responsibilities, how to restore trust in the financial markets, and how countries with badly damaged economies could be supported, resulting in initiatives like the European Economic Recovery Plan. However, already in 2009 there were signs of recovery (see Figure 1.1), and by 2010 there was talk of growth once more:

> **Chinese IPO success comes with a warning.** As a record number of Chinese initial public offerings hit US capital markets, investors may be beginning to step back from the market. The US has seen 34 debuts of China-based companies in 2010, according to Thomson Reuters figures, topping the 31 that issued in 2007, 'It feels like Silicon Valley did in 1996' says Scott Cutler, executive vice president of NYSE Euronext, which by the end of this year expects to top its record of 20 Chinese listings. 'We're are at the beginning of a long growth cycle.'
>
> (*Financial Times*, 9 December 2010.)

So the sudden crisis was followed by a quick recovery, at least in certain areas. And once again, investment banking was at the centre of events.

In the excerpt above, their role is implied in the large number of initial public offerings (IPOs) that typically would be underwritten by syndicates of investment banks.

The observed instability of the stock markets and close involvement of investment banks are important for the issues we wish to address in this book. Acting in an unstable environment places high demands on an organization's ability to adapt flexibly to changing circumstances and successfully exploit change. At the same time, investment banking must have a 'systematic' or 'orderly' character, like any other organized activity. How is investment banking organized to cope with these organizational demands? The omnipresence of investment banking organizations in the events reported above also underscores the need to probe further into their role for the financial markets. Are they passive intermediaries that lubricate the system, or should they be awarded a more active role – placed in the driver's seat of the financial markets, as it were?

Investment banking

The buying and selling of stocks is linked to a number of specific practices, most of which can be subsumed under the label investment banking. By analysing the operations of major corporations, assisting in the issuing of shares in these corporations, and actively trading these shares on stock exchanges, investment banking is truly at the heart of 'stock marketing'. By defining investment banking as those practices that contribute to producing securities transactions, we can identify four groups of experts that regularly engage in investment banking practices. *Traders* execute orders to buy and sell securities on the financial markets. *Brokers* offer advice to investors, informing them about investment opportunities in order to generate securities transactions. *Analysts* support these efforts by conducting research on market and corporate developments, assessing whether a particular security is correctly priced or not. *Corporate bankers*, finally, advise and assist top managers in the creation of new securities, for instance, in connection with mergers, acquisitions and other situations where companies wish to raise capital. These four groups of experts typically perform their tasks side by side within the same organization, which may or may not be called an investment bank.

The focus on securities transactions distinguishes investment banking practices from commercial and retail banking practices (handling payments, taking deposits and lending money). It also links investment banking closely to the financial markets. It is on the stock, commodities and future exchanges around the world that the bulk of the millions of securities transactions take place to which investment banking practices contribute. These exchanges are referred to as secondary markets, since the transactions taking place there typically do not involve the producer or issuer of the security being transacted. In contrast, a company issuing new shares or making an IPO sells these shares on a primary market, which an investment banking organization typically helps to organize. Irrespective of whether the securities transactions take place on the primary or secondary market, then, investment banking practices are involved.

Investment banking practices related to the issuing and trading of securities are an explicit example of how division of labour and cooperation between different professional groups has become accentuated in the financial industry, making the machinery of finance more sophisticated. In contemporary digital stock markets, trading technologies support the adjustment to even more information. The technical systems also facilitate and speed up transactions, allowing more trade to take place, larger numbers of traders to participate and also allowing transactions across the globe. In addition, financial products have become more varied and complex as a result of efforts to generate new ways of handling risks (Millo and MacKenzie, 2009). The financial markets seem to be increasingly complex and 'systemic' in character. In this context, investment banking experts work in collaboration with one another, with investors and with corporations in need of capital, and they are closely involved in the activities that create the characteristic flow of the financial markets (Knorr Cetina, 2006). Of course, investment banking practices are not the only ones involved in this construction process – investors buying and selling securities, regulatory efforts, the provision of trading infrastructure by exchanges and the publication of financial news are all examples of complementary practices – but their role in mediating securities transactions warrants further attention in order to better understand the financial markets.

While it may be difficult to accurately assess the contribution of these practices and practitioners to the wider economy (Haldane et al., 2010), the role of investment banking in the financial/banking/mortgage crisis between 2007 and 2009 – 'the most damaging economic event since the Great Depression' (Turner et al., 2010:1) – left little doubt as to their import. Still, this book is not about the spectacular crisis and its many unfortunate consequences. Rather, it is about the everyday humdrum of investment banking. It is about getting to know what the experts engaged in investment banking do during their working days, and about appreciating the consequences of their doings for the organizing of investment banks and stock markets.

The role and import of experts and their expertise

Our use of the terms 'experts' and 'expertise' is intended to convey that the occupational groups in investment banking use specific knowledge to perform their work: knowledge that is usually shared within the group and acquired through on-the-job training (Brint, 1994; Hasselström, 2004). The choice of terms also signals that investment banking experts do not constitute a profession similar to that of lawyers or medical doctors; they do not monopolize and police the knowledge and technical skills applied in their area of expertise (Reed, 1996). These experts rely on a relatively esoteric knowledge base, a combination of theoretical knowledge, analytical tools and tacit knowledge, and they are usually less concerned about formal credentials and education. Instead, they seek political and economic advantages by aggressively marketing their knowledge/skill base.

The roles and contributions of the specific expert groups working in the financial sector have already received considerable scholarly attention. Traders and their close involvement with markets have fascinated many. Abolafia (1996) studied the work of market-making traders, arguing that their culture and organization was central to the ongoing social construction of institutional arrangements that produce specific trading markets. The role of traders in constructing 'the global economy' has also been brought to the fore (Knorr Cetina and Bruegger, 2000; Hasselström, 2003; Knorr Cetina, 2005). Others have studied the various strategies employed by brokers to become successful in markets (Smith, 1981) and how different approaches to stock brokering may account for performance variation (Blomberg, 2004). The knowledge-producing role of several of the expert groups has been emphasized, for instance, by Hasselström (2004) in her study of how traders, brokers and analysts make sense of the financial markets. Several studies have shown how the specific knowledge work of stock market analysts contributes to construct investment objects out of corporations (Zuckerman, 1999, 2000; Hägglund, 2000; Rao et al., 2001; Mouritsen, 2003; Fogarty and Rogers, 2005). The experts' handling of market uncertainty has also been attended to, such as how analysts seek to handle situations characterized by partial knowledge (Beunza and Garud, 2007) and how relatively stable social networks among corporate bankers contribute to mitigating the effects of market uncertainty (Podolny, 1994). The workplace culture of corporate bankers has been shown to intervene in the booms and busts of markets (Ho, 2009), and their growing status and role as trendsetters in business life has been linked to their social packaging (Svedberg Nilsson and Winroth, 2005). Finally, management issues related to investment banking experts have been brought to the fore, for instance, in discussions about risk management (Clark and Thrift, 2005; Power, 2005) and conflicts of interests (Hayward and Boeker, 1998).

Organizing multiple experts in investment banking

Despite this considerable attention to experts working in the financial sector, few studies have studied the joint involvement of several expert groups in investment banking, or investment banks, as such. One important exception is the study by Eccles and Crane (1988) of management practices in investment banking, which characterizes investment banks as self-designing organizations. Since the financial experts require a high degree of autonomy when performing their work – doing deals – the banks are flexibly organized. Management is adjusted to the circumstances that apply to the experts' work, 'the function, economic characteristics and production process of the business' as Eccles and Crane put it (ibid.: 4). The authors further suggest that the flat structure, the tight management control systems and the subjective bonus determination process within investment banks form a triad of organizational characteristics that compensates for the weaknesses of each individual component. Largely, then, this is a rationalist narrative in which management practices are (soundly) adapted to the task requirements of the experts. Even though their study introduces the work of the experts, the primary objective is to explain how the management practices used within investment banks enable managers to evaluate and direct the experts' performances. In the light of the events in the world of investment banking during the past few years, the need for additional insights into how such organizations can be managed seems to be as great today as it was when Eccles and Crane first published their study.

While our interest is not primarily related to management practices, they certainly enter into our concern for the organizing of investment banking. Specifically, we address how the individual practices that the various experts engage in are coordinated within investment banking organizations. The autonomy of the experts, emphasized by Eccles and Crane, suggests that organizing mechanisms other than traditional hierarchical structures and management control systems may come into play in investment banking. For instance, Engelen et al.

(2010) argue that agents in the financial markets engage in *bricolage* in a Lévi-Straussian sense; that they innovate by making do with the diverse resources that happen to be at hand, constructing fragile, contingent and context-dependent chains of events. Identifying and exploring such organizing mechanisms, by analysing how the expert practices in investment banking become interlinked, is an important step towards further developing our understanding of how these organizations are and can be managed. Specifically, it allows us to identify tensions between different organizing mechanisms and management tools employed within investment banking. In this respect, managerial issues are part of the remit for our first question: How are investment banking practices organized? In pursuing this question, we seek to understand how it is possible to coordinate activities undertaken by members of relatively distinct communities of practice (Wenger, 1998). The specific practices that the experts engage in create 'epistemic differences' and lead the experts to understand given situations in quite different ways (Brown and Duguid, 2001). As suggested by Brown and Duguid, coordinating practices across such communities, despite knowledge differences, remains a central organizational challenge.

Organizing the stock markets?

In addition to the organizing challenges that the multiple expert groups give rise to within investment banks, there is a growing body of studies of 'market professionals' that highlight the importance of various forms of market expertise on the organizing of markets (e.g. Barrey et al., 2000; Geiger and Finch, 2009). As noted above, several such studies address how financial experts are involved in the enactment of the financial markets (e.g. Abolafia, 1996; Zaloom, 2006; Beunza and Garud, 2007; Ho, 2009). The work of MacKenzie, Millo and colleagues has been particularly influential in its emphasis on the role of economic theories and theorists in shaping the financial markets (MacKenzie and Millo, 2003; MacKenzie et al., 2007). Typically, markets are the scenes of multiple examples of such ideological organizing efforts, and thus unlikely to mirror the views, intentions and interests of any one group of experts or theorists (Kjellberg and Helgesson, 2006; Engelen et al., 2010). This multi-pronged character of market processes becomes very clear in the context of the engagement of investment banking experts with stock markets. Traders, brokers, analysts and bankers all actively engage with, and influence, the stock markets, but not in a uniform way. These ideas thus lend further weight to our contention that investment banking experts may contribute to shaping the stock markets, and also underscore the centrality of investigating further how they do so. This becomes particularly important in the light of the tension between the traditional view of investment banking as a relatively passive intermediary lubricating the flow of assets between 'issuers' and 'investors' (Eccles and Crane, 1988) and more recent suggestions that these experts are primarily concerned with exploiting their position and expertise to 'run the show' (Folkman et al., 2007).

Understanding investment banking by studying the qualifying of shares

Conceptually we approach these two issues from a practice perspective inspired by work at the intersection of science and technology studies (e.g. Latour, 1987, 2005), organization studies (Czarniawska and Hernes, 2005) and marketing (Kjellberg and Helgesson, 2006, 2007). In doing so, we join a growing body of scholars who have sought to appreciate the internal logic(s) of financial and other markets in recent years (e.g. Knorr Cetina and Preda, 2005b; Callon et al., 2007; MacKenzie et al., 2007). These constructivist market studies have shown that markets and other forms of economic governance can be fruitfully regarded as outcomes of the many and often conflicting sets of practices that make up economic organizing. From this perspective, then, investment banking organizations and stock markets alike are ongoing accomplishments constructed through a range of practices involving different forms of expertise and material devices (Callon, 1998b; Helgesson et al., 2004).

Based on the assumption that discourses are performative, that is, that they contribute to constructing the reality they describe (Callon, 1998b; MacKenzie, 2006; Callon, 2007), we conceive the world in terms of multiple realities, rather than multiple perspectives on a single reality (Mol, 2002; Law and Urry, 2004). That is, different practices enact different, yet overlapping, versions of the same objects, such as agents, products, markets (Mol, 2002; Kjellberg and Helgesson, 2006). As noted above, the work performed by various market professionals and their expertise is one important influence on this process of enactment (Barrey et al., 2000; Azimont and Araujo, 2007). More specifically, Callon et al. (2002) have emphasized the centrality of such forms of expertise for the *qualification* of goods – the process through which products and services become temporarily stabilized as goods that can be exchanged under specific conditions (see also Finch and Acha, 2008; Karpik, 2010).

For our purposes, these ideas direct attention to how investment banking experts engage with financial products in their everyday practices, in order to render them attractive for potential buyers. Contemporary investment banking involves several different types of securities, such as bonds, shares, futures, warrants. We have chosen to focus on how the experts construct and use one specific type of security, namely shares. While financial products have become increasingly decoupled from the ordinary economy of production, distribution and consumption, through the construction of derivatives and the growth of speculative trade (Knorr Cetina and Preda, 2005a), shares in publicly listed corporations remain a major form of investment. They also constitute the basis for many of the derivative products that are traded on other financial markets. The continued importance of shares is further reflected in the media coverage of stock markets, discussed above. Without the stock markets, the current global financial system would be unthinkable. A final important reason for focusing on shares is the fact that all major expert groups in investment banking actively work with this type of security. The ways in which they do so differ, as do their views of these objects, something that will become increasingly clear throughout the coming chapters. Still, representatives of these expert groups regularly interact concerning specific shares without these differences leading to breakdown. Indeed, their interactions concerning shares go beyond the investment banking organization to other actors on the financial markets, implying that their work with shares may have consequences for these markets. Thus, focusing on how experts work with shares allows us to address both the issue of how expert practices are coordinated within investment banking, and how they influence the stock markets.

Shares as boundary objects linked to an invisible infrastructure

These starting points lead us to borrow the concept of *boundary objects* from science studies as a resource for our inquiry (Star and Griesemer, 1989). This concept was developed as an analytical tool for addressing how cooperation and coordination between different social worlds may be possible without these worlds sharing a single view of the object or phenomenon with which they engage. 'Boundary objects are objects which are both plastic enough to adapt to local needs and the constraints of the several parties employing them, yet robust enough to maintain a common identity across sites' (ibid.: 393). This suggests that shares may be regarded as one type of boundary object that facilitates interaction between the different expert groups within investment banking.

A central idea linked to the concept of boundary objects is that these objects are weakly structured in common sense – affording various readings of them – while capable of becoming strongly structured in specific settings – being understood as very precise things in the various 'worlds' within which they are used. To exemplify, a trader and an analyst may superficially agree on what a share is, but construct very different images of specific shares as part of their expert practices. As Kopytoff (1986) suggests, objects can reveal multiple identities across settings much in the same way that people do. While many objects thus signify different things in different social worlds, a boundary object must be recognizable and useful across such worlds. Among the four types of boundary objects suggested by Star and Griesemer (1989:410), the 'coincident boundaries' category is most relevant for our discussion. These are objects whose boundaries coincide for several actors, but whose internal content differs. According to Star and Griesemer such objects arise in the presence of different means of aggregating data and when work is geographically distributed, as it is in the financial markets. This means that work in different sites and with different perspectives can be conducted autonomously while sharing the boundary object as a common referent. The advantage of this type of boundary object is its ability to resolve different goals, while still enabling communication and interaction between groups of actors that engage with it.

This hints at a core characteristic of boundary objects: their ability to be employed in diverse intersecting social worlds. The central assumption is that consensus is not necessary for cooperation to take place. Rather, each 'participating world' can abstract or simplify the object to suit its demands, that is, 'extraneous' properties can be deleted or ignored as they form their object identities (Star and Griesemer, 1989). The boundary object reduces the need for, or alternatively, affords the creation of, a minimal common understanding across diverse social worlds due to its adaptability to different viewpoints. This adaptability makes the object open to the specific needs and constraints of each social world. By buffering the tension between cooperation and heterogeneity, the object can be simultaneously employed as part of several different practices (Trompette and Vinck, 2009).

Previous work on boundary objects has emphasized how these objects work as mechanisms for knowledge integration and coordination, allowing and supporting heterogeneous translations across sites (Trompette and Vinck, 2009). One particular example of this is coordination between experts and non-experts, a theme highly relevant also for the present study. A less acknowledged facet of the concept is how boundary objects incorporate an invisible infrastructure that 'transports a set of conventions, standards and norms indexed to a community of practice' (ibid.: 4). This suggests, in line with the literature on the co-construction of users and use (Woolgar, 1991; Oudshoorn and Pinch, 2003), that boundary objects not only take on characteristics as part of being employed in specific practices, but also potentially shape those practices. The challenge is the invisibility – that such infrastructures tend to evade attention, only becoming visible as they break down (Bowker and Star, 1999). This becomes a central issue when addressing the organizing of investment banking, since such an invisible infrastructure may interfere with and create tensions that are difficult to pinpoint when encountering more overt organizing mechanisms (Blomberg et al., 2011).

By viewing shares as boundary objects, we implicitly assume that shares may contribute to the coordination of practices across settings beyond those of the experts working in investment banking. Corporations that issue shares, and investors that buy and sell shares on the stock markets, are two such groups of actors that investment banking experts regularly interact with concerning shares. The invisible infrastructure that develops around the shares does not end at some organizational boundary, but continues into the stock markets. This suggests that, by following shares as boundary objects, we can address both the organizing within investment banking firms and the organizing of stock markets.

Constructing share identities

To make use of the concept of boundary objects when studying how investment banking experts work with shares, we need a basic framework for characterizing how these expert groups construct different share identities as part of their practices. In what ways do the share identities that the experts develop differ from each other? What consequences, if any, do these differences have for how investment banking and stock markets are organized?

Shares are particular objects in many ways. First, they are highly abstract entities that lack physical form; instead, owners of shares are simply registered. Second, and related, shares are not worn out by use; there is nothing to wear out. Third, and still related, shares do not age; time itself will not affect the object positively or negatively. Even though a share can be ascribed different qualities and value over time (see the discussion on temporality below), such changes are not the results of the passage of time. Beyond these basic characteristics, shares are regularly ascribed a number of qualities. Along with these qualities, monetary values and prices are attached to them. In some identities, the homogeneity of shares is emphasized, for instance, in comparisons of P/E (price/earnings) ratios. Such share identities, which rely heavily on a limited set of characteristics, often closely or even exclusively related to their price, suggest that shares are 'commodities' (Kopytoff, 1986). In other incarnations, shares are constructed as highly unique entities – 'singularities' (Karpik, 2010) – for instance, in a stock analyst's regular in-depth analysis of a corporation.

Despite these differences in identities, the various experts within investment banking are typically able to both recognize that they are dealing with the same object and successfully interact with one another concerning this object. We suggest that this is due to the share being a boundary object with 'coincident boundaries'. The various identities ascribed to the share have a common denominator, a shell if you will, that can be filled with different contents as part of the specific expert practices. This is not to say that the qualities ascribable to such an object are arbitrary: as is well known from the sociology of science and techniques, ascriptions require differential amounts of work (Latour, 1987). Given the wide range of possible dimensions for characterizing the construction of object identities, we have explored the literature and empirical material in parallel. In this way, we have identified a few general categories capable of capturing important differences between share identities. Still, our proposed conceptual scheme is by no means exhaustive. Inspired mainly by authors taking an interest in the role of objects in social or economic life (e.g. Appadurai, 1986; Latour, 1992, 1994; Pinch and Swedberg, 2008; Miller, 2010), we propose four dimensions for characterizing the construction of object identities: constitutive associations, representations, potential uses and temporal framings.

The first dimension is related to the configuration of the share identity itself: how it is put together. If objects are temporary results of a process of combination (Latour, 1994), then one important aspect of their identity is the *constitutive associations* that are recognized by an actor as forming a coherent whole. These associations explain very literally how specific characteristics become ascribed to an object in a certain situation. If object identities change over time as well as across settings, mapping their constitutive associations will allow us to register such changes. In the context of shares, we expect this dimension to capture the various referents, entities and indicators employed to form a share identity. By doing so, the constitutive associations also allow us to appreciate how various expert groups can form quite different understandings of the same object.

The second dimension concerns what the object identity *represents* to those constructing it: what the object signifies (Kopytoff, 1986:68).

An object that is commonly known and referred to in everyday vocabulary can symbolize quite different things. In some settings, shares are mainly held to represent corporations or ownership in these corporations. In others, shares represent investment opportunities, allowing them to be compared to very different objects, such as barrels of oil, real estate or government bonds. It is important to stress that there is no one-to-one relation between the constitutive associations that make up the object identity and what this identity is held to represent. While traders 'know' that the shares they trade represent corporations, they primarily constitute their identities by associating them with various external forces that can be expected to influence their price.

The third dimension of share identity concerns the *potential and actual uses* of the share that actors include in its identity (Kopytoff, 1986:67). In taking uses into account, we acknowledge the insight from user and consumption studies, that object identities may be significantly influenced by the way in which objects are employed (de Certeau, 1984; Shove and Pantzar, 2005; Shove and Araujo, 2010). This suggests that we can gain additional insights into the construction of share identities by inquiring into the purposes and circumstances under which shares are used. A share may, for instance, be used for investment purposes in one setting, while being used primarily as a means for exploiting power within an organization in another. This dimension thus highlights the practical facet of share identities by attending to what the experts do with shares, rather than how they understand them (Pickering, 1993).

Fourth, and finally, we suggest inquiring into how object identities differ in terms of their *temporal framings*. Drawing on Callon's (1998a) discussion of the temporal framing of economic exchanges, we consider to what extent an object identity takes historical (and future) events and relationships into account. As suggested by Jalas (2009), the temporality of objects can be regarded as a relational phenomenon situated between human actors and the material world. Depending on the temporal boundary traced around the object as part of its identity construction, historical developments and future prospects held to affect the object may or may not be included, thus giving rise to quite different versions of a given object. The temporal framing of object identities is also closely connected to the notion of *durability* (Law, 1986a); this includes considering how stable is the share identity that is being constructed by the experts? Does the share remain the same over long periods or does it change more or less on a daily basis? The durability of an object identity can be expected to affect how experts interact with it and, as Law

(1986a) suggests, the possibility of exerting control at a distance via the object.

These dimensions allow us to capture some of the possible differences that may exist between the share identities constructed by investment banking experts. Investigating how the experts construct their share identities will also shed light on the social worlds in which they are constructed. For our purpose, then, this will generate insights not only about the shares but also about two important contexts that are enacted by these expert groups: investment banking organizations and stock markets.

Studying expert practices in the financial markets

The financial markets rely on a wide range of actors, objects, ideas and activities. This book empirically investigates one particular facet of this complex: investment banking practices related to the primary and secondary markets for shares. More specifically, we have mapped the associations produced by the practices that investment banking experts engage in by 'following the shares' (confer Latour, 1987). That is, we have focused our attention on how the experts engage with shares in their daily work. In this sense, we have studied investment *banking*, rather than investment banks. In doing so, we have sought to answer 'a dual question: what is being done, and how does this connect to other things that are being done in the same context?' (Czarniawska, 2004:784). In short, we have tried to reconstruct the networks of associations, or *action nets*, that link actors and objects as part of investment banking practice. This has allowed us to describe both the work of these expert groups and how their respective efforts become practically interlinked. It has also allowed us to identify a number of other actors that regularly take part in the action net by engaging with shares, including investors, corporations, stock exchanges, various service suppliers, media and regulatory bodies. The invisible infrastructure incorporated in shares in their capacity as boundary objects will be part of this action net along with other associations that contribute to enact investment banking organizations and stock markets. Figure 1.2 provides a simplified overview of the *context* of investment banking, and hence a cursory glimpse at the setting within which we have mapped our action net (see Chapter 10 for a graphic re-presentation of the 'ecological' action net of investment banking).

Three brief clarifications are in place concerning the empirical study reported in the book (for more details, see the Appendix). First, it is

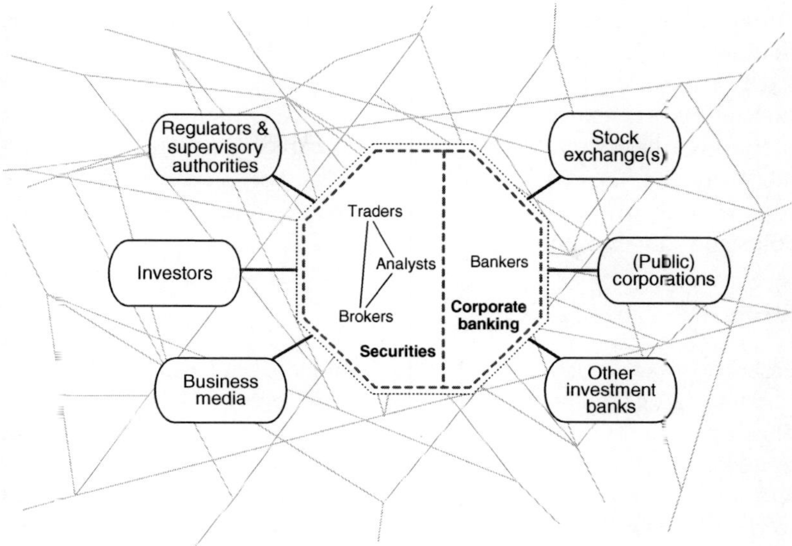

Figure 1.2 The context of investment banking practices

important to underscore that we have sought to map the general ways in which the experts engage with shares, rather than idiosyncratic action nets. Apart from following the birth of a specific share in Chapter 7, no individual shares have been followed in the project. Hence, the chapters will describe a number of ongoing processes of interaction involving shares taking place within and between the expert groups, as well as between the expert groups and other actors.

Second, contemporary investment banking practices are international in character. They have gradually evolved during centuries (see Chapter 2), but they have become increasingly isomorphic during the past decades. Deregulation and intensified international trade in the financial markets are two important factors contributing to this development. This growing isomorphism means that investment banking throughout the world involves the four studied groups of experts (traders, analysts, brokers and corporate bankers). Thus, even though our data concern Swedish practices, it mirrors an established model of investment banking in contemporary (industrialized) economies.

Third, investment banking practices can be performed by experts working within various organizations, such as brokerage firms, investment banks, mutual funds and increasingly also in commercial banks.

There are also firms specializing only in one or two of the expert services that we subsume under the label 'investment banking'. We have chosen to study the practice of investment banking in organizations that include all four expert categories, which means that we have studied investment banks and larger commercial banks. Data on the management practices of investment banking (primarily Chapter 8) emanate from investment banks, since all their managerial control systems are adjusted to investment banking.

Structure of the book

Based on previous studies, Chapter 2 offers a brief history of investment banking, including societal, organizational, technical and legal developments. From its very first instantiations to contemporary global investment banking, its practices have comprised creative adaptations and innovative actions, closely linked to economic ups and downs, and to the ebb and flow of regulatory efforts. Investment banking practices have alternately relied on interpersonal trust in more or less closely knit networks and on more institutionalized forms of trust. Through a gradually increasing global reach, as well as increasing division of labour, contemporary investment banking engages at least four distinct groups of experts: traders, analysts, brokers and bankers. Their respective work is the topic for the subsequent five chapters.

Chapter 3 takes us to the world of traders, the experts working closest to, and sometimes literally in, the stock markets. The chapter describes the main types of activities performed by stock traders: cash trading, market making and proprietary trading. The central role of information technologies for communicating about, materializing and activating contemporary trading markets is highlighted, as well as their role as direct competitors to expert traders. Traders are shown to search continuously for patterns and opportunities in the markets in which they trade. But whereas the possible influences on stock markets are held to be extremely diverse, traders qualify shares primarily as exchange objects in a few standardized dimensions, notably their current and expected price.

Chapter 4 takes an inside look at investment banking's own researchers engaging in 'stock market science'. During the 1990s, the once very anonymous back office expert – the analyst – became the new high-profile star of investment banking. Today, good analysts offer an important competitive edge in investment banking. What do these experts do during their working days and during the 'four seasons' that structure their work (dictated by the quarterly reports of corporations)? With whom and what do they interact? How – and why – do they create their so important cases? Based on the account of the analysts' work, we show how analysts enact shares as knowledge objects whose identities are closely linked to the corporations they represent.

Chapter 5 focuses on the practice of stock brokering. Once the stars of brokerage firms, stockbrokers are now 'just' one of several occupational groups in investment banking. Still, a significant share of investment banking revenues emanates from the brokerage fees charged when clients make transactions. Being sales people, the brokers keep regular contact with their clients, offering advice concerning profitable or suitable investments given the client's preferences. The centrality of the clients is also what stands out in their construction of share identities. In stock brokering, the same share may mean very different things to different clients, depending on their attitudes towards risk, their current investment portfolio and so on.

Chapter 6 introduces the least public line of business within investment banking: corporate banking. In this department, significant changes to industry and company structures are regularly planned and realized. The involvement of corporate banking in large business deals, such as mergers, acquisitions, spin-offs and IPOs makes it one of the more important 'construction departments' for the financial markets. Based primarily on interview material, the chapter provides an in-depth view of the types of activities this expert group engages in, how members of the group perceive their own work and also how their customers perceive it.

In Chapter 7 we provide a detailed account of the role of corporate banking in the birth of a new share. Via an in-depth case study, the chapter traces this process over the course of four years, from the conception of an idea to the introduction of a new share on the stock exchange. By tracing the specific activities of bankers in relation to shares, the chapter complements the general view of bankers at work reached in Chapter 6. The emerging image of the share is one of a product under construction where the question of what parts to include in its construction is open-ended.

In Chapter 8 we turn our attention to the efforts to manage investment banks. The previous five chapters have described investment banking as an arena for expert performances. Managers underscore this image and downplay their own contribution, suggesting that the primary managerial task is to provide a stage for the experts to perform on. However, management does matter, as the administrative tasks involved in investment banking are considerable. Establishing ethical standards, creating systems for risk management and preventing inside trading are all important managerial tasks. The chapter focuses particularly on the practices of risk control and compliance management, and identifies a tension between managerial tools that encourage the experts to be creative and take risks (bonus systems) and tools that seek to control their behaviour in some detail (risk control systems).

Chapter 9 analyses how investment banking is organized and suggests that coordination via boundary objects is well suited to support a heterarchical form of organization. The expert groups are found to be flexible and innovative on the one hand, and observed to co-produce a coordinated and orderly system on the other. The focus of the analysis is on the extreme flexibility of the share as a boundary object and the invisible infrastructure it seems to bring with it. The chapter also expands on the possibilities of other boundary objects as well as other coordinating devices within investment banking. Besides the organization of the expert groups, the management and, in particular, the role of risk control systems and bonus systems are analysed. The chapter concludes that more than one organizational logic is at play, and although this produces friction, they can all be said to make investment banking possible.

Chapter 10 addresses how investment banking practice constitutes stock markets. The action net of investment banking is observed to have autopoietic qualities, containing numerous self-reproducing practice loops. One important source of these loops is the repeated re-qualification of shares that the experts engage in based on their respective share identities. In this way, the experts routinely destabilize the stock markets, prompting market activity on behalf of other experts and investors. The experts' distinct share identities also contribute to their enactment of partially overlapping stock market versions that stand in stark contrast to the uniform and singular image of 'the Market'. This natural(ized) image of 'the Market' offers insiders, like investment banking experts, considerable latitude while relieving them of responsibility for developments they actively co-produce.

2
A Brief History of Investment Banking

The origins of investment banking are many and they reach far back in time. As noted by Fleuriet (2008) few of those working in contemporary investment banking know its origins. In this chapter we approach investment banking by offering a brief account of a long history of organizational developments and innovations that, among other things, produced investment banking as we know it today. This history will show that the analytical stance applied in this book is supported by historical evidence. The history of investment banking is one of interaction between bankers, businessmen, investors, ideas and technical solutions. Through their actions, these actors co-constitute investment banking while enacting exchanges of securities.

Even if this book primarily aims to explore investment banking practices during the first decade of the twenty-first century, it is important to appreciate that these practices did not simply emerge out of thin air. This chapter thus serves as a historical backdrop to our main story about expert groups doing investment banking. At the same time, we should acknowledge that what happens today is part of the history of tomorrow. Thus, understanding the investment banking of yesterday and today is to investigate its future. Irrespective of whether we analyse the secondary stock market in Genoa in the fifteenth century, the bank regulations after 1720 or 1929, the collapse of the Bretton Woods agreement in the 1970s, the birth of NASDAQ and electronic trading in the 1970s, descriptions of traders and brokers in popular culture during the 1980s, the rise of star analysts during the 1990s or focus our attention on the contemporary growth of risk management, our accounts will be influenced by and interact with historical material. As such, our inquiry in this book is one into history in the making.

The medieval roots of investment banking

As a point of departure for our account, we follow the convention of most historians of finance and start with a description of the medieval Italian trading cities. This was where international money transfers and currency trade first took place within banks (Green, 1996), and where government bonds and something resembling shares were first issued and traded (Fratianni and Spinelli, 2006). The most progressive Italian bankers dealt in bills of exchanges, operated with correspondents in different countries, speculated in exchange rates, and invested parts of their deposits in the debts of city-states (a kind of government bond) and equity shares in commercial projects and shipping companies. These bankers were influential actors in the growing international goods trade. Over time, some of these bankers gave up acting as goods merchants and specialized in trading currencies, securities and/or equity investments (Fleuriet, 2008).

The two most influential city-states were Genoa and Venice, where you could also find the most influential bankers. While Venice was originally the stronger of the two, due to its trade with the Far East and a more stable political environment, Genoa was the more financially innovative (Fratianni and Spinelli, 2006). The monetarization of economic activities, the giro system and many other financial innovations can all be traced back to these Italian cities, but here we will focus on the development of investment banking, meaning the issuing of and trading in securities.

Increasing international trade and new financial solutions

As trading volumes and trading distances grew, so did the need for capital and the risks involved for investors. The growth of international trade, and the development of new legal and organizational solutions, enabled more capital to be allocated to these larger and riskier trade ventures. Previously, business projects used to be organized in some version of the Roman corporative form *societa*, in which investors and businessmen took unlimited risks. If the project went bankrupt, so did the investors. But a new form of venture, the *compania*, gradually replaced the *societa* and became the first example of joint stock financing (Basking and Miranti, 1997). This company form introduced different classes of long-term debts on top of corporate capital and discretionary deposits.[1] Entrepreneurs could now attract capital where the risks exceeded the individual investors' personal financial capacities. Now corporations could collect capital from a large number of independent and passive investors, without risking their personal fortunes.

This changed the principles for evaluating business projects. Rather than valuing a business venture by its content and by personal trust in the entrepreneur, ventures were now being valued by how much capital they attracted. This was not only due to the fact that the ventures were financed by actors with limited responsibilities but also because they were financed by greater numbers of anonymous investors who had less insight into their practical execution (Sevenius, 2007). The relative focus shifted from an industrial and entrepreneurial logic, towards a more financial, technical and anonymous one.

The new contractual form can be viewed as a first institutionalization of a relational gap between owners and managers. This gap was a prerequisite for later developments in technical analysis of investment risks and quantitative evaluation models. The development created markets for financial middlemen specializing in connecting, analysing and marketing individual business projects and financiers.

Better organized sea ventures and early corporate structures

These new financial techniques became popular among the Italian merchant banks that now could attract more capital from outside the personal networks of their bank family members. The banks allocated capital from investors to entrepreneurs, allowing investors to invest in something more liquid than land and property. Since the major Italian banks at the times were international, their assets could be moved quickly, which was a major benefit for investors in the politically unstable medieval Europe (Sevenius, 2007). Thus, the new banks filled important functions for both businessmen and investors, linking them to each other and managing their risks.

Most of the business projects were just that – projects. There were no institutionalized organizational forms for how to organize or stabilize the projects into more ongoing operations. The banks were relatively stable, but always governed by banker families and/or city-states. Gradually, however, corporate structures developed that resembled our contemporary joint-stock corporations. By the thirteenth century, a standardized contract had developed that allowed passive co-venturers to invest their capital, while others contributed their time and energy to transporting and selling the wares overseas. This new *colleganza* contract went beyond the existing *compania* by also clearly stipulating the responsibilities for the active manager of the enterprise. It was an early example of a standardized corporate structure, which was also used for organizing manufacturing enterprises by Venetian merchants (Basking and Miranti, 1997). Thus, the corporation as an investment object was starting to assume a more stable and standardized form, allowing it to be categorized, valued and compared. Although the formal theory of portfolio management was explicitly formulated 700 years later, all the ingredients for its practical application were in place.

The first public bank

Another early example of a corporate structure resembling the contemporary joint-stock corporation is the Banca di San Giorgio in Genoa, formed in 1408 by the creditors to the city of Genoa. Instead of paying back city loans, the city gave up part of its financial monopoly by creating this privately owned bank. Via the Banca di San Giorgio, the city-state could finance its spending by lending and thus create a city-state debt, and also increase its tax earnings through the increased commercial activity that the Banca di San Giorgio triggered. In good times the city regulated businesses and raised taxes to pay off old debts; in bad times the bank helped the city-state along with credits. Thus, Banca di San Giorgio functioned as the world's first central bank, enabling a sort of fiscal policy in line with much more recent economic theories.

Banca di San Giorgio had both Genoese and foreign stock owners and its shares were traded on a secondary market that was active, and relatively liquid. Through its public ownership, the bank was regarded as more stable than the city-state itself, and was able to supply the institutional stability that Genoa lacked (Lopez, 1964; Fratianni and Spinelli, 2006). A dividend was paid to the owners four times a year, but the actual payment was often delayed, sometimes for many years. As a consequence, a secondary market developed also for the dividends. The shares and dividends were issued and traded in *lire di paghe* as bank money. This was Genoa's money market and for then a major innovation. In the late fifteenth century the Banca di San Giorgio share was traded internationally, it was a market maker in the Genoese money market, and took positions in both the city-state debt and *colleganza*-like securities (shares). The Banca di San Giorgio can thus be viewed as the world's first full service investment banking organization.

The major Italian city-state banks like the Banca di San Giorgio in Genoa and the Banca di Rialto in Venice operated as central banks. Exploiting a positive relationship between institutional reputation and trust and low cost debts, they were used as tools for the city-states to borrow money at low cost. The banks transformed public debt into capital, or as we say today, they swapped debts for equity. They also served the evolving new national states by offering payments to soldiers in different countries and currencies. The different currencies were then traded through bank notes to yet other actors. The banks could thus benefit from arbitrage through their 'global' reach. The governance and management structures were still quite primitive and the enterprises often temporary and unstable investment objects. There were still no large-scale secondary stock markets. The Genoese bankers did set up 'exchange fairs' to clear and reissue international credit letters during the sixteenth century. But these letters did not have the standardization, marketability or liquidity of the financial instruments found in Amsterdam, London or New York in later centuries. Consequently, trading in them was never very intense (Fratianni and Spinelli, 2006). But all the important components were there: the passive investors, the shares, the bankers, and even budding secondary securities markets.

The new world and the genesis of securities markets

The Italian dominance in international trade gradually decreased as the Atlantic states turned their attention westwards. Despite their knowledge of international trade and finance, the Mediterranean city-states were surpassed as financial centres, both in size and power, by the young national states further north. During the sixteenth and seventeenth centuries, new trading companies were formed supported by national monopolies and armies. From a trade and banking perspective, the Dutch 'Vereenige Oost-Indische Companie' (VOC) and the British 'East India Company' were the most prominent. These companies were used as tools by their national governments to conquer the new world and were given monopoly rights to trade with different continents. As trade projects, they brought wealth to both private investors and nation states (Sevenius, 2007). They were partly financed by issuing stock to the general public, and the VOC is regarded as the world's first publicly owned corporation. Besides representing a new form of investment object, these trading companies contributed directly to the emergence of investment banking. First, they issued securities to buy government debts, thus creating securities markets similar to those that had existed in Genoa. Second, these securities markets were large-scale, creating a need for continuously open exchanges.

The first stock exchanges

When trading securities, clearing and settlement is the process by which payment is collected from the buyer and transferred to the seller, while the securities are transferred the other way. In Genoa, moneychangers took deposits and offered a transfer as a means of payment between accounts. The brokers for these transfers used to clear and settle bills at fairs, but gradually began to gather regularly in the same places (Fleuriet, 2008:29). In Bruges, Belgium, traders met at a house owned by the *van der Beurse* family to clear and settle bills of exchange and trade various commodities during the fourteenth century. The Antwerp Beurse for financial and commodity trading was formed in 1460, making Antwerp the financial capital of Europe. While the secondary market for national bonds was concentrated to the Antwerp Beurse, no stocks were listed there.

At the somewhat younger Amsterdam Bourse, trading involved wheat, fish and spices, but no securities. But when the VOC was formed in 1602 and the Amsterdam Bourse became its exchange, it became the world's first stock exchange. In 1609, the shares of the British East India Company were quoted on what would become the London Stock Exchange. The VOC was successful and the Amsterdam Bourse grew and became the world's largest exchange in the eighteenth century, trading debt and equity in cash and even futures. There were foreign debt instruments quoted there and foreign equity issuers, including for instance the English East India Company and the French South Sea Company. In 1725, nearly all the large bond issues were offered in Amsterdam. Several corporate banking practices we still have today developed here, such as the use of syndicated issuing of securities, with underwriters and managers (today's corporate bankers) issuing the bonds, and brokers selling them.

A British semi-hostile takeover

The nation states emerging in Europe in the seventeenth century tied politics and finance together even further. Their new banks were political tools within, as well as between, nations. The creation of the Bank of England was a direct consequence of the 'Glorious Revolution' of 1688 led by the Dutch *stadtholder*, and later King of England, William III. The revolution was a victory for Protestantism over Catholicism, an important step towards democracy and ended the British attempt to conquer the Netherlands through war (Jonathan, 2003; Morrison and Wilhelm, 2007a: 104–106). The new Dutch-British alliance shifted the centre for trade and finance from Amsterdam to London. The Bank of England was formed in 1694 and made the British state much more dependent on the rising merchant class and the idea of property rights, and less dependent on wars and the divine right of kings and noblemen (Pincus, 2009).

The Bank of England was important for the development of investment banking due to its ability to issue promissory notes to finance the English national debt. The credit of the bank was so good that the notes started to be used as means of payment. Thus they were not only traded on a secondary market but also became the first paper money in widespread use outside China (where they had been used for at least 600 years).

In early eighteenth-century England, all components of modern investment banking practice were in place. There was a major stable banking institution issuing and trading securities. In addition to the book-keeping practices developed in the Italian city-states, more advanced quantitative techniques had been developed for analysing financial practices. In addition, there was relatively high physical security and social stability, and ideas about the common man's democratic and property rights and the protestant work ethic were beginning to take hold. All these changes helped the financial sector expand and fuelled the development of broader and more anonymous financial markets. These developments in England affected all of Europe. By the early eighteenth century, negotiable commercial papers and swaps of national debt into shares in corporations (banks or trading companies) were all traded on the international exchanges in Amsterdam and London. These exchanges were regarded as more stable than others due to the protestant, parliamentary and trade-friendly environment. By now the financial sector employed brokers and stockjobbers, and mathematical calculus, accounting rules and financial theories developed to provide a basis for the practices of these financial workers.

Major setbacks and bursting bubbles

Kings and churches had traditionally regulated finance. If a state defaulted on payments to its creditors, it was not uncommon that the state, or rather the king, solved this by killing the creditors. This made credit expensive and dependent on personal trust between lenders and borrowers. This would become a major problem for the French state, since such trust was very much absent between the monarch and the wealthy merchants. Also the church, and especially the Catholic Church, was a major regulator of finance since it had banned the use of financial loans with interest.

When merchant classes, Protestants and democrats promoted their various interests, they did so with the help of growing economic power, thus also promoting a more influential financial sector. During the late seventeenth and early eighteenth century, the English state became increasingly dependent on the new social class and on a growing financial sector. The ability of the Bank of England to raise capital on credit for the British state was badly needed. England's wars, particularly against France, drained the state of resources and incurred costs far beyond what it could amass through taxation. The ability to draw on the financial markets became a decisive factor in defeating France. But this also made England more dependent on the workings of the financial markets. This became apparent through a number of financial setbacks and bursting bubbles, caused more by financial logics than by regulations, religion or war. Most of the medieval banks had gone out of business due to political instability. Now, with increased state dependence on the purchase of the national debt by the banks and on secondary securities markets, the relationship was reversed. States were shaken by setbacks created within the financial sector, often by investment bankers.

The south sea bubble

The successful handling of the British national debt through the Bank of England, and the increased trading in securities in Amsterdam and London, triggered French efforts to catch up. Drawing on Scottish financial expertise and experience from Amsterdam, the so-called Law scheme was launched in 1717. Its purpose was to swap the excessive French national war debt for stock in the newly created *Compagnie des Indes*, managed by the equally new French central bank, *Banque Royal*. The plan was initially successful, due in part to systematic exaggerations of the new company's possibilities and early successes. The French national debt problem seemed to be resolved. This caused concern in the British Parliament. Thus, a second major British trading company, the South Sea Company was formed, once again to reduce the national debt (Basking and Miranti, 1997:105–110).

This second major British swap of government debt obligations for shares in a joint stock company initially seemed to work. But the new South Sea Company did not have the same substantial business success as the East India Company. The East India Company was well managed and had good connections at the far-off destinations in which it operated. The South Sea Company did not. Further, plans to diversify the South Sea Company into other industrial activities were halted by the Bubble Act of 1720, which stipulated that no corporation was allowed to do business outside its original charter. The South Sea Company was initially able to sell its stocks for prices above realistic values by spreading rumours and false information about success. When reality caught up, or rather, when the hopes of future business did not materialize in France or in England, the biggest financial crash ever was the result (Carswell, 1960; Basking and Miranti, 1997:110–117).

A return to personal networks

The South Sea Bubble had extensive consequences for the future of investment banking. In France, a desperate run forced *Banque Royal* to close, the Paris Exchange to shut down and the new national currency to collapse. Louis XIV banned joint stock corporations and locked France into a quasi-feudal society where the financial sector would remain in the hands of small family firms and limited partnerships for more than a century. In England, the South Sea Company was saved by its portfolio of long-term low-risk government securities, and also through harsh negotiations with financiers and the support of the Bank of England. After a reconstruction, it became the manager of a large portfolio of government securities, much like a modern-day mutual fund. The Amsterdam Bourse collapsed while the Royal Exchange in London survived. The pound sterling was saved through the intervention of the Bank of England.

In England, several regulations had been devised for the financial sector before the South Sea Bubble burst. The Bubble Act of 1720 was in fact intended to support the South Sea Company by limiting competition from other joint-stock corporations. The activities of the stockjobbers and brokers at the Royal Exchange had been regulated in 1697 when brokers were required to sign written pledges to deal honestly and avoid conflicts of interest with clients. The official number of stockjobbers was also limited to a maximum of 100 (Morrison and Wilhelm, 2007:117). Finally, all trades in stock had to be registered with the Bank of England. In 1709, these rules were sharpened and a committee for market oversight was created. In 1734, after the collapse of the York Building Society, option dealing was prohibited (Carswell, 1960; Basking and Miranti, 1997:115–122).

The policies regulating the financial markets and joint-stock enterprises became more restrictive and the attitudes towards large anonymous financial markets changed from appreciative to critical. States, bankers and investors reverted to dealing informally within small circles of enterprises led by individuals with proven reliability. Despite the fact that trading had an increasingly global reach, with banks and merchant houses in London as the centre of the financial world, social networks once again became more important relative to contracts and legal frameworks (Hancock, 1995:80–85; Morrison and Wilhelm, 2007:112).

Another important lesson from the South Sea bubble was that to try to retire national war debt as fast as possible was a poor strategy. Establishing an adequate revenue base for interest and gradual amortization became the new ideal. This made the economic environment more stable and changed the ways in which national debts were retired. Instead of swapping debts for shares, the use of underwriters capable of raising large amounts of capital from wealthy investors grew in importance. The Bank of England also began to sell government securities directly to individual investors (Basking and Miranti, 1997:116). Thus, by the end of the eighteenth century, there were not only brokers and stockjobbers but also bankers with personal contacts among wealthy investors, enabling the financing of state or quasi-state enterprises. Accounts that place the birth of corporate banking in the United States a 100 years later may have missed these European banking activities during the eighteenth century. It is not far-fetched to claim that a financial revolution (and investment banking) preceded the Industrial Revolution, at least in terms of the existence of secondary security markets, traders active on exchanges and bankers issuing securities. To fully appreciate the emergence of contemporary investment banking, however, we need to take the Industrial Revolution into account.

The new industrial joint-stock corporation

The major joint-stock trading companies created in the seventeenth and eighteenth centuries all had important functions for the state. Even if they were created in collaboration with wealthy financers, they had all been vehicles to expand state power. Until the early nineteenth century, the preferred investment objects for investors had always been related to government spending and debt. Nation states were held to be more stable and less risky than private business ventures. Government bonds were also easier to value since they often had a fixed interest rate and regular dividends. Thus, government bonds (or joint-stock shares closely linked to state-legislated monopolies) dominated trade on the international exchanges.

In England, the first half of the nineteenth century was characterized by deregulation of governmental monopolies and acts hindering private business. The legislators were inspired by the ideas of Smith, Ricardo and Mill – free trade, the principle of comparative advantage and social liberalism. The development was also affected by the complete colonization of the world; there were few opportunities to further expand the national economies by importing resources from new colonies. Instead, the new paradigm for supporting a growing population involved more efficient organization and management of goods production and distribution. New technologies like the steam engine made industrial production plants and reliable transportation by railway possible. New regulations fostering private financing of industrial joint-stock companies and lowering the cost of controlling them followed the deregulations in the mid-nineteenth century. Gradually, the perceived risks involved in owning shares were lowered and the number of registered joint-stock companies grew quickly (Basking and Miranti, 1997:128–130).

The centre for these developments was still England, but the American continent with its similar cultural and legal traditions soon took off. America attracted both people and capital. But there was yet no consistent legal framework across the US states concerning limited liabilities, annual audited reports, investors' property rights and financial activities. This created a need for highly known traders and bankers who could handle their own credit and underwrite the credit worthiness of others. The lack of institutionalized trust created an opportunity for established merchant houses like Barings, Browns and Rothschild to shift their business into becoming the first modern investment banks (Morrison and Wilhelm, 2007:129, 142).

Construction projects for canals and railroads drove the development of how to value industrial joint-stock companies. The lower the population of the area that the new means of transportation was going to connect, the harder it was to finance the project through local government and business life. The need to attract capital from far away put pressure on standardized accounting, auditing and other types of reporting, but was also complemented by trustworthy local bankers acting as underwriters. These early investment bankers gradually started to market corporate securities. The investment bank houses, the investors specialized in industrial sectors, as well as the banks, grouped themselves together in new financial centres. The railroads became the most important sector in Boston's financial centre, but other industries also started to make use of the joint-stock company form. The two leading US banking houses for railroad financing were JP Morgan, with strong connections to London and Paris, and Kuhn-Loeb Company, with contacts in Amsterdam, Paris and Frankfurt. The investment banks were now taking the lead in counselling wealthy investors making investments in Europe and the United States (Basking and Miranti, 1997:138; Morrison and Wilhelm, 2007: 1[illegible]3–170).

Several defaults, frauds and collapses in the nineteenth century temporarily reduced the investors' trust in shares of joint-stock companies.

The most notable setback was the American panic of 1847, which among other things shifted the US financial centre from Chicago to New York (Morrison and Wilhelm, 2007:152). By the early twentieth century, however, the trend towards increasingly commoditized financial products was clear. By then, company debt instruments (usually with fixed interest), preferred stock (a fixed-income instrument that was easier to price than common stock), and common stock were all regarded as legitimate investment objects. By this time, investment bankers had also become heavily involved in shaping industrial structures. Not only did they issue and market shares (through syndicates involving a lead underwriter and a list of syndicated banks) and counsel investors, but they also actively assisted in corporate restructuring during the periods of consolidation that most new industries went through (Morrison and Wilhelm, 2007:175–182).

According to Baskin and Miranti (1997:138–143), the development was fuelled by: (1) legislation which was more friendly to joint-stock companies, including the possibility of negotiating credit; (2) standardized rules regarding equity ratios, information provision, accounting and auditing; (3) the development of management techniques for better company control; (4) advances in communication technology such as the telegraph (1837), the trans-oceanic cable (1866) and the telephone (1876); and (5) the establishment of professional investment banks. These and other factors made the secondary markets for securities grow on all major exchanges around the world. Common stock became perceived as an investment object with a high but manageable risk and possibilities of high returns. Investment banking activity grew in terms of issuing shares, offering financial advice and trading on secondary securities markets. By the early twentieth century, the investment banker sat at the very heart of the US economy (Morrison and Wilhelm, 2007:184).

The bankers' own panic of 1907

By the time of the 1907 crash, Wall Street had become the financial centre of the world. The US financial sector was fully populated with commercial and savings banks, investment bankers, brokerage houses and trust funds. It was also truly deregulated with no American central bank and with President Roosevelt, at least rhetorically, seeking to reduce the power of trusts. Although the increasing power of the investment bankers and their syndicates were a source of concern (Morrison and Wilhelm, 2007:185), 'laissez-faire' was still the dominant ideology among legislators. But it was about to become dented.

The 1907 panic differed from previous crises in that the bankers and brokers themselves primarily caused it. The panic developed in as free a financial market as there has ever been. Some of the details of this crisis have special interest with regards to the history of investment banking. The crisis developed during a general economic contraction and was affected by the earthquake in San Francisco in 1906, which transferred capital from New York to the rebuilding of San Francisco. But the specific cause of the crisis was an attempt by Wall Street bankers to manipulate the stock price of United Copper Company, by aggressive and timely buying, selling and re-buying of stocks. The bankers had been successful in similar schemes before, but this time they misinterpreted the market and the scheme failed. It created several bank runs (with the banks directly involved in the scheme going bankrupt), caused major increases in interest rates (making the brokerage houses unable to finance their trading) and sent the stock market plummeting (Tallman and Moen, 1990; Bruner and Carr, 2007). The whole American bank system was on the verge of collapse. The US banker JP Morgan was instrumental in avoiding this, by amassing capital from John D. Rockefeller and others, and drawing on support from the famous European banker Lord Rothschild (Carosso, 1987:535–549). After desperate negotiations between the most influential bankers, trust funds and brokerage houses, and a last-minute visit to President Roosevelt to convince him to set aside the Sherman Antitrust Act and allow US Steel to buy shares in another major steel company, calm was finally restored (for a similar description of the events linked to the 1987 crises, see MacKenzie, 2006) (Figure 2.1).

There are many similarities between the 1907 panic and more recent crises, including the credit crunch of 2007, regarding both the events leading up to the crises and their aftermaths (Bruner and Carr, 2007). After studying the European financial sector, the US investment banking industry itself proposed new regulations including the creation of a federal bank. The aftermath of the 1907 panic is a good example of how the actors within the financial sector turn to regulations to restore trust and functionality to their industry. It raises doubts as to the possibility and desirability of a free financial sector, unhampered by regulations and civil society.

Investment banking in the twentieth century

Previous sections have highlighted several re-occurring themes in the history of investment banking: the tension between entrepreneurial

Figure 2.1 The 1907 panic starts on the curb outside the New York Stock Exchange

capitalism and political regulation; advances in the handling of risk and periods of speculative gambling; a growing global economy; and recurring setbacks. The history of investment banking until the mid-nineteenth century was more about the circumstances under which it came about than about its actual practices. Even if there were stockjobbers, underwriters and bankers in Amsterdam and London in the seventeenth century, investment banking was not an industry before the mid-nineteenth century. From then on, investment banking is a phenomenon of its own, and thus our history can now focus on the practices of investment banking *per se*. Regardless of how one structures such an account, there is no way around the crash of 1929.

The big crash

The most (in)famous economic setback so far is 'the big crash' and the 'Great Depression'. It is usually said to have started on black Thursday, 24 October 1929, with the collapse of the stock market on Wall Street (followed by black Monday 28 October and black Tuesday 29 October). Still, the empirical evidence indicates that there were economic problems well before those days, but also that market optimism endured well into 1930. Economists have disagreed concerning the causes of the crash and the depression that followed. Explanations are polarized between a Keynesian demand-side view of free market failure, and a monetarist view of too much government intervention (Bernanke, 1983, 2000).

Macro-level explanations aside, history shows that investment bankers and stockbrokers played key roles in the crash. The credits offered by stockbrokers to both small and large investors were extreme. The brokerage houses on Wall Street lent up to 90 per cent of all investors purchases of shares. A one-dollar deposit could thus be used to buy ten dollars worth of shares. When the stock market fell and the brokerage houses started to call in their loans, the debtors usually failed. When the debtors failed or sought to withdraw their deposits, the banks began to fail. This triggered multiple bank runs and a large number of bank failures. Almost 1000 US banks failed during the year following the crash and a total of 9000 failed during the 1930s. With borrowers struggling to repay their loans, banks failing *en masse* and forecasts indicating shrinking economic activity, the surviving banks became extremely conservative in their lending. The price of money soared, investments were halted, industrial production dropped and so did consumption, while unemployment grew rapidly. The rapid decline in the US economy was the factor that pulled down most other countries at first, then internal weaknesses or strengths in each country made conditions worse or better. The protectionist policies introduced by many governments reduced international trade even further. The result was a long-lasting depression affecting most economies in the world (Blum et al., 1970).

There has been considerable academic debate as to why and how the depression became so deep and lasted so long. One conclusion is that the fixed rate of national currencies to the gold standard made the supply of money too short (Temin, 1990). During the depression, every major currency left the gold standard, starting with Great Britain in 1930, followed by the Scandinavian countries and Japan later that year. In terms of unemployment, the depression lasted until the massive rearmament a few years before the Second World War increased the demand for workers. The war itself can be seen as one of many consequence of the depression. For investment banking the depression had a more direct consequence – new regulations of financial and banking activities, first nationally and then internationally.

New legislation then de-regulation again

Both the South Sea Bubble of 1720 and the black Tuesday at NYSE in 1929 were caused by a mix of naïve beliefs in economic rationality, greed, high-risk speculation and fraud. Both were also followed by major waves of national and international legislation to recreate functioning markets and to prevent similar developments in the future. In the case of the 1929 crash, this legislation included the Glass-Steagall Acts of 1932 and 1933 (in force until 1980 and 1999, respectively), which separated commercial banks from investment banks. The acquisitions of Merrill Lynch by Bank of America and of the bankrupt Lehman Brothers by Barclays and Nomura in 2008 would thus not have been possible prior to 1999. Another major US regulation was the Chandler Bill passed in 1938, which required a trustee to take over management of the ongoing business during corporate reconstructions due to bankruptcy. Until then, investment bankers had made good money on assisting managers during this kind of reconstruction (Morrison and Wilhelm, 2007:213).

Even if the regulation of the US security market had, and still has, worldwide implications, there are of course other national legislations, as well as truly international regulations. The most ambitious international legislative programme so far is the Bretton Woods agreement of 1944. This agreement between the major Western countries aimed to control international financial activity so as to prevent the financial disaster of the 1930s from being repeated. For the first time, the leading nations explicitly agreed on a set of rules for collectively managing international finance. The system of fixed but adjustable exchange rates lasted until the mid 1970s, but the two major international institutions, the International Monetary Found (IMF) and the World Bank, still exist today (Pryke, 2008).

The regulations introduced during the 1930s and after the Second World War were extensive. The depression convinced both Americans and Europeans that the world economy could not be left to its own devices (Strange, 1994). Many influential authorities viewed the Second World War as a consequence of the crash and the financial turmoil that followed. In the opening speech at the Bretton Woods meeting, the US Secretary of the Treasury addressed the representatives of 44 nations with:

> All of us have seen the great economic tragedy in our time. We saw the worldwide depression of the 1930s. We saw currency disorder develop and spread from land to land, destroying the basis for international trade and international investment and even international faith. In their wake, we saw unemployment and wretchedness – idle tools, wasted wealth. We saw their victims fall prey, in places, to demagogues and dictators. We saw bewilderment and bitterness become the breeders of fascism, and finally war.
>
> (Panic, 1995)

In the 1940s and 1950s, the regulations around investment banking made volume security brokering more interesting. The advisory role concerning mergers and acquisitions was still not very developed, while the underwriting of new issues was more regulated and relatively less profitable. The regulation of international financial activities also made the costs of transactions between national exchanges higher. Thus there were good reasons for developing the brokering side of investment banking. As in many other cases, less established firms initiated the change. New and more local stock brokerage houses were established around the world. The most successful of these new investment banks was Merrill Lynch, which also specialized in industries that had been relatively neglected by the established investment banks, such as retailing and moviemaking (Morrison and Wilhelm, 2007:219).

By the end of the 1970s, the major actors within international finance had learned how to redirect the international financial flows to escape legislation and international agreements. Offshore financial centres and 'tax havens', such as the Cayman Islands and Mauritius, allowed international finance to circumvent regulations. By the end of the 1970s, the conduct of the banks had led to the collapse of the Bretton Woods system. When nation after nation moved from fixed to floating exchange rates during the 1980s and 1990s, the international financial flows can be said to finally have been 'liberated' (Hirst and Thompson, 1999) or, less positively, dissociated from governmental political process and hence from accountability to the people (Patnaik, 1999). The deregulation radically increased the space within which financial actors, including investment banks, could conduct their business. These deregulations, combined with the other developments outlined below, help to explain the growth of investment banking over the past 20 years.

Rapidly increasing trading volumes

For centuries the issuing and trading in stocks revolved around personal reputation and trust. Up until the 1960s, the business models of brokerage houses and investment banks relied on personal networks and tacit knowledge and trust between experienced bankers and brokers and their clients. This limited their ability to handle a large number of clients. The business model was hard to scale up, even though there were market opportunities (Morrison and Wilhelm, 2007). Instead, traditional savings banks took care of the general public, while commercial banks catered to the capital needs of business firms through traditional loans. Especially in Europe the practice of taking loans instead of issuing new stock has been enduring.[2] During the 1970s and 1980s, this changed. Due to changes in tax regulations, the US pensions funds grew rapidly and became important securities investors. Business firms increasingly saw the possibility of attracting capital through stock issues instead of re-investing profits or taking loans. As we saw above, this was not a new practice. Corporations had issued new stock with the help of bankers since medieval Italy (Michie, 2006), and this practice started to be a more prominent feature of business life during the nineteenth century (Carosso, 1970; Basking and Miranti, 1997). But with the rapid growth of the pension funds during the 1980s, the securities markets grew much faster than before. Both primary market banking and secondary market brokering grew rapidly. This growth was also supported by the development of new information technology and by the emergence of modern financial theories.

The development of information technology

The pressure on the stock exchanges and their members to handle the increased trading volumes was high already in the 1960s. The volume of shares traded at NYSE hovered between 3 and 4.5 million shares per day during the first half of the twentieth century. In 1965, the average daily volume exceeded 6 million and by 1968 it was nearly 13 million (Morrison and Wilhelm, 2007:233). The administrative workload and the related costs became prohibitively high for the brokerage houses. The administrative overload escalated in what the New York Times described as a 'mass confusion' (23 December 1970:35). NYSE responded by shortening the trading day and closing down every Wednesday to allow members to process and backlog transactions. But these changes also hurt trading; the solution became the first wave of computerization in stock brokering and investment banking. When the computers became advanced and inexpensive enough to be used for back office administration of the exchanges and their members, they allowed the security markets to grow even faster. The major consequence of the introduction of modern information technology was the ability to handle effectively many more clients and much higher trading volumes. But this also had secondary consequences: it lowered the spreads of security prices and increased the need for capital to be able to invest in the new technologies (Wilhelm, 1999; Morrison and Wilhelm, 2007:224–225). This in turn led to concentration among the brokerage houses and investment banks; fewer and larger firms handled more and more money.

The development of the mini computer during the 1970s had just as much impact on investment banking. The mini computer and the computer spreadsheet moved to the trading desks, enabling real-time calculations. The mini computer could track positions and preferences of institutional investors, reducing the value of the networks and tacit knowledge of experienced bankers. The mini computer also allowed automated trading and furthered the development of markets for new types of derivative securities (Pryke, 2008). This second phase of computerization rendered the administration of trading cheaper and made back office staff more redundant. It also changed the very practice of banking, advising and trading, making it less dependent on the experienced bankers, brokers and traders, and more dependent on sophisticated computer software.

Modern financial theories

A third development that had major consequences for investment banking practices is the emergence of modern financial theories. Although portfolio management can be traced back to medieval Genoa, its impact on security market practices was starting to be seen in the 1970s with the gradual spread of the ideas presented by Markowitz (1952). The primary investment strategy of the funds of the institutional investors is to maximize their risk-return ratio compared with established indexes. With the development of normative portfolio models, this strategy could be quantified and optimized, and thus replace more tacit and network-based knowledge of various investment objects, risks and returns. What had previously been the personal know-how of experienced bankers and brokers was increasingly turned into objective scientific knowledge.

Another important development for investment banking practice was the diffusion of the Black–Scholes–Merton framework for valuing options (MacKenzie and Millo, 2003). This theory influenced the strategies used in existing security markets and promoted the development of more complex financial products to be traded. The Black–Scholes–Merton framework spread internationally, not only to members of different securities markets, but also to the world's business schools where bright students were educated in modern finance theories (Wilhelm, 1999; Morrison and Wilhelm, 2007:242–245). The large institutional investors; the increased volumes of trade; the new information technology and the new sophisticated 'basket'; 'combined' or 'structured' product securities markets; modern finance theory as well as the mass education of professional investment bankers at the world's most prestigious business schools – all contribute to constitute what we see today as the global investment banking and security markets industry.

New regulations and a contemporary organizational model

A new phase of regulative activity can be observed in the recent decade. These new regulative efforts are typically made on an international level and, in contrast to the Bretton Woods agreement, in collaboration between financial business organizations and governments. A major part of these new regulations consists of soft law (Mörth, 2004). The two regulative bodies which have had most influence on investment banking are the Bank for International Settlements (BIS) and the International Organization of Securities Commissions (IOSCO).

The BIS states as its mission to make international monetary and financial policy more predictable and transparent among its 57 member banks. The most important role of BIS for investment banking is as the administrative home for the Basel Committee on Banking Supervision. The Basel Committee was formed by the G-10 nations as an answer to messy and even fraudulent currency trading by German banks during the early 1970s involving an illegitimate use of the time lag between New York and Europe. BIS is best known for its international standards on capital adequacy, the Core Principles for Effective Banking Supervision and the Concordat on cross-border banking supervision. The most influential parts of the committee's regulative recommendations are the 1988 Basel Accord (also known as Basel I), the 2004 Basel Accord (Basel II) and the 2010 Basel Accord (Basel III). These accords purport to avoid major bank collapses by setting up rigorous risk and capital management requirements including rules on minimal capital reserves that banks need to hold to protect themselves against the risks to which they are exposed. The Basel Committee makes recommendations on bank supervision, diffuses industry advances in risk measurement and management, engages in research on financial stability issues, explores trends and innovations on securities markets, develops knowledge and regulations on how to monitor banks exposures from its trading activities, amongst other responsibilities. It also hosts coordination meetings with other international organizations with similar or complementary interests.[3]

The most influential regulatory body for investment banking is the IOSCO. The history of IOSCO is one of how large US exchanges, investment banks and trading houses became global role models during the latter part of the twentieth century. Originally created in 1974 by 11 security regulatory agencies from North and South America, IOSCO decided to become a global cooperative body in 1983. Since the mid 1980s, regulatory agencies from all over the world have joined the organization, and today its members regulate more than 95 per cent of the world's security markets. In 1986, IOSCO created its first permanent General Secretariat and during the 1990s and 2000s it has provided technical assistance to its members and adopted comprehensive securities regulation principles. Many exchanges still have different regulations, but they are converging. IOSCO develops principles not only for how authorities should supervise exchanges but also for how the internal processes of market participants, such as investment banks, should be managed. Everything from what constitutes prudent analysis, forms and timing of information, to the organization of so-called Chinese walls, is subject to investigations, recommendations and evaluations from IOSCO. For instance, their code of conduct suggests that Chinese walls should exist not only between corporate banking and securities trading but also between both of these businesses and the risk and compliance management function.[4]

Even if the US influence on investment banking has been significant for many years, the development of the European Union has to some extent altered this. In many areas, the EU directives are stricter and more influential than those of IOSCO. Still, the regulatory frameworks are far from harmonized across Europe, and many nations implement the directives with a certain amount of modification (Stichele, 2008). Thus, banks with activities on many exchanges across many countries may have to follow quite different and sometimes conflicting regulations and directives. As previously, these regulatory efforts can be seen as responses to major financial scandals, whether caused by individual banks (e.g. Bank Herstatt, Barings Bank, Goldman Sachs), by corporate management (e.g. Enron and Arthur Andersen, MCI WorldCom) or by a number of actors in society, as in the recent sub-prime mortgage crisis. These and other setbacks have once again strengthened the regulatory efforts of various supervisory authorities, national legislative bodies, and European, American and international soft and hard regulators.

The death of the investment bank?

The standalone investment banks have become fewer and fewer due to increased concentration and the relaxation of regulations keeping commercial banks from trading on both primary and secondary security markets. Today all the major US-based investment banks have been incorporated by less specialized banks, and investment banking is commonly executed within large financial holding companies or universal banks. Since this has been the case for many decades in many European countries, one could interpret this development as the global diffusion of a European bank model. This is also supported by the fact that many major European (and some Asian) commercial and universal banks today own major American investment banks.

If we look at less global investment banking activities, we still find a number of standalone investment banks, even if they are getting fewer. Starting in the 1990s, these banks have also complemented their traditional corporate banking and trading businesses with a fast growing fund and asset management business. The 'pure' investment bank is not dead, but is getting more difficult to distinguish from other types of financial organizations. Irrespective of whether the pure standalone investment bank is dying or not, investment *banking* practice is expanding, in terms of both volume and the number of people involved. Investment banking – issuing and marketing securities, introducing new securities in the form of complex 'structured products', engaging in corporate restructuring and other advisory activities – is bigger business today than ever before.

Along with the general expansion of the financial markets, share trading on the world's stock exchanges has undergone considerable growth and turbulence during recent decades.[5] Whereas total share trading in the world saw an exceptional peak in 2001–2002, this positive development has continued in the Nordic region (the setting for our empirical study), at least in terms of the number of shares traded (see Figure 2.2). One outcome of this is clear: the market for equity-related investment banking services has increased enormously.

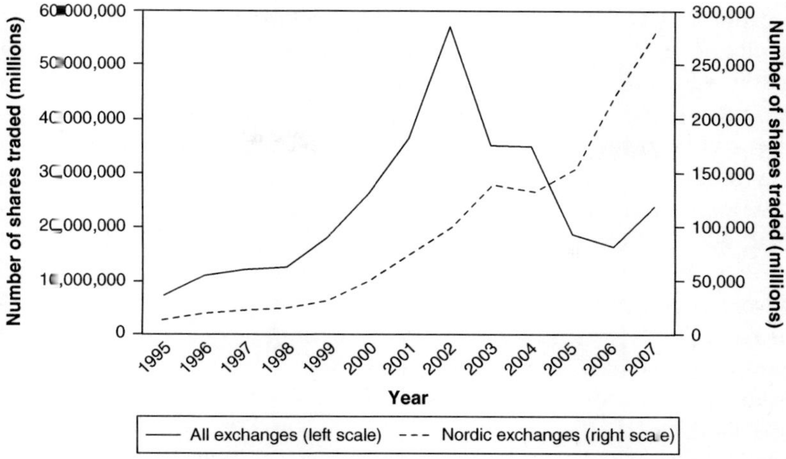

Figure 2.2 Total number of shares traded on the world's stock markets, and on Nordic stock markets, 1995–2007
Source: WFE 2009a.

Towards investigating contemporary investment banking

The history of investment banking suggests that its development is intimately connected to the development of securities markets. The organizational and institutional innovations, the new information technologies, the theoretical developments as well as the waxing and waning of regulatory efforts have contributed to turn a once truly innovative way of financing business ventures – the joint-stock company – into a specific and carefully regulated organizational form, in which ownership rights can be traded on increasingly global securities markets. This process shaped and was shaped by intermediaries in the form of bankers engaging with primary securities markets, and brokers and traders engaging with secondary securities markets.

Legislation with roots in the 1929 crash separated the commercial banks from the investment banks in the United States, and corporate banking activities from securities trading through the creation of Chinese walls. When the post-war global financial system collapsed in the 1970s, financial capital flows were once again liberated, this time at a much larger scale and with technologies making transfers much faster and less expensive than before. This enabled the investment banks to grow in size and make more money than ever. With the repeal of the Glass-Steagall Act in 1999, there were no real obstacles left to prevent the creation of large financial holding companies offering a complete range of financial activities at a global level. The world's major commercial banks waited for just the right moment to step in.

Growing trading volumes on securities markets and new information technologies put pressures on investment banking to reduce costs on increasingly standardized products by investing in technological systems to simplify trading. Economies of scale became more important, relative to the experience and personal networks of the individual bankers. But, coupled with modern financial theories, the technological developments also enabled innovations in the form of more advanced products, which at least temporarily could improve margins. Over recent decades there has been a strong tendency in investment banking to innovate by introducing new types of financial products to maintain profitability.

Even if there are many types of securities involved in investment banking today, the share stands out as the most fundamental one. The move from primarily issuing and trading governmental debt instruments, towards issuing and trading shares of private joint-stock corporations, took place quite some time ago. The more recent development and exploitation of increasingly complex financial instruments, such as derivatives and structured products, are typically linked directly or indirectly to shares of joint-stock corporations. Also, the share is the fundamental link between the issuing practices of corporate banking and the trading practices of brokers, traders and analysts on secondary markets. Thus if one were to pick one product, one object to follow, to be used as a way into the practical worlds of investment banking experts, the share stands out as the primary choice.

The history of the financial industry is largely a story of rapid and turbulent growth, big business with major societal influence, and our major interest here: a story of increased specialization, organization and professionalization. The growing division of labour can be most clearly seen in the so-called securities line of business: trading on the secondary securities markets. Gradually, the traditional stock brokering has been split into trading and brokering (sales). In addition, with an increasing share of trading being executed by computers rather than experienced traders, analysts have become the new stars of investment banking in the 1990s, experts who sought to calculate potential hidden values in shares as investment objects rather than trade such shares. Today, the machinery of finance and the practices of investment banking involve a large and increasing number of experts, complex technological systems, national and international regulatory bodies, and financial flows linking every corner of our world. Recent years show that regulatory efforts are not a thing of the past, however. Repeated scandals and setbacks have prompted national and international legislators, as well as the industry itself, to initiate new rules, codes of conduct and laws. This has given birth to yet another occupational group within investment banking: the risk and compliance manager function, or 'middle office'.

The history of investment banking explicated above lends support to our contention that, by following the share into and through the practices of the various expert groups engaged in investment banking, we could improve our understanding of investment banking, and maybe also of the financial system. We start this journey in Chapter 3, by visiting the first of the expert groups in investment banking: the traders.

3
Traders Activating the Stock Markets

> To be a good trader you have to be on fire about the market, to really enjoy trading. It's multidimensional, you need to understand the psychology, and you need to be there when something happens. You need a feeling for the market – it is somehow not possible to explain.
>
> (Head of Trader Group)

Many of the financial experts interviewed for this study have brought up the complex personality needed to be a successful trader. In the literature, traders have been compared to test pilots in the US Air Force, which implies that both categories either 'have it' or not; that they need to be made out of 'the right stuff' (Bruegger, 1999). For traders, the central abilities seem to be to comprehend the rapid shifts occurring in the various markets with which they engage and to have the nerves to function under pressure. Due to their close and frequent involvement in transactions on specific financial markets, traders are seen as operating at the centre of the market mechanism (Abolafia, 1996). Their role has been further accentuated by the rapid growth in both the number of financial transactions executed and the value of the securities transacted. Even though there is a wide range of securities on sale in contemporary financial markets, the stock markets remain central to the financial industry. Figure 3.1 illustrates the value of shares traded annually on the global stock markets since 1995. The periods of rapid growth leading up to the dot-com crash in 2000 and to the global financial crises in 2008 can be clearly seen.

Trading is not the only expert activity involved in the buying and selling of shares. In the business line of securities, traders work side by side with brokers and analysts. These two expert groups offer investment

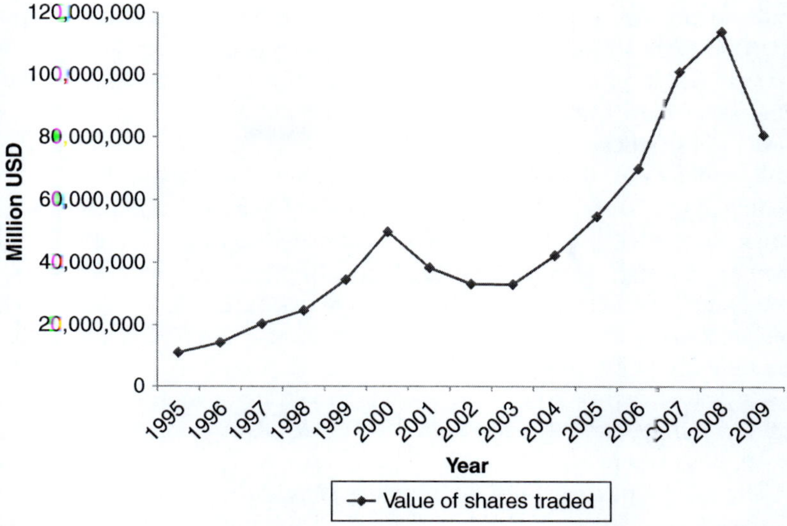

Figure 3.1 Total value of shares traded on the world's stock markets, 1995–2009 (based on statistics from the World Federation of Exchanges)

advice to clients, in this way seeking to generate orders to buy or sell securities, and hence they generate work for traders. But in this chapter we focus on trading practices alone, seeking answers to questions such as: What activities do traders perform? How are traders involved in the 'market mechanism'? What does this involvement imply for their enactment of stock markets?

The work of trading

Traders are the people who actually transmit orders and conduct transactions on the secondary securities markets. They broadly perform three types of activities: cash trading, market making and proprietary trading. *Cash trading* is the least complex of these activities, as it simply involves executing orders that the brokers have generated (sales). The brokers are the ones who work directly with the clients; however, when a client wishes to conduct a transaction, the broker will need a price for the specific security in question – which might be a share, a bond or a derivative. (For the sake of simplicity, we will focus on shares throughout the chapter.) Since share prices vary over the course of the day, a trader has to set the momentary price at which this customer is offered to buy or sell. For smaller deals, the price can be 'taken out of the markets', meaning that there already is a corresponding offer to buy or sell that volume of shares at a certain price in the market. If the client accepts the price, the trader places the order, which is then matched to a corresponding order at the stock exchange.

In other cases, the customer order may be so large that it cannot be matched to corresponding orders at the stock exchange. Then the trader must set a price at which he or she is prepared to buy the shares, temporarily 'storing' them in the bank and then selling them off during the course of the trading day. This type of pricing activity is also called *market making*. It is regularly performed in most markets, but becomes particularly important in markets that are less liquid. For securities seldom traded, it becomes more difficult to assess a market value. But traders are generally trusted to 'know' what a reasonable price is also in markets where trade happens to be scarce.

The third type of activity performed is *proprietary trading*. This activity is the most complex of the three, and also the most profitable. Proprietary trading means that traders are allowed to exploit their knowledge and abilities in the markets by trading 'for the house', that is, by buying and selling securities on behalf of the firm in which they work. By continuously analysing prices of securities and flows between various markets, these traders are expected to conduct transactions with the aim to 'beat the market' consistently. In this type of trading, traders are allowed to hold positions also overnight, which is not permitted in cash trading. This allows the prop traders the possibility of acting strategically to a certain extent. Proprietary trading grew rapidly during the 1990s and today involves substantial amounts of money. At times, it has added considerable revenues to the business line of securities. However, this type of trading also involves considerable risks, as became evident in connection with the financial crisis of 2008, when Lehman Brothers and other prestigious Wall Street investment banks ended up in acute trouble which was directly due to their propriety trading activities (Gandel, 2010).

While proprietary trading is all about generating revenue for the firm, cash trading and market making are often presented as ways of 'lubricating the financial machinery'. Cash trading is primarily about mediating customer orders, and, even though this operation does involve some risk, the risk is much lower than in taking positions for the bank itself. The three types of trading activity often overlap, so that one trader performs more than one type of trading (Fenton-O'Creevy et al., 2004). Since Scandinavia is a medium-sized market, traders working there typically perform at least two of these activities.[1]

To summarize, the work of traders includes (1) pricing securities in the markets; (2) conducting transactions on behalf of customers; and (3) speculating on behalf of the traders' own firm. Trading is in many respects the core of the securities business, since it is directly related to revenues. Trading revenues include (1) fees for completing customer transactions; (2) profits from cash trading – that is, 'buying the risk' from customers successfully and turning it into profitable transactions during the trading day; and (3) making profit from proprietary trading. This suggests that, even though the services of analysts and brokers are important, the profitability of the securities business is based on trading (but see forthcoming chapters for other views on what it is that generates profit in securities).

Exotic Expertise

The characters involved in trading and their gambling-like work have lent traders an exotic image, mirrored in renowned movies and novels.[2] This is further emphasized by stories about traders who have caused major disruptions for their employers – such as the story of how Nick Leeson's proprietary trading in Singapore took down Barings Bank in 1995.[3] As we noted in Chapter 1, traders' close involvement with markets has also fascinated many scholars (Abolafia, 1996; Bruegger, 1999; Willman et al., 2001; Knorr Cetina and Bruegger, 2002b; Beunza and Stark, 2005; Zaloom, 2006). Themes that have been addressed include how traders contribute to the enactment of 'the global economy' (Knorr Cetina and Bruegger, 2000; Hasselström, 2003; Knorr Cetina, 2005), how they construct knowledge about financial markets (Hasselström, 2003), and how digitization of these markets has changed the culture of trading (Zaloom, 2006). Much attention is devoted to examining how the trading activity – for instance the pricing and qualifying of shares, or their actual buying and selling – takes place in close proximity to, and even in, markets.

The setting for trading activities has been described as an informational universe (Knorr Cetina, 2005), a site where materiality is of less concern than information. In this setting, changes are said to be caused primarily by new information, and traders suggest that 'everything' can influence the markets. Hence everything, from world politics to local events, might have consequences for how the markets evolve. Since any information might affect the market, at least temporarily, irrespective of its correspondence to external events, the imagery of an informational universe underscores the fact that, from a trader's point of view, financial markets are continuously being reshaped. Markets are in constant flux; their lack of completeness, or of real being, turns them into moving images. These markets are inherently temporal, characterized by flows rather than by products and geographies; they materialize through the *scopic systems* that depict them (Knorr Cetina, 2006).

Comprehending an information universe

> The financial market is like a creature. So many things are involved in how it moves, you cannot judge it only by analysis, you need a feeling for it. The moves depend on so many events and various flows. The market is just like a wild animal.
>
> (Trader)

A trading room is dominated by information screens mounted on the walls around the room and a long trading desk offering working space for traders. Supplementing the large wall-mounted screens, all traders have in front of them a number of screens offering their personal choices of information sites. At each seat there are at least three phones for external communication, one or two often being headphones. The desks are positioned towards each other, so that everyone can talk to the people on the other side while standing up – a common working position. The screens on the walls offer prices of raw materials, indexes of various shares and markets, currency prices at any given moment and news from Bloomberg and Reuters. As a complement, BBC news shows the latest in world politics from a television set placed in a corner close to the ceiling.

To provide a more detailed description of trading work, we will follow a trader at one of Sweden's largest investment banks. Marcus, as we call him, is an experienced trader. After studying psychology, philosophy and sociology at university, he started at one of the Swedish banks and traded there for some years. He has also worked at two large American investment banks in London for a couple of years, before returning to Sweden. During all of these years he has been trading telecom shares. At present Marcus performs cash trading, market making, as well as proprietary trading. Marcus describes his work as a continuous search for information:

> A normal day starts by me reading the papers and listening to the news. I update myself on what has happened in the world during the night in politics and in the market. Then, when I arrive at work this updating actually continues throughout the day.
>
> (Marcus, Trader)

Marcus uses the term 'scanning' when describing his information search, and he indicates that this scanning covers a wide variety of sources. After reading the papers and listening to the morning news, Marcus focuses on indexes. During his working life he has developed certain criteria – in his case, indexes that he checks every morning. Marcus describes himself as being 'graphics oriented', and he explains that he focuses especially on different graphs describing indexes and shares. Other traders can be 'oriented' to other sources. When these indexes reach certain levels, or when the graphs take on certain shapes, Marcus interprets these facts as specific signals. Depending on how these signals combine, they make him focus on certain issues, so that his morning analysis becomes a basis for his trading activity during the day.

Being located at the trading desk, Marcus also uses the 'buzz' among the other traders when he assesses possible future movements on 'his' markets. In the trading room, rumours indicating possible changes are discussed and shared throughout the day. Marcus has also developed personal relationships with contacts 'in the market' – other traders, whose judgements he appreciates. So, by keeping in touch with these people over the phone, he includes traders from other banks in his web of communication. In addition, he also suggests that the brokers can be a useful source of input when he tries to comprehend the markets. They add information concerning the interests of the investors and how they might react to the latest news, thus signalling possible changes in the markets.

Using these various sources of information, Marcus tries to visualize the markets and their movements throughout his working day, asking questions such as: What are the prices, and how have they changed lately? Are there big interests on the buy or the sell side? How will this or that piece of news affect the market? How will changes in the derivative market influence the cash market? The answers to these questions provide guidance on when and how to trade.

Experimental strategies

The work of trading is described as individualistic. Traders are responsible for their own accounts, and some present their work as entrepreneurial. They receive instructions concerning what trading activities to perform (cash, prop and/or market making) and what securities they are responsible for; but deciding how to relate to 'their' markets and what strategies to use when trading is typically left to the traders themselves. The promotion of individual strategies lets traders use their differing talents in various ways and supports innovative approaches in the markets. This heterogeneity is further evidenced in the variegated educational background of traders: some have no higher education at all, while others can hold, say, a PhD in physics. Differences aside, most traders suggest that the search for patterns in the flow of information is at the heart of their work. This search for opportunities in the markets raises questions about how to recognize patterns and spot opportunities before others do. As argued by Beunza and Stark (2005), the trading desk becomes a place that allows traders to experiment with ideas and theories directly in the markets:

> You can't learn this from books. You can learn from theory how to value an option, how to value a share, but that does not necessarily need to be true. There are no rules in this world; there is no absolute truth.
>
> (Trader)

To comprehend the market fully, though, there is a need to calculate how other traders and important players in the market will act and react. The 'psychology' of the market is often used to explain why actual market developments differ from theoretically derived predictions. Willman et al. (2001) suggest that traders use two strategies when relating to markets. First, they use financial theories of markets for understanding 'how the world works'. These theories offer a perspective for understanding markets and the various instruments traded, and for communicating in the financial language. Second, and in contrast with these theories, the traders also use their everyday practical experience of 'how to work the (financial) world'. Here, an intuition and a flair for the market are required, usually accompanied by mathematical reasoning. To understand the markets, you need to understand how other traders will act. And traders do not necessarily act like the rational economic man of financial theories:

> There are a lot of feelings involved in trading; you try to be cool and so on. But if you have a good day [...] 90 per cent of the people I've worked with get hubris. This hubris gets to your head, and then you break yourself – that is classic. You can be a millionaire in the morning and then poor again in the afternoon.
>
> (Trader)

Since traders are allowed to develop their own strategies in trading, Beunza and Stark (2005) compare the trading floor to a laboratory, suggesting that the traders use the trading room to explore core problems of value, equivalence and calculation. It is as if the traders were conducting experiments throughout their working days, deploying an array of instruments to test the markets. Let us take a closer look at how a proprietary trader integrated information from various sources into a speculation strategy, and how this affected trading one late afternoon when the exchange was about to close.

Closing time – Trading time

> I closed more than 100 deals in the final seconds of that trading day. All of them were part of a long-term strategy where I had successively built up a position to make money on an expected downturn on the stock market during 2007. The reason why I closed these deals at the end of the trading day is that the option market closes at 17.20 and I counted on the stock market turning down during the final minutes of trading.
>
> If you look at the statistics from the stock exchange, you can see two things: First that the volumes are the greatest towards the end of the trading day; everyone wants to trade towards the end of the day. It's like when they play the final song at a dance. Second, the graphics from Reuters show that the index was almost at its highest when the options market closed, 1153, but that it collapsed like a house of cards in the remaining ten minutes, closing at almost its lowest that day, 1147.5. This is an extraordinary movement for a trader. I think I even cried out: Are you allowed to do this? If I bought options at 17.20 or just before that because I thought this movement would occur, then that is precisely what my job as a trader is about; to identify trading opportunities; to buy as cheaply as possible and sell as dearly as possible. During the remaining ten minutes of trading I bought massive amounts of shares in the 30 largest corporations on the stock exchange, happy that the market was falling and that I could buy cheaply. I speculated in a downturn, and when it happened I bought. If I hadn't, the market would have fallen even further.
>
> The reason why I thought the stock exchange would drop during the final minutes of trading had to do with a phone call I received a few hours before. I was offered to buy futures for €9 million from a seller via the brokerage firm Etrade. This can be seen from the compilation of my transactions during that trading day: the transaction at 15.00 that says 'ETR'. I knew Etrade was dealing exclusively with

> large institutional clients. When they offered to sell a block in this way, it was neither the first nor the only sale that this client wanted to make during the day. It was a way for them to start softly by selling one block and get a good start. Of course, I couldn't know this for sure, but I had good reasons to believe that the customer had more to sell. I had a hunch about who was behind the sale and knew that it was a customer that would sell until closing time and push the course down as far as possible to make their decision to sell look as good as possible. We also have computerized sales programs programmed to sell shares in large corporations and purchase shares in small companies, which I was involved in. This also gave me good reasons to believe that the stock market would fall.[4]

The strategies used by proprietary traders can be both short term and long term (which is not to be confused with being long term from the perspective of an analyst or an investor). Various sources of information, some of them only hunches, build up the image of where the market is going. When combined with the strategy that the trader has developed, this is turned into direct trading activity. But, as this trader hints towards the end of the story, trading is no longer exclusively performed by traders. Today, traders face severe competition from computers equipped with various trading algorithms.

Computer trading

Within the contemporary financial industry there is considerable amount of computerized trading. This is often called 'high-frequency trading' (HFT) and involves computers executing trades based on specific parameters. The computers are programmed to trade when certain index or price levels are reached. Using specific algorithms for trading, the computers take advantage of small price differences between markets. By trading large volumes of securities, firms can generate considerable profits from small prices differences, since the computers can keep trading as long as there are inequalities between the markets (which may be a matter of fractions of seconds). Some argue that computer trading makes the financial markets more efficient by balancing differences between them. One commonly recognized effect is the reduction in trade sizes. The volume of trading conducted by computers is hard to measure. Some sources estimate that computers perform about 50 per cent of the trading in Europe, and even more in American markets (Grant, 2010). This figure is expected to rise in the near future. One reason for this expectation is that computer trading can reduce risks compared with human trading, since profits are related to volumes traded rather than to few but large deals.

Information about computer trading is rare in our interviews. One trader describes it as being 'a bit hush-hush in the business'. Even though the presence of computer trading is common knowledge, there are few discussions about it in the industry. Larger banks and funds use both human and computer trading, as described by the trader above. There are also some firms working exclusively with computer trading. Despite the relative silence on the matter within the industry, the media has shown considerable interest in computer trading. Articles in morning newspapers try to explain HTF and how this form of trading has evolved into such a profitable strategy. But firms focusing solely on computer trading often prefer to be anonymous and discreet, since they have no interest in gaining clients. Their trading activity is simply not dependent on customers in the same way as a regular investment bank is. The secrecy around computer trading makes it hard to evaluate it, both in terms of market shares and in terms of possible consequences.

The digitization of the financial industry has changed conditions in many ways, one being the increased competition from computers. The trading floor is a story from the past for most traders, since trading nowadays is conducted primarily in cyberspace, markets being embodied on screens. This has subtly changed 'life in the markets', and the culture of speculation has transformed to adjust to digitization (see Zaloom, 2006). Technology has, however, also affected the objects exchanged in the financial markets. A number of more complex financial instruments have been introduced during the last decades, not least as a consequence of financial crises, when risk exposure created considerable losses. As a consequence, the products become refined, but also harder to analyse for those involved in marketing them. Due to the complexity of the products and their ability to hedge future scenarios in the markets, it has been suggested that some of these derivative instruments affect our understanding of time and space (Pryke and Allen, 2000).

Information squeezed into a price

One key task for traders is the qualifying of shares. The qualification process involves stabilizing the qualities ascribed to a particular share, which makes it possible to set a price for it and thereby to offer it for exchange. In financial markets, the pricing of an exchange object comes across as the result of some 'magic formula' and is expected to represent all the relevant information about an asset (Fenton-O'Creevy et al., 2004). As new information appears continuously, prices will vary also in the short-time perspective. Thus financial news and trading firms provide figures on how specific shares vary in price during the day.

Returning to the trader Marcus, he explains that a share has no true value. On the other hand, he says that shares always have a price 'in the market'. However, when a transaction involves a substantial volume of shares, the pricing will be more complicated, since risk calculations will enter into the price. As an example, Marcus uses the telecom company T and invents a case where the current ask price is 6.05 (the price at which you can buy the share), and the bid price is 6 (the price at which you can sell the share). If a hypothetical client contacts Marcus and wants to sell 40 million shares in T, Marcus cannot quote the current bid price. Rather, he will have to assess what consequences such a large transaction will have on the market. Is the context nervous? Is there liquidity in a transaction as large as this one? As a conclusion, Marcus might offer the price of 3, instead of 6. If the customer wants to go ahead with the transaction, Marcus becomes responsible for a large position, not knowing at what price he can actually sell these shares. Another trader suggests a similar type of reasoning:

> Ok, let's say that H&M has presented a report today, and quite a few sellers have contacted us. The German Index, the London Exchange is on their way down, and we already have a big seller of H&M since the report was not received very well. So, if a customer wants to sell a large amount of shares, I will value all these aspects and come to the conclusion that this does not feel very good. Everything points downwards. Then my price will be relatively low, or I will 'price me out' as we say. If he sells at this low price, I will try to work on these shares and work the risk out in the market. And hopefully earn some money on it.
>
> (Trader)

Marcus underlines that one critical issue in pricing is to assess the direction of 'the flow' (the psychology of traders). There is a herding instinct in the market, and therefore indicated trends often accelerate. The reasons behind changes in the flow are far from logical all the time, so an unexpected transaction can create a chain reaction leading to volatility without any sensible explanation:

> If the price of oil increases, just as an example, then the stock market might respond to this and investors think 'well maybe we ought to

> sell some'. It is not really that often that the stock market is rational. It's a bit like the chicken and the egg – what comes first?
>
> (Marcus, Trader)

Since traders' actions will affect the market, part of the game in trading is to scrutinize other traders' activities. Zaloom (2006) suggests that traders are constantly 'watching and being watched'. Movements in the markets affect the possibility of profiting from a position, and consequently all the moves need to be recognized. But, even though all the traders watch one another, some are more interesting to follow than others. Successful traders are given most attention. To some extent this is due to the fact that they are the most challenging competitors. But if everyone follows them, they are also the most beneficial ones to follow, since their activities will be the ones that others react to, and hence the ones that initiate market movements. Therefore there is no need for external information to set off market movements; by engaging in speculative trading, traders are perfectly capable of setting off their own market movements.

In these flow markets, the most interesting pieces of information are the ones concerning the future. What actually turns out to become the future, however, is often less interesting:

> It is a lot about expectations, what people expect will happen. We say that the market 'prices in' what is going to happen. If you expect an economic recovery in, say, about a year, then the market is already ahead when calculating risks [...] But what is going to happen is never given, even if you have all the parameters.
>
> (Trader)

Risky business

Risk is a concern when one is pricing shares, but also when one is trading. While proprietary trading involves the largest risks (using the bank's resources to speculate), cash trading also involves risks, for example when securities are 'stored' in the firm. Traders' relation to risk varies, as do their strategies for coping with it (Fenton-O'Creevy et al., 2004). Some are hesitant about becoming involved in risky positions and activities. Others aspire for the most prestigious and risky trades, striving to take proprietary trading responsibilities. The ability to handle risk is also a key characteristic in evaluating traders, according to a head of securities. Traders will experience both significant profits and significant losses in markets, and their ability to manage these shifts is regarded as crucial for their success as traders. One kind of behaviour considered directly dangerous is to 'double out' in times of loss – that is, to double your risk in order to regain the losses made. When this behaviour is observed, the head of trading will typically discuss the matter directly with the trader, and if he/she does not change, the trader is likely to be fired. However, since trading is a risky business, traders need to be daring:

> They need to be brave enough to do the transaction before everybody else grasps the possibility. They need a go, a self esteem, and still let the market make them humble.
>
> (Head of Security)

The risks involved in trading are a concern not only for traders and for the securities business, but also for investment banking at large. Since investment banking practices are intimately connected to risks – even try to benefit from 'buying' risks – there are overall risk concerns, as well as specific concerns about individual trades. The business lines of asset management and private banking (see Chapter 8) also include risks that have to be monitored and adjusted. However, trading practices (particularly of the speculative kind) are the ones that are most exposed to market volatility. The value of trading positions can vary considerably even during one day (as the trader quoted above put it: 'you can be a millionaire in the morning and then poor again in the afternoon'), as will the risk in these positions. So risk controllers are concerned with trying to estimate the risk and value of a position of shares whose price changes repeatedly during a day. The difficulties surrounding the estimation and control of risks becomes clear when risk controllers wish to limit trading to certain risk levels (see Chapter 8). However, these efforts to control risks interfere with the traders' ability to play the market and are typically perceived as disturbing. Irrespective of the accuracy or inaccuracy of the results of risk analyses, their practical consequences for trading appear to be a central stumbling block – to which we will return in Chapter 8 (see also Millo and MacKenzie, 2009). Here we will move from the issue of risk assessment to the situation in which traders actually assume risks – when they enter into the stock markets.

Traders engaging in markets

Traders typically enact stock markets by (1) qualifying shares and quoting momentary prices and (2) conducting transactions. Knorr Cetina

(2005) notes that the material infrastructure of contemporary financial markets includes electronic networks, satellite connections between banks across continents, as well as trading floors. The transfer of the markets onto screens means that traders are now able simultaneously to position themselves inside the markets, in the sense of becoming players in their overlapping networks, and to relate to the markets on screen as an exteriorized 'other'. Thus the work of trading is at the same time performative and reflexive. In addition, these technologies have changed financial markets from their being communities of space (like trading floors) to their becoming communities of time.

But even though global connections are of vital importance, the local trading desk is still an important site for information and innovation. Being close to colleagues means having informed co-workers to test ideas on, as well as direct access to information about various markets and market activities. The intensity around the trading desk is often underscored when one describes the environment in a trading room. The everyday work of traders is about being a winner in the market, which sometimes makes the trading desks very temperamental sites. In their work, traders display a mixture of aggressiveness and control, and they present outbursts of anger as 'part of the working culture'. In this frequently tense environment, timing becomes crucial. A trader's success in the market depends on having the nerve to trade at the right moment. As a result, one of the most striking aspects of trading is its relation to time. One broker sitting next to the traders described them in the following way:

> They have to be like tennis players, every second means a new business decision. If you have lost a ball, you have to concentrate on the next one. These people *eat* in front of their computers; they hardly have time to go to the bathroom.
>
> (Broker)

In ethnographic studies of trader culture, a common ingredient is its abusive and often sexual language (Bruegger, 1999; Hasselström, 2004; Zaloom, 2006). Irritated outbursts are common and expected. When deals go wrong, expressions like 'I got raped' or 'killed' are common. In trying to monitor some of this energy, a head trader underscored the importance of having conflicts out in the open and of trying to address issues as they occur. Since the competition is severe, conflicts are recurrent. Bringing them out becomes a way of resolving tensions around the desk – which is regarded as important, since the traders perform better when they are able to use information from one another. Being dependent on the 'buzz' in the trading room means that longer conflicts are not wanted. To support the team spirit and an open dialogue, traders often socialize after work, in restaurants and pubs. It is suggested that this is a way of handling emotions between traders and of stabilizing the group (Zaloom, 2006):

> We spend a lot of time together, see each other socially after work. We go out eating, play golf and so on – and of course without our girlfriends. It is important to socialize, it makes it easier to solve things if conflicts turn up. It is crucial that the group works well together. I have to watch out for signs of 'core meltdowns'.
>
> (Head, Trader Group)

In this environment marked by temperament, information flows, noise and competition, traders are still expected to trade with discipline and control. The market will sometimes be stormy and unpredictable and at other times boringly calm. During periods when next to nothing happens in the market, the traders still need to focus on the screens and potential opportunities. These periods are described as irritating and annoying by many traders. In a nervous and action-oriented context, tranquillity can be quite frustrating.

Above, Marcus suggested that the 'buzz' around the trading desk was an important source of information. In fact, this kind of input is not limited to the trading desk, and Marcus claims to speak regularly with other traders whose 'judgement he appreciates'. Knorr Cetina and Bruegger (2002a) emphasize that traders perform markets through conversations, since sequences of utterances do not only convey information but also accomplish economic actions. The information contained in prices, for example, not only helps traders to make decisions but also stimulates deals. In addition to this, the information, knowledge and judgements conveyed in conversations with others also become commercial entities of sorts. While trading involves traders in the exchange of goods for money, their communication with other traders involves them in a sort of reciprocal gift exchange. Traders can offer information to others without requesting immediate payback, but they rarely give out the same information to everyone. While the 'buzz' may extend beyond the trading room, market information is still differentiated.

There are several reasons for traders to search for profitable strategies in the trading room. First, their individual compensation is divided into a fixed salary and a flexible bonus, which depends on their trading results. Successful trading will thus significantly affect the financial situation of the individual trader. Second, the profits made around the trading desk affect the overall bonus within the firm. All experts working in securities are compensated via bonuses calculated on the yearly return from this business line. These annual bonuses vary greatly over time but, as an indication of their overall import, one of the investment banks in our study paid 10 per cent more in bonuses than in fixed salaries over the ten-year period 2000–2009 (see Chapter 8). Third, since the trading desk often generates an important share of the revenues, it contributes significantly to the overall bonus paid. Thus successful trading will also give traders personal status within the firm.

The share identities constructed by traders

Having described the work of traders, it is time to focus our attention on how traders construct share identities as part of their work. As we argued in Chapter 1, various forms of expertise contribute in the enactment of markets, not least by qualifying goods – that is, by ascribing to products specific characteristics, which allow them to be exchanged in markets (Callon et al., 2002). In the stock markets, the goods in question are shares. Even though all the experts in investment banking work with shares, they use different dimensions to qualify them (Winroth et al., 2010). Still, the experts are able to communicate and interact with one another in tasks that concern shares, which suggests that the shares may work as boundary objects that travel between the different expert communities. The adaptability of the shares may then buffer tensions between expert practices. In this chapter we have described the work of traders, but what do the practices in which they engage reveal concerning their construction of share identities? To answer this question, we will now explore systematically the four dimensions proposed for characterizing the construction of share identities: *constitutive associations, representations, potential uses* and *temporal framings*.

Shares as exchange objects

Stories about 'the invisible hand' of the market or about prices being given 'in the market' represent considerable simplifications of stock market practices. For shares to be turned into goods that can be exchanged on the stock markets, they need to be qualified in specific settings, their characteristics and price determined, at least momentarily. The qualification of goods in general can involve several types of actors; but, in settings characterized by complexity, uncertainty and repeated re-qualifications of the object, experts often assume an important role (Callon et al., 2002). This is very explicit in the case of stock market trading, where traders are exclusively relied upon to qualify shares. As a result of their relatively narrow concern with shares as exchange objects, the re-qualification of shares becomes highly intertwined with the attribution of prices in the market.

Most significantly, traders construct shares as exchange objects. In their world, shares do not *represent* anything in themselves, and traders ascribe them little or no internal content. There are very few indications to suggest that traders systematically differentiate shares from one another. Instead, they engage in general discussions about shares as commodities: objects whose sole purpose is to be exchanged and which lack internal attributes that deserve to be acknowledged. Shares become mass products with non-interesting substance. Instead, the re-qualification process focuses on external forces that are likely to affect the share. Traders seek information that will allow them to predict future developments in the markets, so that they can engage in profitable trade.

Constitutive associations and the qualifying process

What specific entities and referents do traders use when they form share identities? Our account suggests that they use numerous and widely varying constitutive associations to construct share identities. Potentially, 'everything' affects (the price of) the share. Sources as varied as international political events, current supplies of raw materials, interest rates, the latest quarterly reports, statements made by important financial institutions, macro-level indicators and 'expectations about market developments' can influence their re-qualifications. All of this information is thought of as being represented in the momentary *price* of the share, which is also the most important characteristic of the share by far. A second important characteristic of the share is its *liquidity*, in other words how much of it you can buy or sell at any moment in time. This is important primarily because it affects directly the stability of the price and is assessed by looking at the level of trading activity. Taken together, these characteristics mean that traders construct shares from the outside rather than from the inside. Forces external to the share determine both its price and its liquidity, at least in the short run (which is the only run relevant to a trader).

One other important point of reference contributing to the trader's construction of share identity is market development. For traders, this means that the 'psychology of traders' becomes important. Rapid changes in prices are often caused by traders trying to take advantage of price movements. Thus traders will try not only to assess objectively how a piece of information is likely to influence the price of a particular share they are trading in but also to second-guess how other traders will respond to this information. This further accentuates the unpredictable and fluid character of the stock markets. Can traders turn this unpredictability into an advantage in their use of shares?

Using shares

Traders *use* shares as a commodity that can be exchanged and for speculation purposes. Even though the exchange of shares seems to be an uncomplicated use of the object, the practices related to it present various degrees of complexity. When traders exchange shares on behalf of investors, this primarily means pushing a button. The trading system takes care of the rest. At times, if the share in question is less liquid, the trader also needs to quote a price. When deals involve larger volumes of shares, the trader may need to buy the shares, temporarily 'store' them and subsequently sell them in the market. These transactions demand assuming a certain amount of risk, for which the customer also has to pay (by being offered a lower price). Even though this form of transaction requires more judgement, and hopefully a return of the risk taken, it is still primarily a service for clients.

But traders also use shares to speculate. The basic rationale behind proprietary trading is to generate profit by speculating in price changes. Instead of a transaction service, the trading desk becomes a casino where you can win or lose. The exchange object is turned into an object for speculation. While shares are repeatedly re-qualified due to the complexity of their constitutive associations, using them to speculate places even further emphasis on re-qualification. Whereas volatile markets might be frightening to the average investor, they represent profit opportunities for professional traders (Abolafia, 1996). Hence the traders' repeated re-qualification of shares is not only due to the stock markets being volatile, but also fuelled by speculative motives. This has consequences for the stock markets as such, and suggests that traders contribute to the performance of stock markets by conducting transactions, and also actively shape these markets by engaging in speculation.

Momentary identities

The fluid and elusive character of the stock markets leads traders to re-qualify repeatedly the shares they trade. This results in *temporal framings*, which are momentary and oriented towards the future. The qualification of shares is a repetitive process that involves identifying patterns and opportunities in an information universe where any

Table 3.1 Summary of the major aspects of the share identities constructed by traders

Constitutive associations	Potentially to 'everything', filtered by the individual trader and the (emotional) interaction between traders.
What the share represents	A share does not represent anything 'in itself' beyond an opportunity to trade.
Potential uses	A commodity that can be traded for short-term gains.
Temporal framing	Momentary. Each transaction is a new situation.

rumour or fact could become important, but where only some actually do. The stock markets are continuously being re-shaped, in a process intertwined with the qualifying of the shares traded. This turns the qualification of shares into a full-time job and awards traders a major role in the process. Potential other actors that could have been involved in the process typically lack both information and the possibility to be updated at every moment. Indeed, the growth of computer trading suggests that even professional traders fall short of keeping abreast. The durability of any specific qualification is extremely low. In principle, a share needs to be re-qualified after each transaction. In this context, minutes may be too long a time frame (even seconds can be too long, as indicated by the growth of high-frequency trading).

Given this momentary context, it is hardly surprising that traders rarely take historical events into account when constructing their share identities. They may very well appreciate that such events affect the share, when regarded as an investment object. But to a trader shares *are not* investment objects; they are commodities that can be used for speculative purposes, and this makes all the difference.

Table 3.1 summarizes the key points concerning how traders construct share identities. As we argued in the introductory chapter, the different expert groups working in investment banking are likely to construct qualitatively different versions of the shares as part of the practices in which they engage. In Chapter 4 we take a closer look at one of the remaining two expert groups active in the securities business: stock analysts.

4

Analysts Doing Stock Market Science – Sort of

> The analyst team has invited investors – clients and potential clients – to a one-day 'industrial sector seminar' at the bank. From breakfast to lunch the invited professional investors are listening to 15-minute corporate presentations by CEOs, CFOs, and IR directors. The analyst team is responsible for the programme and has invited corporations it regards as especially interesting. Each presentation is followed by questions from the investors and ends with brief comments by the analyst team to explicate their view of the situation. There are some recurring themes: The US market is not very hot, but given the correct strategic focus, there are still profit opportunities. Environmental issues seem to be the thing for the future, but it will soon be too late to join the bandwagon, the analysts caution. China, on the other hand, still has great potential according to all the invited managers. And so the discussion continues. After (an excellent) lunch at the bank, 'one-on-one' meetings follow. The corporate managers sit down individually with potential investors, often with one of the bank's analysts as a third speaking partner. If all goes well during this 'speed-dating' (in many cases it does), the investors commit to making new or additional investments in the industry and/or in specific firms, the managers attract new capital to support their business ventures, and the bank's analysts add to their own, as well as their bank's, brand value. Bottom line result for the bank: the investors will trade more of their securities via the bank's trading desk in the near future.

Basically, stock analysts try to calculate the value of shares and relate that value to the current price at which the share is traded in order to identify interesting investment opportunities. As noted by Beunza and Garud (2007), this means that analysts regularly deal with situations characterized by Knightian uncertainty. For many analysts, this is also what motivates them:

> Brokers and traders want to sell and make money; analysts want to be right.
>
> (Head of Analyst Group)

Analysts are active in all business lines within investment banking, but their major role is within securities. This is where they spend most of their time, residing next to the brokers and the traders. Since the analysts regularly interact with people outside their own occupation, as well as outside the bank, they are an informative group on which to focus if one wishes to understand what goes on between the different experts in investment banking, as well as between different actors in the financial sector. Describing the work of stock analysts will shed light not only on what they do themselves but also on what they do together with others.

Very simply put, analyst work is about convincing investors to trade more via the investment banking organization that the analyst works for. The main activities they engage in to achieve this are (1) producing and communicating 'theoretical' target prices on shares, which differ from the prices at which the shares are currently traded; (2) communicating views and recommendations (sell, hold or buy) to investors; and (3) producing and arguing for cases regarding under- or overpriced corporations (investment objects).[1]

Another star of finance – The stock analyst

Going back just a couple of decades, the attention given to investment banking was mainly focused on corporate banking practices and securities trading. This applied equally to practitioners, researchers and media. While traders and brokers were being given leading roles in Hollywood movies (*Wall Street*) and ethnographies (Abolafia, 1996; Bruegger, 1999), analysts were rarely noticed. The number of studies of traders and brokers well exceeds that of analysts, and it is quite symptomatic that one of the most impressive recent books on investment banking (Morrison and Wilhelm, 2007) fails to mention analysts even once.

But things *have* changed. During the late 1980s and 1990s, analysts were increasingly acknowledged in financial practice as well as in the financial press. After another decade or so, they also started to interest researchers (Hägglund, 2001; Mouritsen, 2003; Gasparino, 2005; Beunza and Garud, 2007; Fleuriet, 2008). Today, having highly ranked analysts is one of the most important competitive factors for investment banking organizations. The analysts have moved from an anonymous back office expert position, to a front stage selling and marketing function in securities services. With growing status, they have become stars, during the late 1990s maybe even *the* stars, of investment banking:

> Well, we have taken the fast elevator upwards in the hierarchy, straight up to the work of CEOs and investors.
>
> (Analyst)

But the higher you climb, the further you may fall. As a group, the analysts experienced such a fall in connection with the dot-com boom and bubble in the late 1990s and early 2000s, especially in the United States where top-ranking analysts were held responsible for systematically making misleading recommendations. Instead of putting their clients first, they made recommendations that benefited their employers (Swedberg, 2005). When people like Jack Grubman and Henry Blodget were accused of boosting shares without substance, the result was that the high-profiled analysts, their banks, but most of all their clients, suffered considerably (Fleuriet, 2008:151–153). As a result, the trust in analysts, as well as in investment banking, deteriorated in the first years of the new millennium. The information that became publicly available in connection with the settlement between Merrill Lynch and the State of New York, and also Eliot Spitzer's 'global settlement' with Wall Street in late 2002, certainly contributed to this.[2] So, what is it that analysts do?

Collect data, analyse firms, present views

The content of the work of the analyst has changed radically in parallel to their growing importance. Twenty years ago the analysts worked mostly alone, their main task being to collect information and analyse the financial accounts of public corporations when a trader or broker so requested. The analysts constituted a support function for the high-profile experts. They did not interact much with anybody else, while doing their analyses:

> It's 10.45 am. One of the analysts is sitting in one of the smaller meeting rooms in the securities department, where the banks front office employees usually have meetings with their clients. She looks

> up and down a spreadsheet on her laptop, browses a few sheets of paper, and turns pages in a sector report. She has moved away from the large trading room to get some peace of mind. The questions, the sometimes quite loud discussions, and the general noise in the trading room are important for everybody working there, but sometimes it can be distracting. Sometimes analysts need to work on their own. In the meeting room, the analyst works in solitude with the bank's formal analytical model. It is, as in most banks, a version of the DCF-model (a 'discounted cash flow' model). 'Her' sector had its last round of quarterly reports a month ago, and since she is 'in between cases', that is, she presented her latest case this morning, and there is no major turbulence in her sector, she has time to adjust some parameters to improve the fit of the model to her sector. If everything runs smoothly, she should be done before lunch.

As implied above, analysts still collect data and analyse firms and industries, but today their work is much more structured, involves many more sources of information and is analytically more advanced. Another important change is that analysts work more proactively today: their analyses are not primarily responses to requests made by brokers or traders. Instead, their work is governed by the increasingly structured approach to doing business within securities at any investment banking organization. Their work could be seen as a consequence of the demands placed on investment banking by more and more professional investors, or of the fact that all competing analysts are doing it:

> Today every investor sits two pushes of a button away from executing a trade. We cannot live on only doing that pushing. We have to add value. That's where we come into play. Our analysis has to be something more and different than what the investors can do themselves.
>
> (Head of Analysis)

Most of the analysts are focused on a specific industry sector, and they are expected to know more or less everything about what is going on in and around that sector.[3] Some investment banking organizations work strategically with the sectors they cover, trying to create, define and specialize in new sectors like 'environment' or 'betting'. In the larger organizations, the analysts work in teams specialized on particular sectors. Each team of analysts comprises a sector analysis manager, a few senior analysts and some less experienced assistant analysts. Typically the senior analysts have more contact with clients and the less experienced ones (who are educated in the latest calculus) are doing the bulk of calculative work.

Although the calculations require both initiative and skills, there is a clear trend towards increasing standardization as far as the actual number crunching is concerned:

> The common way of working with company valuation is to collect industry and company information, anything really that can be used to build up an analysis product. Then you use that info to project future results and balance sheets. Usually these figures are discounted in a DCF. Values pop out and one argues for that value and the estimates behind it.
>
> (Analyst)

But while analysis has become increasingly standardized in terms of the use of DCF-models, for instance, the models employed by the analysts still constitute an important differentiating factor. The analysts use several models, some of which are specifically tailored to the corporations they follow:

> We use a number of different models in our work. First, we have models to estimate the corporation's turnover and profitability. Then we put that into a standard model that all analysts here use. This second model gives us a profit and loss statement, a balance sheet, cash flow estimates, etc. And then we put that into a standardized cash flow model. So the only model that is unique for the analyst is the one used to estimate some kind of turnover and profitability for the corporation in question. Then that estimate is standardized into models that we can save in our databases and use as data for various purposes.
>
> (Analyst)

Seasons, views and flashes

Today, analysts' work is totally dominated by the so-called four seasons. These seasons are the few weeks when the corporations in the industry sector publish their quarterly reports (see Figure 4.1). They are the most hectic time periods during the year for the analysts. Within limited time frames, the analyst has to write previews, reviews and other comments that have to be grounded in in-depth analyses of the firms, their industry, global economic trends and so on. Even though the analysts produce written comments throughout the year on all possible news

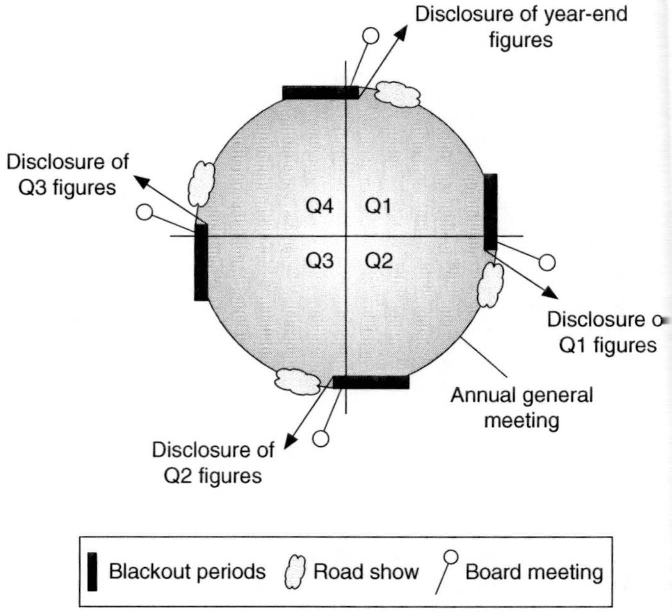

Figure 4.1 The four seasons
Source: Adapted from Grunberg (2007).

related to the industry and the firms they follow, their work is highly intensified around the quarterly reports:

> Today everything is centred on the four seasons. If you're working with a sector where the reports are presented in close connection to each other, it's enough to work yourself to death during a few weeks, for those covering sectors where reports are more scattered, it becomes worse.
>
> (Analyst Manager)

Different banks have different policies, but all have policies about how and when an analyst is expected to write comments and reviews. Usually the analyst checks the financial news early in the morning before arriving at work. If there is news concerning his/her sector or the corporations therein, s/he writes a comment – a flash – straight away, usually on a PDA or cell phone, and sends it into the intranet. This first comment regarding specific news consists of a short statement stating whether the current recommendation on a specific share is to be reconsidered (buy, sell and target price). Later this comment is followed by a slightly longer reasoning – an on-the-spot analysis – for the current recommendation and, if the news is regarded as important for the future valuation of the investment object, a more in-depth analysis will follow.

The main product – Cases

Even if analyst work is structured in time by the four seasons, the analyst's main products are not the previews, reviews, flashes or on on-the-spot analyses. The main products, according to the analysts, are the cases. When they are not working with the quarterly reports, it is up to the analysts to find, or rather create, interesting cases that impress investors enough to want to trade via the trading desk at the analyst's bank:

> There is an old saying: Good firms are bad shares. This is where a lot of firms belong. Then there are bad firms that are good shares. When things are totally dynamic or open. But what cuts straight through these dimensions is of course the case. The case is our main product. Everything is about producing better, more convincing cases.
>
> (Analyst)

The cases have many similarities with the previews and reviews performed in connection with the quarterly reports; they consist of large quantities of quantitative data and in-depth analyses concerning the focal firm, its industry and related global economic trends. A major difference for the analyst is that the work of preparing these business cases is less stressful than their work with the quarterly reports. It is possible to collect data in one's own way and the deadlines for finishing the cases are not as strict. When preparing cases, there is more room for the analyst to do what s/he wants and to let one's personal style as an analyst shine through:

> You need a creativity of your own; you can't search for information via directives. The thing is to find your own ways, your own sources. Because you need primary information. But it is up to each person to decide what kind of primary information.
>
> (Analyst)

Working on cases also differs from working with previews in that it is easier to get information from the corporations you analyse when doing a case. During a few weeks before the release of a quarterly report, it is more or less impossible to get any new information from the corporate top management or IR people (the so-called black-out period in Figure 4.1). After the release of a quarterly report, the 'door gradually opens' into these important sources of information, and the production of new interesting cases can start again. Some analysts do not hesitate to use relatively unconventional methods to get a feeling for the sectors and the corporations they follow. This is how an analyst of the clothing and retail sector went about it:

> I have a habit of walking up to NK [Stockholm's premier department store] and go through all the different clothing brands. I look at their pricing and the quality of the goods. It gives me a feel for what the different companies are doing.
>
> (Analyst)

Based on present-day figures, analysts anticipate future scenarios for the sectors and corporations they monitor. By generating a number of scenarios, they try to illustrate what can be expected to happen in the market in the mid- to long-term. Analysts collect a considerable amount of information, compress it, and present it in forms that are meant to be easier for the brokers and investors to understand. Usually this means modelling and talking figures, activities that most analysts seem to enjoy:

> Of course figures are fun. To sit there with the models and find out some smart model for guessing what the sales volume will be. To collect different types of market data, like sales statistics from different countries, and try to build them together into some sort of market figure.
>
> (Analyst)

Organized social interaction

Even if the cases themselves do not generate trade, they are often used as a point of departure for the subsequent interaction between the bank and the investor; thus it is important that the analysts are able to make an impression. The interaction that follows typically involves brokers and traders, and hopefully results in trade and hence revenues for the bank. Today, the analysts are highly involved in this interaction with investors, as well as with other experts, both inside and outside the bank.

Inside the bank

There is both formal and informal division of labour between the analysts. There are a few macro analysts, specialized in interpreting macro trends and their implication for specific sectors and firms, but the majority of the analysts focus on the corporations within specific industry sectors. The analyst teams specialized in different sectors sit next to one another to enable both more structured communication and small talk among all analysts. They continuously exchange ideas on everything from the quality of a specific piece of information, how to interpret macroeconomic trends, how to develop their models, to specific cases. Most of the analysts' working days are focused on the securities business of the bank, but at times they also help out in corporate finance projects.

Within securities, the analysts are located next to the brokers and usually quite close to the traders as well. Most securities departments have an open office landscape, and the analysts interact frequently with the brokers and the traders. Most often, brokers ask analysts for opinions or advice, but the analysts also ask brokers questions concerning everything from where they feel the market is heading to a query about a specific corporation or client:

> We serve them with information, we present our thoughts concerning what has happened since yesterday, and concerning what will happen during the day. Sometimes we have a short company presentation, we might believe that a specific share will go up or down due to some new information. Whether the brokers and the traders are attentive to what I have to say depends largely on which corporation I'm talking about. If it is HM, everybody listens, and I get a lot of questions. If it is 24Hpoker, maybe one is listening. It also depends on who is talking, like if Lars is talking, there will usually be discussion, most brokers are interested in his sector, and he is also a top ranked analyst.
>
> (Analyst)

The analysts' interaction with the corporate bankers is regarded as sensitive, both ethically and legally. The investment banking practices related to securities trading (recommending and enabling investors to buy or sell stock and other securities) and the corporate banking practices (helping top managers finance their corporations) must be kept apart to avoid conflicts of interest and unlawful use of information. Hence the use of so-called Chinese walls (see Chapter 2).

From the analyst's point of view, the relation to bankers is generally seen as unproblematic. Their interaction is usually initiated by the bankers who seek assistance with some specific analysis, often before they have sold their services to a specific firm. At least, the analyst's task in the corporate banking area has very little to do with his own work within securities. Virtually all analysts say the same thing:

> One has to have integrity. If you start to compromise your own valuations and give in to some pressure to raise a target price on a stock, you will not last long as an analyst.
>
> (Analyst)

At the same time, some analysts have no problem in pointing out how competitors in other banks have done just that, that is, made recommendations that fit some ongoing corporate banking project a little bit too well:

> Well, there are cases, for instance one quite obvious one a few years back, when Deutsche Bank, or rather the analyst at Deutsche Bank here in Stockholm, overnight and without any real new information, raised their buy price on Saab quite a bit. This happened just before their bankers started to distribute a new issue of Saab shares. That one was a little bit too much.
>
> (Analyst)

The interaction between the analysts and the corporate bankers is of special interest for other reasons than the legal issues concerning inside information and conflicts of interest. All experts within securities are to some extent dependent on the work of the corporate bankers. The bankers can be said to produce new investment objects that the experts within securities can analyse, recommend and trade (see Chapters 6 and 7). Among the experts in securities, the analysts are the ones who work most closely with with the bankers, contributing with their expertise to specific projects. But some of the analysts seem to regard this cooperation as somewhat problematic and even disturbing:

> Well... it [being involved in a corporate banking project] is not really my real work, it could be interesting, but no, it is actually rather disturbing. It takes my focus from my shares and... it is difficult to explain, but it is somehow disturbing.
>
> (Analyst)

We will return to the issue of the interaction between the expert groups in Chapter 9 as we address the question of how investment banking is organized. Here we will instead turn our attention to the various other people that the analysts meet as part of their work.

Meeting people outside the bank

The analyst's work also includes direct communication with investors and clients over the phone and face-to-face. Analysts are in frequent contact with professional investors and their contacts with them can be characterized as ongoing discussions. According to Fleuriet (2008:136), the analysts typically spend one to two weeks in a month visiting the offices of their buy-side clients to pitch their cases and latest investment ideas. Our material might indicate a little less time for this interaction, but it also shows high variation between analysts. Some customers, of the large institutional investors, are primarily interested in the analyst's future scenarios rather than in their views on how these scenarios will affect the value of the share. This is a consequence of these clients having become more sophisticated, developing analytic competences themselves (see also Hägglund, 2001; Beunza and Garud, 2007; Fleuriet, 2008). Nowadays, portfolio managers and buy-side analysts working for large institutional investors typically use information from several analysts, comparing their different scenarios and making their own assessments of share values. Other customers, like hedge fund managers, are more interested in the analysts' opinions of the value of specific shares:

> Some customers only want to talk estimates and industrial data, others want to go all the way, discussing the arguments for a specific valuation.
>
> (Analyst)

> They [institutional investors] know how to calculate. More and more they want to use us analysts as speaking partners to access our industrial knowledge. To sit down and bandy ideas around. My industry isn't that big on a global scale. The clients that follow it have maybe

> done so for a year or so, while I sit here and have been following it daily for ten years. So there's some kind of value in that, which they perceive.
>
> (Analyst)

Today, then, the analyst's work is very much about communicating, via texts but also face-to-face, with investors. Meetings with investors take on many shapes. Investors come to the bank, invited for seminars, breakfasts or lunches, or just by appointment with 'their' analyst. Also, the analysts visit the investors for one-on-one appointments, or in connection with more or less extensive 'roadshows'. But they also organize more elaborate events to attract investors:

> I have regular contacts with 'my' corporations and at times I set up visits at their facilities for interested investors. This is not to give them inside information or anything, but hopefully they become more knowledgeable about the business, the unit, their market etc. It provides them with a 'flavour' of reality, shows them that it's not just a spreadsheet in Excel, you know, but allows them to see what it really is. Verbally, the investors are very interested in these events. But it takes a lot of time, of course, so in the end we typically have only a small group with us.
>
> (Analyst)

The information between analysts and investors does not flow in only one direction. The investors are an important source of information for the analyst that complements sources like written reports and public accounts. Their conversations are interactive, interpretative and productive. They are not only about exchanging information, but could be said to allow the analysts and investors to enact their views of the corporation and the value of its share. The investor's and the analyst's investment objects are to a large extent created in their communication with each other.

Besides meeting with investors, the analysts also interact with others outside their organizations. One important such group is the corporate managers. The analysts interact over the phone, via media and face-to-face, with CEOs, CFOs and investor relations (IR) staff of public corporations. These contacts are initiated both by the managers and by the analysts or brokers at the bank. One occasion for interaction between analysts and managers is when the analysts and/or brokers invite investors to seminars and meetings. It could be a breakfast meeting or a one-day seminar focusing on a particular sector, for instance. The main reason for the analysts, the brokers and the banks to initiate these kinds of meetings is to market themselves to investors. The experts act as facilitators, but the listed corporations and their managers are the main focus. What is important for the analysts (and their employer) is to be able to present managers who are as prominent as possible. A CEO is preferable, a CFO is good and an IR manager is OK. If the analysts and brokers can produce occasions for investors to meet top managers, the likelihood that the investors will trade via their trading desk increases, as does their future ranking of the analysts. Similar meetings between analysts, managers and investors take place when the corporate managers go on 'roadshows' after publishing their quarterly reports:

> As a general rule, I meet all the corporations I follow in connection to their quarterly reports. Plus I call them whenever there's a development.
>
> (Analyst)

In contrast to the seminars and the 'study visits', the corporate managers are the ones who initiate the meetings in connection with the quarterly reports. Their choice of bank to facilitate a meeting with potential investors in a specific area, like London, Frankfurt or Stockholm, depends on what the different banks can offer in terms of contacts with investors in that specific area. Thus, the roadshows can be seen as a method for corporate managers to pitch to and pick investors, just as much as the other way around (investors choosing corporations to invest in).[4]

Analysts' construction of share identities

Based our empirical material concerning the work of analysts, we raise the question: What kind of share do they construct as part of the practices they engage in? In Chapter 3 we argued that traders construct shares as standardized and fairly empty exchange objects that are constantly affected by a large number of forces. As a result, traders were noted to constantly re-qualify the shares that they trade. Viewing the share as a boundary object that potentially can be ascribed quite different identities as part of different expert practices, we now look at how analysts construct their share identities. Once again we employ the proposed four dimensions for characterizing their construction of share identities: constitutive associations, representations, potential uses and temporal framings.

A knowledge object representing a going concern

Analyst work is to a large extent about creating specific knowledge about individual corporations and the industries to which they belong. As suggested by Hägglund (2001), analysts construct investment objects out of corporations. In this constructive work, they use a variety of sources of information and interact with many different actors. The main outcome of their work is an understanding of the corporation as an opportunity to invest or de-invest. The firm is constructed as a unique investment object. In order to do this, analysts forge links between the internal operations of the corporation, its relation to other organizations within the sector and to the markets in which it operates. All this boils down to an estimated theoretical value of a share. This value is then compared with the share's current price on the stock exchange, and results in a buy, hold or sell recommendation in a mid- and long-term time perspective. This is a process of abstraction that translates knowledge of the corporation into quantitative value assessments in terms of a theoretical price presented in the shape of written and oral reports.

The translation of a corporation into an investment object with a forecasted theoretical value ascribed to its shares is in no way a neutral reduction. It is rather a creative act of transformation. Thus this work is best described as process of knowledge creation in which the corporation and the share become (loosely) coupled to one another. The construction of an investment object is both social and calculative and results not only in the investment object per se, but also in the models that the analysts use. As shown earlier in this chapter, the analysts do not use one and the same standard DCF-model, but rather use several models and employ the DCF to construct a specific model for the corporations and sectors they follow. The ongoing construction of models can thus be seen as a second outcome of analyst work in addition to their construction of investment objects (as expressed in cases, views, recommendations).

According to Beunza and Garud (2007), analysts primarily build interpretative devices (calculative frames) that bracket the situation facing a corporation, so as to make it manageable and allow a value to be attached to the share. This, in turn, allows investors to make trading decisions. Although analysts certainly contribute in this way, our empirical material indicates that analysts primarily construct investment objects, but that the calculative framing of these objects is an important outcome of their practice. Analysts enact models that they use when constructing investment objects. In addition, it seems clear to us that analysts are not the only ones engaged in framing shares as investment objects. On many occasions, the construction of investment objects is a joint effort between the analysts, the investors and the corporations, such as during their various conversations at seminars and roadshows.

These differences aside, the practices that analysts engage in clearly suggest that they construct shares as objects of knowledge that depend on both the calculative frames (models) they use and the specific pieces of information that they associate with these objects. Taken together, this suggests that analysts ascribe shares a distinctly epistemic identity. Shares are knowledge objects, and the quality of your construction depends on how well you link them to an underlying physical reality of production units, resources, customers and so on.

An object gradually evolving over time

Perhaps the most significant aspect of the share identity constructed by analysts concerns the inner life of the share. To analysts, the share represents the operations of the listed corporation, which means that they are full of life. Importantly, the inner life of the share is materially heterogeneous. It includes facilities, sales offices, patents, formal contracts and administrative rules. But it also includes key knowledge workers and managers, not only in terms of 'intellectual capital' (Mouritsen, 2003), but also in terms of physical bodies and social representations. This inner life of the share implies an entity with content and with some 'weight'; this means that the analyst share has a relatively stable identity with carefully specified spatial and temporal boundaries. As a body it includes and excludes; it is filled with specific content by the construction work of the analysts. Thus, it cannot be reconstructed at a whim. The material and social life of the share, and the structured work of the analysts gives rise to a distinct, stable and relatively closed identity.

As a consequence of the way analysts construct share identities, each share is ascribed a history and a future. The share is temporally framed in accordance with its contents. It can change, but usually not radically from one moment in time to the next. Fleuriet (2008:139) estimates the typical temporal horizon for analysts' intermediate-term investment ratings to be around 12 months, and for the long-term investment ratings roughly three years. Beunza and Garud (2007) imply a similar temporal frame when they discuss an analysts' three-year investment horizon as long term. But here we have also shown that the very practice of analyst work implies a temporal frame, also characterized by content, weight and relatively long-term temporal horizons. A less-experienced analyst has to put a lot of work into creating her first cases, to get to know her sector, to fill all the models with data. Once this is done, there is still a lot of work, but the work is less dynamic, concerned with updating models, information and views on each share. Again, the share has a body, a weight consisting of structured knowledge, humans, machines, contracts and so on. Thus, it has a recognizable and meaningful history that is important to account for when assessing its future. Rather than the momentary flux of the present, as in the traders' concern for market prices and volumes, the analyst share is temporally framed as having a mid- to long-term identity.

Constitutive associations

Although the analysts develop their own (versions of) valuation models or calculative frames, the models used are still fairly well structured and rather standardized, not only within the organization they work for, but also across the financial sector at large. An individual analyst interacts with several different groups of actors, both inside and outside their immediate working context. Thus, his/her construction of share identity is not only about the share's inner life and the constitutive associations forged with such elements as production facilities, key figures within the organization and formal contracts. The share identity is also constituted through the associations with formal valuation models, managers with an interest in attracting capital to their corporation, and professional investors who seek information and interesting cases of over- or underpriced investment objects. All these actors have their particular interests in the share, and since they are interacting with the analysts, they also influence the analysts' construction of share identity. The corporate managers might want the share to be priced at a high and stable level, enough to keep and attract capital needed for their business endeavours. The professional investors are primarily interested in knowing things that everybody else (the market) doesn't know, so that they can make good investments (Fleuriet, 2008:145). At the same time, they need to be able to create their own knowledge base to be able to evaluate what in the analyst's message is worth taking into consideration. They are looking for new information, but are not ready to blindly accept the marketing messages by the analysts or the managers. These examples shows the analysts' share identity could be said to be constructed both from within (its body) and from the outside (its association with actors and artefacts).

Using shares to appear reasonably different

Despite the importance of accepted valuation models and conventions, analysts also need to apply their subjective judgements and use information in ways not directly prescribed by method or convention. The analysts must offer some added value, something unique. This is what their construction of cases around specific investment objects is about; constructing an estimated value of a share that is neither the same as the current market price, nor the same as the other analysts' mid- to long-term target prices. Thus, there is a motive for analysts to produce cases, opinions and views that are different from all other analysts' cases, opinions and views. Analysts need to stand out in order to be interesting and generate trade. To stand out is important for the individual analyst, but their work is just as important for the bank and the investment banking industry:

> Today we have reached a level similar to or not far away from the brokers in that we assume a lot more responsibility for selling our ideas ... that are both in short, middle and long term so much more important to generate trade, because you cannot ... only be an order central, that doesn't work any more. Then people go to the net-brokerage houses and trade on their own. This has created a metamorphosis of the analyst trade. We are needed in order to differentiate, not only our selves, but also the whole investment banking industry.
>
> (Head of Analyst Group)

But there are also limits to this differentiation, as well as external pressures to conform to what other analysts recommend:

> One can put it like this, it's not bad to be right, but there is also ... it's hard to pinpoint, but if I do an analysis of a large well-analyzed share and comes up with a 200% up side. Then I will put, let's say 30 or 40%, and people still will say that I'm crazy. Even if you want to be a little provocative, you cannot disagree too much or too often with consensus.
>
> (Analyst)

So, the shares constructed by analysts are used to differentiate them as interesting – but sane! – researchers in the science of finding hidden values in investment objects. At a more collective level, their share constructions, views and recommendations are used to profile their

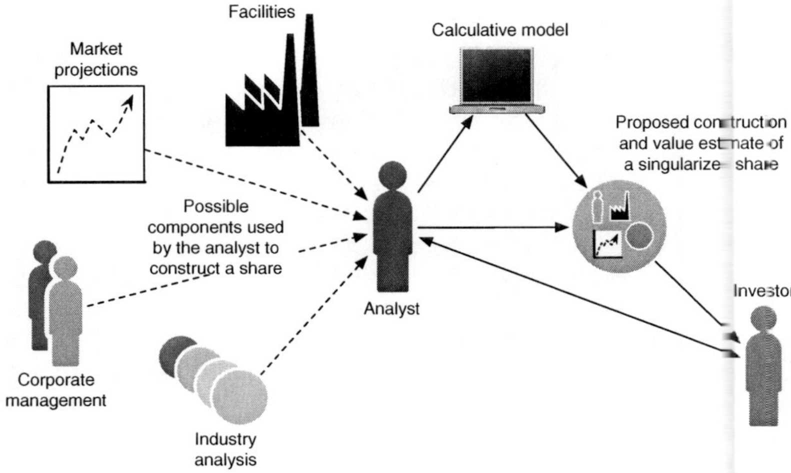

Figure 4.2 Constitutive associations of the analyst's share identity

occupation in relation to other experts within investment banking. Well-regarded analysts cost a lot of money, and the analysts use the share identities they construct to show that they are worth it. In addition, the analysts use their share identities as a way of differentiating their analyst team and securities services as interesting in terms of being both unique and well-researched. An investment bank without high-profile analysts is in a difficult competitive situation. On an even more aggregated level, the analysts' construction of shares is used to legitimize the investment banking industry as a whole, in the eyes of other stakeholders. By constructing shares as investment objects through careful analyses based on theoretical models and thorough empirical data, the analysts counteract a view of stock trading as high stake and high-risk gambling. Instead, they suggest a view of stock trading as science – sort of (Figure 4.2).

Conclusion – A singularized good

The analysts' constructions of share identities comprise evident elements of commoditization. They routinely reproduce the sector categorizations that have become the standard way of describing global stock markets. They also enact the valuation models that are used by financial professionals more or less globally. Finally, they strategically position their views and recommendations at a 'reasonable' distance from both market prices and consensus views within the analyst collective.

But despite these indications of commoditization, the core activities that stock analysts engage in are still geared towards singularization, of themselves, of their employers and, maybe most importantly, of the shares. It is the unique theoretical price of a single case, a single investment object, and a single share that is the focal object for the analyst's share construction. The analyst reproduction of the industry sectors, and use of widely established valuation models are side-effects, or prerequisites, and not the primary focus of the analyst's attempt to create interesting cases concerning over- or underpriced, singularized, shares.

From the account above, it is clear that the share constructed by the analyst is a singularized good. It is constructed as having not only a current price on the market but also a value that depends on an underlying investment object and its context. Indeed, a central task for the analyst is to construct scenarios concerning this underlying object and context, and work out their implications for the value of the share. The share's price-to-value relation can then be compared to other shares' price-to-value relations as part of an investment decision. In this sense, the analysts construct shares as objects of knowledge.

Perhaps the most significant aspect of the share identities constructed by analysts concerns the inner life of the share. The identity of the share is intimately connected to the operations of the noted firm. This means that the analysts construct shares with content and weight. The central aspect of their identity construction concerns what content will fill the share. As a result, these shares have bodies with a history and a future. The shares constructed by the analysts are thus not only objects of knowledge but also seen as representatives of materially heterogeneous collectives.

Closely related to this identity construction is a temporal profile that differs significantly from that of the traders. Whereas traders constructed a share identity that was transitory and highly dependent on external forces, analysts construct an identity where internal forces afford the share some inertia. The analyst's share does change, but usually not radically from one moment to the other. Again, the share has a body, a weight consisting of humans, knowledge, machines, relations between analysts, valuation models, investors and so on. Thus, these shares have a recognizable and meaningful history that is important to account for when assessing their future. Rather than the momentary flux of the present, these shares are framed to exist in a mid- to long-term world.

In terms of uses, finally, the analyst primarily draws on the share to produce well-researched, singularized investment opportunities that generate attention and thus attract investors. At least three beneficiaries

Table 4.1 Summary of the analysts' share identity characteristics

Constitutive associations	With 'data', valuation models, investors, managers and (business) media.
What the share represents	Represents an investment object with a materially heterogeneous body.
Potential uses	A singularized good constructed to attract investors and to legitimize analysts and investment banking.
Temporal framing	Medium- to long-term. Historical events affect the future of the share, which changes gradually over time.

can be identified from this use of shares: the individual analyst, who gains reputation (and arguments for increased pay); the securities department employing the analyst, which can increase trading volumes and hence revenues; and the investment banking industry as a whole, which comes across as less casino-like (Table 4.1).

5 Brokers Selling Investment Advice

> Once there were no investment banks, only stock brokerage firms. There are still some small stock brokerage firms around, but many of them, maybe most, have grown or merged into full house investment banks. In the brokerage firms we [brokers] dominated, in the investment bank we're just... just sales – a significant part, but still just one of many parts in the system.
>
> (Stock Brokerage Manager)

Twenty-five years ago, the stockbroker was literally in the centre of the stock market. Standing on the actual market floor, following the stock prices on large notice boards, moving physically between telephones used to contact investors and the trading zones in which they shouted out their 'desires and intentions to buy or sell' (Baker, 1984:789). This was the familiar open-outcry auction system. Although these markets may have come across as chaotic – at times they probably were – Baker's classic study suggested that they nonetheless contained relatively stable patterns of social interaction among the brokers. Behind the scenes, away from the bustling trading floors, you could also find a few analysts providing support to the brokers in the form of in-depth analyses of firms and industries. The brokers would assign specific tasks to analysts working for their brokerage firm when and if they felt that this was called for. Typically, however, the broker's own knowledge of the firms and industries behind the stocks they traded was sufficient to get the work done.

Starting with the Toronto Stock Exchange in 1977, the execution of trades at stock exchanges was gradually automated (Nasdaq having opened as an electronic stock market already in 1971). This meant that the process of matching orders to buy and sell, determine market prices and allocate shares was computerized (Muniesa, 2004). In the case of the Stockholm Stock Exchange, automation happened in 1989. As a result of automation, the typical site for market activity (buying and selling) changed from the physical market floor of the stock exchange to the inhouse trading desk at a brokerage firm or investment bank. Still, even after exchanges had become automated, brokers remained in charge of both communicating with investors and executing trades; not by shouting, but by typing orders into their terminals connected to the electronic stock exchange. Although there are still a few brokers who execute their own (or rather their customers') trades, this is very much the exception nowadays. Brokers working in investment banking today are specialized in recommending investors to enter into specific transactions (still mainly by phone). The execution of trades, however, is now in the hands of specialized traders, who also execute trades for the investment bank itself (see Chapter 3).

While brokerage fees are but one of several sources of revenue in investment banking, it is typically the most important source. The relative importance of brokerage revenues varies over time, as illustrated in Figure 5.1. For this major Scandinavian investment bank, brokerage fees accounted for 56 per cent of the turnover in 1998, were down to 43 per cent in 2001, and have since then risen well above 50 per cent again. Of course, not all of these revenues emanate from the buying and selling of stocks; they also include fees for the exchange of other types

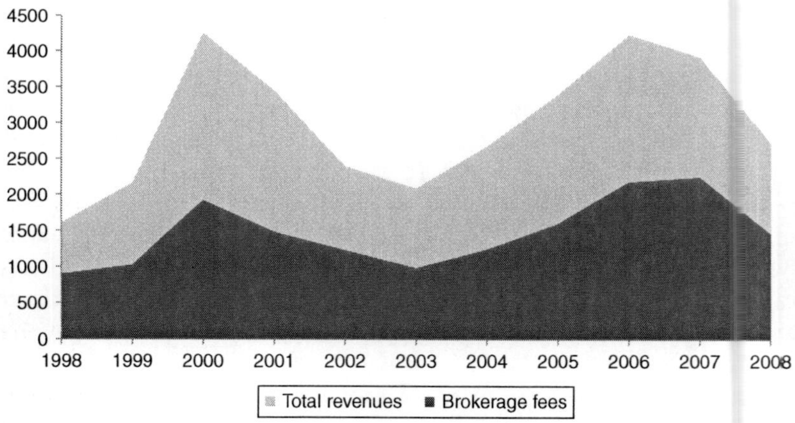

Figure 5.1 Brokerage fees in relation to total revenues, 1998–2008 (annual reports)

of securities. Still, it is clear that brokering is an important generator of revenue in investment banking.

Despite their continued importance, the brokers' position gradually changed as the brokerage houses developed into investment banks. In Chapter 4, analysts were said to have become the new stars of investment banking during the 1990s. A growing demand for corporate financial services – during initial public offerings, mergers and acquisitions towards the end of the 1990s – complements this story. Together, these developments had major consequences for the brokers, including perhaps a decreasing stardom and relative degradation into 'just sales'.

What brokers do

Stockbrokers are salesmen, although they sell a peculiar type of good. As salesmen, their work involves a considerable amount of direct interaction with customers. Indeed the customers are important enough for stockbrokers to be categorized according to the type of customer they are working with. The brokers working with *institutional sales* serve relatively few, but typically very important, customers (in terms of generating revenue). These customers are institutional investors; organizations making large investments, such as banks, hedge funds, insurance companies, pension funds and large corporations. Over the past two decades there has been an increasing professionalization of these customers, who now often employ their own analysts as well as sophisticated theoretical models for determining asset allocation. Brokers working with *private sales*, on the other hand, serve a much larger number of customers, while each such customer makes more modest investments as compared with the institutional investors. Among these customers you find wealthy individuals (the reason why it is called *private* sales) but also trade unions and various foundations.

The categorization of brokers according to the customers they serve is not only employed by the investment banks, but is also reinforced by regulatory frameworks. Since 2004, firms working in investment banking within the EU are required to distinguish between professional and retail clients (of investment services and activities) as part of the MiFID regulatory framework (Directive 2004/39/EC). Whereas a professional client is assumed to 'possess the experience, knowledge and expertise to make its own investment decisions and properly assess the risks that it incurs' (ibid. :43), retail clients are regarded as less well equipped. Consequently, they are protected by rules prescribing certain behaviours on behalf of those who provide investment advice, for instance, concerning what type of information they must provide in connection with a transaction. Indeed, the rules require suppliers of investment services to investigate each client's level of knowledge and experience in the particular investment field their recommendations concern, and inform the clients of the risks associated with a particular investment.

Irrespective of whether brokers work with institutional or private clients, their task is to keep the customers informed about actual and expected changes in the market. In particular, brokers seek to tailor the information they provide to their customers based on what they regard as important for each customer's investment portfolio. The broker's aim is to make individualized recommendations that will make the investor decide to either buy or sell shares (or other securities). Every such transaction that the broker is able to trigger will involve a commission fee to the investment banking organization executing the trade (which is not necessarily the one that the broker is working for). By convincing investors to trade shares, brokers thus generate revenues for the investment banking organization.

The brokers and their assistants are typically located around a few large desks situated closely to both traders and analysts. Much of their daily activities consists in placing and receiving phone calls. The brokers regularly call their customers to discuss the latest developments on the stock market, any news that might affect, or have affected, specific shares, new insights reached by the inhouse analysts and so on. During these calls they try to pinpoint what these developments specifically mean for the customer and hence what the customer ought to do in terms of buying and selling shares. The calls are usually short, maybe a minute or two. Occasionally, they stretch into a quarter of an hour. If the customer decides to trade according to the broker's recommendation, an order to buy or sell is handed over (electronically) to a trader to be executed. If the customer is an institutional investor, the broker is usually talking to a fund manager, and then the fund manager will issue an order to buy or sell to a buy-side trader, that contacts the salestrader at the broker's investment bank. Thus, to execute one trade, as many as four individuals may be directly involved. As should be obvious, however, these repetitive interactions are not face-to-face, but rely on technical devices that mediate the interaction, including the trading systems supplied by the stock exchange, the telephones that occupy the brokers' desks and the scribbled notes on pieces of paper that tend to be scattered across these desks (Muniesa, 2008). That is not to say that brokers never meet their clients in person, quite the opposite.

As mentioned above, one important source of input into the recommendations made by the brokers is the company and industry analyses performed by the inhouse analysts (discussed in Chapter 4). In the best of worlds, their research provides brokers with strong and unique arguments in favour of a certain investment decision. Nowadays, brokers do not assign tasks to the analysts as they used to do in the brokerage houses. Rather, the analysts work proactively and have a highly structured approach to the various sectors they cover. Besides producing research that the brokers can use in their sales efforts, the analysts also help the brokers generate trade by interacting directly with investors. Hence, the work of brokers and analysts is not only complementary but also overlapping. In Chapter 4, we saw how the analyst interacts with investors through their written reports and cases, through establishing their bank's official valuations of individual shares, and through face-to-face interactions during roadshows and seminars. At times, large customers also ask the brokers to set up meetings with the analysts.

This suggests that today, three occupational groups working in securities jointly perform the work of generating and executing trades of shares, a task that used to be performed by brokers alone. Through growing specialization and division of labour both within and between the expert groups, as well as through increasing technical mediation, stock brokering has become a socio-technical machinery in which traders, brokers, analysts and IT systems work side by side with different, yet overlapping and mutually supportive, activities. Perhaps as a result of this increasing sophistication, the work performed by the individual brokers looks relatively similar. The brokers also describe their working days similarly: they attend the morning meetings; they talk to customers over the phone; they keep abreast of market developments and scan their monitors for news; and they discuss among themselves which news to focus on, which development to expect during the rest of the day and many other things besides.

A working day in stock brokering

The working days of stockbrokers remain more or less the same throughout the year and are structured around a few fixed points in time. Brokers spend the early mornings updating themselves on current events in the financial and business world. This includes reading national and international financial papers, watching Bloomberg or some other business news broadcast, and finding information via the Internet. Some brokers have breakfast together at the bank; others join in later for the first formal morning meeting at 7.30. This meeting gathers all the brokers working at the office, as well selected analysts to present updates on sectors or corporations. In most banks, it begins or ends with a video call from the New York office to sum up the most recent day of trading there. If there have been events that have had, or are expected to have, effects on macro trends (like a change in the interest rates), a macro analyst will make a brief presentation. Most of the meeting, which typically lasts for half an hour, consists of sector analysts presenting in-depth analyses of a few firms. Some of these presentations are planned in advance, others can be 'thrown in' in response to some new development, such as 'how do the price changes on raw materials affect our recommendations on company X'. The brokers comment and ask questions, and there are usually a few short discussions about what to expect and what to recommend during the day. If the bank has several offices across Europe these typically have their meetings in parallel. In some banks, the other offices are online and can participate in the discussion. In others, a separate Nordic or European morning meeting is held afterwards.

After the formal morning meeting, the brokers exchange ideas about what tactics to use during the day, such as who to call first and what to say: 'We decide what to make money on today,' as one broker put it. Then they hit the telephones and a period of intensive communication with customers ensues. Every important customer must be contacted before the stock exchange opens, to inform them about major changes in the bank's recommendations and the arguments for these changes. 'That's what they pay us for!' one broker exclaimed. Given that trading starts at 9.00 a.m., there is not much time:

> I just have to have informed my important customers that we have changed our recommendation and why. The most embarrassing thing that can happen is that the customers read on their screens at nine [after the stock exchange has opened] that we have changed our recommendation on Ericsson from buy to sell.
>
> (Broker)

After the stock exchange has opened, the brokers keep contacting clients, working their way through their list of customers. Every broker is responsible for a number of specific clients and their accounts. With some of these customers, the broker communicates several times a day, with others, only once or twice a week. Sometimes the broker calls the customer; sometimes it is the other way around. Relatively inexperienced brokers usually have to be more active, making many calls, while established brokers also will have customers who call them up. The major institutional investors constitute a relatively stable group of organizations, and new actors rarely appear. This means that successful brokers in institutional sales tend to develop long-term relationships with their customers, including close personal relations with, for instance, fund managers in the customer organizations. Similarly, in private sales, individual clients often remain with the same broker for many years.

The brokers also meet their clients face-to-face. In fact, many brokers know their clients quite well. Lunch meetings with clients are common and sometimes the brokers also attend breakfast meetings and seminars for invited clients arranged by the analysts. Many sales departments also host lunch meetings for their most important customers. Dinners with clients also feature frequently in the brokers' calendars. Finally, sales departments often organize international conferences focusing on specific industry sectors for their institutional investors. Since informing customers about interesting investments is a way of maintaining an ongoing conversation, these events can be seen as both a service and a possible networking arena. Presenting interesting cases along with a nice lunch or dinner becomes a way of supporting a continued dialogue between the bank and the investors (see the account of such a lunch meeting, below).

After lunch, around half-past-one, the brokers in some banks have a slightly less formal meeting during which they try to summarize what has happened so far during the day. During these meetings, they also try to establish a common view concerning what needs to be done during the rest of the day, possibly adjusting the tactics decided on after the morning meeting. Then more of the same follows; more phone calls, more discussions with analysts, more newsflashes, more sales pitches, and hopefully more orders placed with the traders. At 5.30 p.m. it is over; the broker's work is done for the day when the stock exchange closes.

For the specially invited – Lunch at the bank

The Head of Institutional Sales, Erik, hosts the recurring 'Lunch for Institutional Investors'. This time a French corporation, RRA, has been invited for a presentation. RRA is internationally well known and has been listed at the Paris Stock Exchange for many years. They are now looking for Scandinavian investors.

The lunch meeting is held in a large and nicely decorated conference room at the bank. Above the large mahogany table and 12 matching chairs in the middle of the room, there is a cut-glass chandelier. Oil paintings in gilded frames showing landscapes and ships cover the walls. Most impressive, though, is the beautiful view of Stockholm in sunlight seen through the large windows, a view the long white curtains do not hide. Today the room looks even more stylish, with the table set for ten, with silver candelabra, elegant covers and crystal glasses.

To an outsider, the people entering the room may appear rather young for this setting. Most of them are in their thirties or early forties, serious-looking men and women. The dress code is strict and very much 'business'. The men wear well-fitting and expensive-looking suits; a few women wear dark blue or grey skirts; the jewellery and watches signal exclusivity. The man representing RRA is the only one who has added some more years, a distinguished man of about 50. By his side, also representing the corporation, is a woman in her thirties. When entering the room, the guests shake hands and only the representatives of RRA seem to be new to the group. The other guests all represent various institutional investors and seem to have met before. When everybody has taken their seats, Erik says a few words of introduction:

We at the Bank are happy to see you all here for this lunch and I hope this will be a fruitful meeting for us all. Our friends representing our Institutional Investor clients are as always very welcome here. Today we are happy to introduce you to RRA, here presented by the director Francois Chandrée and by his side Francesca Laurant. We are all looking forward to hear what you have to say, so please . . . let us start.

Francois leaves his chair and walks down to the end of the table where Francesca joins him. They start their presentation. The slides are also found in print at each seat.

Thank you very much Erik for this invitation. We are glad to be here and also glad to meet you all' he says looking around the table, trying to greet everyone by looking them in the eye. 'Francesca and I have been looking forward to coming to Stockholm and today it is even more beautiful than we remembered it. But let's turn to the reason why we are here' – RRA.

Francois continues his presentation by introducing RRA briefly. This part is kept very short. All guests are specialized in the industry and general knowledge of RRA, which has a number of established brands in luxury garments and sports equipment in its portfolio, seems taken for granted. Francois rapidly moves on to show slides of figures and discuss numbers. What is particularly interesting about RRA at the moment, he suggests, is the growth prospects of the firm, making it an attractive investment with potential financial gains in the future. The slides suggest that the bases for this growth are organic as well as external. There are also increased synergies to be had at group level of the corporation. One of the investors wants to know more about these plans:

How do you balance organic growth versus acquisitions? What is the historical picture of this strategy, and what are your plans for the future?

Francois provides additional details on the historical path of the firm, and why the current strategy is held to be attractive. Illustrating with numbers, he informs the guests about the strategy and presents facts to convince them about its potential. Francesca enters the discussion when the slides illustrate various key figures. The guests are guided through revenue figures, share price performance, market share gains and acquisitions, all illustrating the growth and strategy of the firm. The performances of some of the larger brands are exemplified, one being slightly disappointing, others showing strong developments. By asking questions the guests add an air of familiarity to the presentation, while also making it more informative.

Towards the end of the presentation, a couple of waitresses enter the room to serve lunch. Francois and Francesca take their seats and the discussion continues during the meal. The last slides describing performance ratios, valuation details, cash flows and balance sheet are commented upon. One guest in particular poses new and interesting questions that Francois and/or Francesca try to answer. There are some brief exchanges between pairs of people but most of the conversation involves the whole group. Being the host, Erik leads but keeps a low profile; the purpose of the meeting is to let the guests get to know one another. The atmosphere is serious and the only one who allows himself to be more personal is Francois. Whether due to his French origins, his industry background or his senior position it creates a contrast to the rather figure-oriented discussion. There are occasional smiles and laughter, usually caused by Francois, but most of the conversation is focused on figures.

The discussion continues over coffee and cakes: What is the debt structure like, and how is it to be related to cash flow? Where is the growth actually expected – is it to come from certain geographical areas, specific divisions or special markets? The questions continue. An hour and a half after entering the room, the guests are getting ready to leave. Business cards are exchanged and hands are shaken once more. Before heading off for the next item on their agenda, the guests politely thank Francois and Francesca for their presentation about RRA and also Erik for hosting the event.

Inter- and intra-professional exchanges

Throughout the working day, the brokers keep discussing news and developments on the market with one another and with the other professionals in securities. For an outsider, the jargon can be quite difficult to decipher, with many specialized expressions and codes being used at a rapid pace. The brokers seem to have no such difficulties and suggest that just listening to the general buzz in the trading room, and exchanging thoughts with traders and analysts, is important for their work. In this respect, the support they receive from analysts is put forward as particularly important:

> We run over to each other's desks all the time. I guess we are more 'contact-seeking' than the analysts are. For instance, we ask them for help when we cannot answer a customer's question.
>
> (Broker)

> Every morning when I get in, my mailbox is full of messages from our analysts. I need to be on top of what they're doing to use them in the right way, to take them to the right customers.
>
> (Broker)

These close contacts between brokers and analysts are easily observed in most securities departments. Some brokers further underscore the importance of the analysts by likening them to the production department in a more traditional manufacturing firm:

> We have 23 analysts here in Stockholm. That's our engine. Without them, we'd have to think ourselves. They produce our products.
>
> (Head of Sales)

Continuing the analogy with a manufacturing firm, brokers also suggest that it is important for their production department, the analysts, to understand the customers:

> There has to be contact between the analysts and the fund managers. So the analysts need to be customer oriented, service minded, able

> to communicate. We work in teams, although there are no stable constellations.
>
> (Broker)

Although most brokers acknowledge that traders also are important for their work, they emphasize that their contribution differs from that of the analysts. Traders are useful because they can execute trades in an efficient way, and not because they can help generate trade. As a consequence, the analysts are regarded more as partners, whereas the traders are seen as extended hands:

> We, the brokers, are the people who generate business; we are deal-makers. Then we need some help from the analysts to get in-depth knowledge, and we need the sales traders to push the button.
>
> (Broker)

Besides the execution of trades, traders also provide brokers with a second type of service: the quoting of prices on shares. If a client wants to sell a large position, the broker needs to offer a price at which his or her bank is prepared to buy. The broker will then contact a trader to get a price quote. Although the sales traders can have direct customer contacts themselves, the brokers suggest that these contacts are completely different in character from their own:

> Traders are fairly uninterested in company-analyses; they want to trade. How much? At what price? If a customer wants to talk, then he needs his broker, or an analyst.
>
> (Broker)

As a whole, the brokers convey an image of three specialized expert groups jointly performing a service for their clients. As part of this collective undertaking, the brokers broker shares, but perhaps primarily offer information or advice.

Individuals, groups and their performance

Since brokers have their own customer accounts, many express themselves as if they work for themselves and their customers, rather than for the investment bank which happens to be their employer:

> Our business is almost like a franchising operation. We all have our own clients, and the strategy for how to relate to them is our own concern. Well, within the frame set by the Financial Supervisory Authority, of course. We work far too much, about 65 hours a week. But you can't keep this job if you don't spend that much time on it. Unfortunately. Otherwise, you won't be able to handle the internal competition.
>
> (Broker)

The individual character of stock brokering is further pronounced by the fact that there is no specific educational background required to become a broker. Without a formal educational route, and without a professional association stipulating requirements that brokers should live up to, it is not surprising to find differences in how they work. Still, brokers often have some kind of business education, sometimes even a degree. A common trait among the majority of brokers is a strong personal interest in the financial markets, an interest that they usually have had for many years:

> I am 35 now, and have a degree in Business Administration. Or, well, I never actually completed the degree. I've been working in this industry for 11 years, but have been dealing with shares since I was 16. I started working back-office in 1997, which is quite common. But if you have your degree it's an alternative to start as an assistant doing analyses. Later I became an assistant in portfolio administration, and in 2001, I became responsible for a portfolio myself. In 2002 I started to work for a large corporation, being responsible for their share holdings, and in 2006 I came here.
>
> (Broker)

There are some signs suggesting that the relative heterogeneity found among brokers is starting to decline. In particular, the regulatory frameworks for investment firms now include specific clauses concerning proficiency requirements that personnel offering investment advice must satisfy (e.g. being familiar with relevant legislation). According to the Swedish Financial Supervisory Authority's general guidelines regarding financial advice to consumers (Finansinspektionen, 2004), personnel providing financial advice to non-professional investors must pass a suitable proficiency test. Irrespective of background, then, a certain measure of standardization is being imposed on brokers, at least on those working with private sales.

In terms of internal assessments, some banks evaluate their individual brokers every week in terms of their generation of trade and brokerage fees. This strong focus on individual performance creates a competitive atmosphere. Even though the brokers are engaged in long-term customer relations, they are expected to continuously generate trade. For all brokers, but especially for the less experienced ones, this poses a problem – they have to make large numbers of phone calls and be highly focused on generating trade, sometimes at the expense of nurturing long-term personal relations, both as part of their jobs and personally:

> The worst bit is that you can't be away even for an hour. That would mean losing about four calls. It's hard to get enough time even to sole your shoes. Nowadays having lunch with a friend is extremely rare.
>
> (Broker)

Interesting pastimes like soling your shoes aside, the use of 'tight control systems' to monitor individual performance has been put forward as an important characteristic of investment banking (Eccles and Crane, 1988). Most investment banks also evaluate their brokers using less formal techniques. In some banks the formal evaluations of individual brokers based on the revenues they generate have been abandoned altogether. One important type of soft evaluation is the ranking of brokers by customers, both formally and informally. Conversations between brokers and customers often relate to these more qualitative evaluations. During lunches with customers, potential investments are not the only topics discussed, but the services offered by the investment banks are often brought up as well. Customers continuously rank the banks they work with, measuring the outcomes of recommended transactions. Successful recommendations will then increase the possibility of generating additional business with that specific customer:

> I meet customers sometimes during lunches and ask how they view us – what we are good and bad at. My task is to improve our performance. Every year we follow up our qualitative goal – how we ought to be ranked – and our quantitative goal – profitability.
>
> (Sales Manager)

Many stockbrokers emphasize that they work in a very competitive environment and that they are under considerable and constant pressure to perform well in the short term. They stress the internal competition between the brokers and the hard long hours they need to put in to be successful in this competition. They also describe their work, and their relations with other brokers, as highly emotional including aggressiveness and outbursts of anger. This is a strongly individualistic narrative implying that only a few are cut out for the job:

> There is tremendous competition between the brokers. The ideal I think, being brought up in team sports, would be to have it 'all for one...' but that is not the case in this business. On the other hand it can be quite good. When I was working at another bank, I saw how a situation without pressure made people under-stimulated. Here we have straight and honest manners. There is pressure, so the adrenaline can start flowing, but it is cleared out at once. There are a lot of people with temperament in the business. Outbursts are a natural part of everyday practice. One of my colleagues actually keeps a cap by the desk and sometimes, when discussions are getting heated, he puts it on and says: 'it is starting to get chilly in here...' Sensitive persons shouldn't work here. It can be really tough sometimes.
>
> (Broker)

Our interviews suggest that there are considerable differences between investment banks in this respect. In some broker groups, the characterization above appears valid, in others the brokers seem to work more like teams, less focused on individual short-term performances and more on the bank's long-term reputation among its customers. These brokers describe their work as a team effort and the atmosphere as rather relaxed. The competitive and even aggressive accounts of brokering are even commented as mythical creations:

> That picture is just wrong. We're a group of fourteen gifted but still normal persons working together in a competitive environment. The work is systematic and almost always calm. It can be intense but it doesn't work that way, we're not psychopaths. If you are away from the desk an hour, like I am now, it doesn't make that much difference. We're a group; we have infrastructure and systems that take care of that.
>
> (Broker)

In some cases brokers sitting next to each other at the same desk can express these differing views of what stock brokering is like. More often, though, they are expressed by brokers working in different offices or in different banks. The different accounts seem to be a question of both individual conceptions of work, and of differences in how stock brokering is actually organized at different banks.

Selling shares?

If stockbrokers are salesmen, then what is it they sell? Although brokers obviously trigger sales and purchases of shares through their actions, they are not precisely selling shares. A first clue as to what they offer for sale is linked to how they view shares:

> *Interviewer:* What's a 'good share'?
> *Respondent:* A good share . . . Well . . . that's a strange question.
> *Interviewer:* OK, what's a 'good investment object' then?
> *Respondent:* Well, that's the same question you know – if you ask a broker, it's the same question. (Stockbroker)

Equating shares with investment objects signals that brokers work with a time perspective that goes beyond the actual buying or selling of a share. The character of their contacts with clients also underscores our contention that brokers do not primarily sell shares. It seems more accurate to say that they sell investment advice. This is linked to the changes in the broker role over the past decades, noted at the outset of the chapter:

> In the old days, you *had to* trade through the guild, so to speak. You *had to* use a broker. Now, you can push buttons yourself, without a broker, so we need to sell something more. The customers can use net brokers and trade themselves, but they have to be our customers to access our research.
>
> (Broker)

With the advent of automated trading, and with increased specialization, the traditional brokering associated with investment banking has had to face competition from low-cost trading. In response to this, the investment banks have sought to add value to their offering by transforming brokers from relatively passive market intermediaries connecting buyers and sellers to more active mediators and advisors. This development is coupled with, and further underscored by, the brokers' view of analysts as producing their product, noted above.

The imagery of analysts as the production department and the brokers as their sales organization is complicated by the fact that the product in question appears to be radically heterogeneous in character. That is to say, that the product's characteristics depend on whom it is for:

> The customer needs the broker and the broker definitely needs the customer. It's like a good marriage. You need to understand the customer. The customer cannot be secretive, that is the worst situation, a customer that doesn't tell you what his portfolio looks like. Then they call you and say: 'Why the h*ll didn't you tell me you were lowering H&M when I have so much?' How am I to know? So that would be the bad relation.
>
> (Broker)

> A good share . . . well that changes so damn much all the time. . . And it depends on the client. I work with very different institutional customers. If you compare a hedge fund to a pension fund . . . one needs to trade profitably every day while the other has an average of 17 years on the debt side. You need to take that into account. Their views of a good deal will differ a good deal.
>
> (Stock Brokerage Manager)

If the quality of the broker's offer depends on the customer, then developing a thorough understanding of your customers becomes central to successful brokering. As we saw above, brokers typically have their own customer accounts. In institutional sales, brokers will typically interact with fund managers representing the customers, whereas in private sales the customers are wealthy individuals with deposits at the investment bank. Irrespective of which, each client communicates mainly with the broker responsible for her/his deposit or account. Through repeated contacts with each customer over relatively long periods of time, brokers get to know their clients, their preferences and their portfolios. In the ideal case, this allows them to tailor their advice to each client.

Most of the time brokers will know (or more accurately: *over* time brokers will *learn*) whether particular customers are risk-prone or risk-averse; whether they have particular preferences concerning firms or industries; whether they wish to make long-term investments or seek short-term gains; how many recommendations they act on in a typical day; and many other characteristics. Insights of this kind concerning customer preferences are generally held to be important. Brokers working in institutional sales will learn what kind of investment policy their clients use for a particular fund as well as the current distribution of assets in that fund. Brokers working in private sales will typically have a good overview of the customer's current portfolio. This allows brokers to make suggestions not only based on the general development on the financial markets and specific developments concerning a particular share but also on the fit between that share and their clients' current portfolios. This will also affect their efforts to book meetings between clients and analysts, such as by matching the analyst specialized in the retail sector with managers of funds that have large holdings in that sector. In producing their investment advice, then, brokers mix together two important ingredients: the analyses of specific shares produced by the inhouse analysts, and their own knowledge of their customers. Brokers thus emphasize that their job is about developing and communicating an understanding of the economy at large, of shares in specific firms as potential investment objects, and of their clients as investors:

> When you try to figure out what will happen, you actually put yourself in a specific company's management team's shoes... Or you try to see the company or companies from a customer's perspective: How would I, as a customer react on... let's take an example, a change of a CEO. How will that affect Ericsson? Should I buy or sell?
>
> (Broker)

Still, understanding these things is not enough to become a successful broker. You also need to become a credible advisor. And for this, you need to earn the trust of your clients:

> Our business is all about trust. I've been building relations for 20 years. My clients trust me. That is more important than whether or not I'm the best broker at the moment.
>
> (Broker)

The importance of trust suggests that the type of relationship that these brokers seek to establish with their clients is not one of passive intermediation, but of active mediation. The sender matters when judging what is being sent, or so they seem to suggest. Of course, this is linked to an important characteristic of stock brokering, namely, that it deals with a subject matter that is steeped in uncertainty. To compensate for the fact that future events may overthrow predictions and result in their advice backfiring, brokers work hard to establish trusting relations with their customers. A certain empathic capacity, the ability to put yourself in your customer's shoes, seems to be one quality that the brokers believe is conducive to this.

But the uncertainty of the subject matter and the development of close and trusting relations with clients also allow brokers to take shortcuts in their sales work:

> Quite often I don't need to say very much at all, and not at all put forward any arguments. My customers hear straight away in my tone of voice that I am pretty certain on my case. It is in these occasions that the decision to trade is swift.
>
> (Broker)

> My work is really simple. I don't really understand why it is so well paid. All you have to do is give the customer the impression you know something they don't. The work runs itself.
>
> (Broker)

> I sit in front of the Reuter screen, I listen to the 'noise' in the trading room, and I talk to customers over the phone. What to say is evident from what my colleagues are saying, doing the same as myself. I don't need any specific information; it's like selling vacuum cleaners.
>
> (Broker)

These brokers suggest that at times their work is not very intellectually demanding or knowledge intensive; it is simply about 'selling'. The advice offered does not have to be very complex or very sensitive to individual customers. This brings us back to the view of brokers as relatively passive intermediaries. Or does it? It suggests that brokers at times may disregard some of the complexity in their offering and still be able to do their job. Some market developments, world events and corporate news are simply held to be important enough to be relevant for every customer. Thus, brokers seem to carry a set of taken-for-granted ideas about things that are important regarding shares. The quotes also hint at a rhetorical element in stock brokering that we recognize from other studies of sales situations (Prus, 1989; Pinch and Clark, 1995).

Share identities in stock brokering

While brokering practices differ between banks, and even within the same bank (see also Smith, 1981; Blomberg, 2004), a number of common themes can be identified in the construction of share identities. One such common theme is directly linked to the observed variation in brokering practices; these seem to depend on differences between the brokers' customers, such as their characteristics, objectives and current investment portfolios. Hence, while it produces variation, the centrality of the customer is common for most brokers. A number of more specific commonalities follow from this and can be observed across the share identities constructed by the brokers.

Investment objects for sale

A first common trait is the view of shares as investment objects, which underscores the importance of the customers in the brokers' identity constructions. The main use of the share for the brokers is as a means to generate trade and hence brokerage revenues. To this end, the brokers must be able to make specific trading recommendations to specific customers. Such recommendations are based on an assessment of the fit between the share, as characterized through analysis, and the investment portfolio of the individual customer. Only through such assessments can brokers generate credible arguments as to why specific customers should change the content of their portfolios. The reason for recommending a specific share is not of primary interest to the broker – it could be price movements on the stock market, a macroeconomic trend, some industry-specific news, an analyst's conclusion regarding future market values – as long as it makes it possible for the broker to argue that a specific customer should change her investment portfolio. Thus, the brokers could be said to construct extremely idiosyncratic share identities; to brokers, shares are singularized goods made for trading but with unique features in relation to each customer. Hence, brokers regularly construct a number of partially overlapping share identities for each share (see Figure 5.2).

Constitutive associations

The construction of overlapping versions of shares is directly linked to differences in constitutive associations. Although the brokers' share identities resemble those of the analysts, in that they are constructed as singularized goods, they are singularized in a different way. As a potential investment object for a client, the relevant characteristics of the share are determined as much by that client's portfolio and situation, as by the corporation that the share represents. It is the relation or fit between the share and the specific customer (portfolio) that matters. For one customer, with a certain attitude towards risk-taking, developments relating to a particular share might make it a highly interesting investment object today, but not tomorrow. For a second customer, the

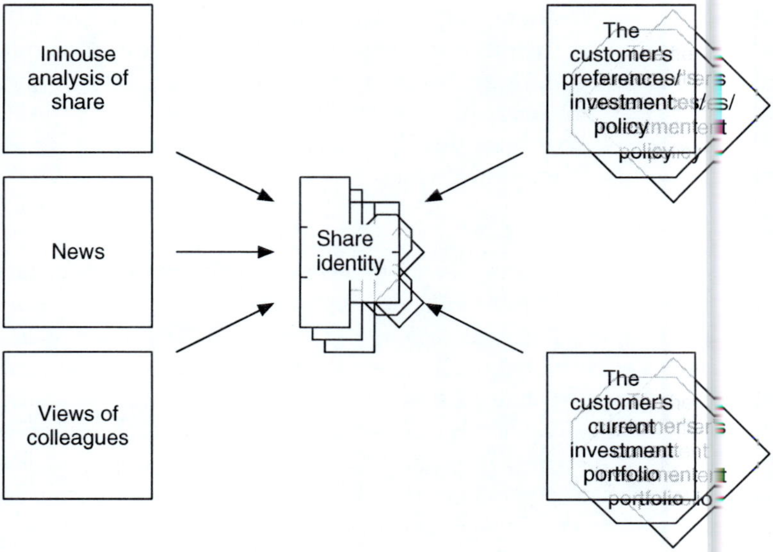

Figure 5.2 Constitutive associations forged in the brokers' construction of overlapping share identities

same share might be highly uninteresting on both these occasions. For a third customer, with a large current position in that share, the same developments may be taken as an indication to divest. What is at stake for the broker is thus not to assess objective qualities in a share, but to assess its subjective qualities for particular customers. Thus, the broker singularizes the share in a situated and customized way that produces multiple overlapping share identities. While one share is ascribed certain common characteristics based on analysts' recommendations, news and discussions among the brokers, the centrality of the associations between that share and customer specifics makes it difficult to speak of the share as having one identity across customers (see Figure 5.2).

Temporal framing

This identity construction allows for flexibility in the temporal character of the share. The inhouse analyses that partake in constituting the share identities afford an extended time frame and durability beyond how the share is currently being traded on the stock market. Newsflashes, the buzz of the trading room and a quoted price from a trader, on the other hand, afford a much shorter temporal perspective, emphasizing the volatility of the share. Whether one of these temporal perspectives is allowed to characterize the share and, if so, which one, is once again determined by the association between the share and a specific customer. Here, the customer's explicit or implicit investment policy becomes important. Associating the share with a customer who is very active and seek to profit from short-term buying and selling, such as a hedge fund, is likely to result in a temporally unstable share identity. Associating the share with a pension fund is more likely to produce a share identity whose temporal perspective is aligned with the quarterly analyses. It is also quite possible that the customer has a temporal perspective that differs from both, such as an industrialist with a time horizon far beyond that of the quarterly analyses. Finally, the character of brokering practices also influences the temporality of the share. Since brokers need to inform their clients about changes in recommendations to maintain their trust, they cannot reconstruct the investment objects too frequently. The account above suggested a rhythm of message adjustment to customers of once or maybe twice per day (morning and mid-day).

Variable share identities

Beyond the variations in share identity that are attributable to the brokers' individual customers, brokers also seem to construct different share identities depending on the situation. On the one hand, brokers emphasize that shares are highly complex products, arguing that successful brokering calls for both a 'deep industrial understanding' and a fair amount of knowledge concerning the customers. This type of reasoning results in the construction of multiple share identities in accordance with Figure 5.2. But at times, stock brokering is 'like selling any simple product'. In these situations, the underlying complexity of a share, which is highlighted through analysis and amplified by customer-specific information, can be dramatically reduced in contacts with customers. This leads brokers to construct less complex share identities primarily constituted through discussions with colleagues and by incorporation of external events. This reductionism also makes the share identities more similar across customers. Although individual customers may still influence the share identity, their specific preferences become less important and the share identity attains a more objective quality.

These different identities have consequences for how the brokers conduct their work. The complex, subjective share identity is linked to cooperation with analysts to explore possible interpretations of a given piece of news, and to engaging in far-reaching discussions with

Table 5.1 Summary of the brokers' share identity characteristics

Constitutive associations	With analyses of corporations and sectors, news and intra-professional discussions, and with customer characteristics and portfolios
What the share represents	Shares represent investment objects for sale, but as such they signify different things to different clients
Potential uses	(Changes in) Shares are used to motivate clients to make transactions and hence generate brokerage revenues
Temporal framing	Variable, spanning day-to-day adjustments, quarterly updates and long-term projections

clients. The reductionist identity, on the other hand, emphasizes discussions within the expert group followed by quick and standardized sales pitches to clients.

Concluding remarks on share identities in stock brokering

While the work of brokers has been divided into three distinct occupations over the past decades, brokers remain an important group in investment banking. They are no longer alone, but they are still responsible for generating a considerable part of the business through their active pursuit of customers. By acting as mediators between these customers and the more specialized analysts and traders, they also seem to perform an important function in the machinery of the financial markets.

The share identities constructed by brokers are once again different from the ones constructed by traders and analysts. An important conclusion from this chapter is thus that the brokers construct yet another type of share identity (see Table 5.1 for a summary of the identity characteristics). At first, this share identity can come across as something inbetween the singularized share of the analyst and the commoditized share of the trader. But our analysis shows that there is a unique and qualitatively different share identity constructed among the brokers, constituted by (relatively weak) associations to the underlying firm and (relatively strong) associations to the customer's specific investment situation. This results in a proliferation of different versions of shares. But our material also shows that brokers at times construct less complex share identities based on strong ideas concerning what constitutes important developments, and how to present such important advice to generate trade.

6
Bankers – Matchmaking and Midwifery

Where do they come from, the shares that populate the stock exchanges, the Reuter-screens, and the pages of the financial press? It is time to go back stage and visit the 'construction department' of investment banking: corporate banking. Such a visit is problematic, however, since corporate banking practices are much less public than the practices of the expert groups discussed previously. Indeed, corporate banking practices are highly insulated even from these other parts of investment banking. Nonetheless, we will not only provide an overview of how these experts work (in this chapter) but also follow corporate banking expertise at work in a specific project involving the introduction of a new share on the stock exchange (in Chapter 7). This will allow us to examine the role of corporate banking in structuring contemporary business life and in organizing stock markets by constructing and reshaping shares.

The expert business advisers

Even though several expert categories can claim to be carrying out investment banking, the experts in corporate banking are usually the ones referred to as 'the bankers'. This signals both the historical heritage of contemporary investment banking and the prestigious position of corporate banking within it. As we noted in the historical overview of investment banking (Chapter 2), corporate banking is a direct descendant of the activities of the famous private bankers and partnership firms of the nineteenth century, from which clients sought assistance when seeking to finance or restructure their business ventures (see Morrison and Wilhelm, 2007a, b). Today, the corporate banking departments are by and large service providers for top managers regarding financial transactions, and their role has been characterized as one of 'information brokerage' (Wilhelm, 1999:26). Although most firms engaged in investment banking have transformed into full service financial firms during the past decades, corporate financial services remain a core aspect of their operations, irrespective of size.

The experts working in corporate banking provide financial analyses and advise to corporations that either seek new ways of financing their operations or seek to buy or sell specific operations. In most investment banks, the corporate bankers are divided into two major groups. The largest of these, sometimes referred to as 'Equity Capital Markets', offers expertise and hands-on assistance in completing different types of equity fundraising transactions, including Initial Public Offerings (IPOs) and new share issues. That is, they offer advice to managers of corporations that want to finance their operations by either noting their shares on the stock exchange for the first time or, if the corporations are already publicly listed, by issuing more shares.

The second group consists of bankers providing advice on 'Mergers and Acquisitions' (M&A), that is, how to restructure corporations. As the name indicates, cases developed by this group often include the restructuring of one corporation in relation to other corporations in the industry. The directors working with these issues tend to have good relations to the upper echelons of the business community, giving them opportunities to exchange ideas with potential clients on possible future scenarios. Common advice they give is to acquire, divest or merge a specific part of operations in order to reap benefits of scale or scope; free capital resources; improve financial efficiency; or simply gain a more advantageous power position within an industry. Since acting on this type of advice may result in major changes in the corporations (e.g. introducing a completely new line of business into a corporation), M&A projects typically affect the shares of the corporations (e.g. triggering re-evaluations).

Corporate banking activities also involve two smaller sub-groups of experts, sometimes referred to as 'centres of excellence', who construct the financial instruments used by the two major groups. The first of these smaller groups consists of experts that tailor financial instruments for specific customers. These experts describe their work as 'financial engineering', focusing on the financing of a corporation, including the arrangement of various forms of loans, or combinations of loans and private funding. The second of these smaller groups of experts, sometimes referred to as 'Restructuring and Valuation', develops standards for evaluating corporations. These standards are used by the experts working in

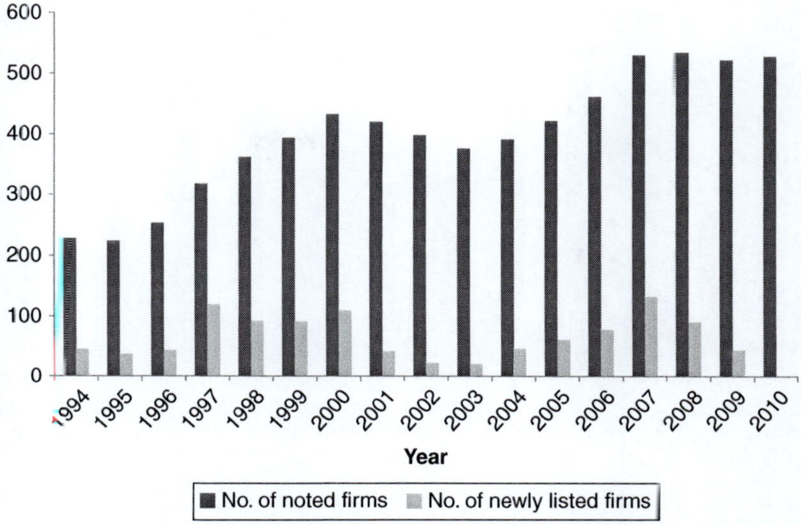

Figure 6.1 Changes in the number of publicly listed corporations on Swedish stock exchanges, 1994–2010
Source: Statistics Sweden, series FM0201.

'Equity Capital Markets' and 'Mergers & Acquisitions' in projects that involve public transactions.

Without claiming a unidirectional causal relation between corporate banking and overall stock market activity, we suggest that there is at least a correlation. The number of publicly listed corporations on stock exchanges around the world has increased considerably over the past 20 years. In Sweden, the number of corporations noted on the stock exchanges more than doubled over the period 1994–2010 (from 228 to 528, see Figure 6.1). Still, the implied net increase of 20 listed corporations per year vastly underestimates the actual stock market-related corporate banking activities over this period. Between 1994 and 2010, 1069 companies were listed anew on the Swedish stock exchanges, suggesting a much larger, albeit varying, number of IPOs made each year. Internationally, we also find considerable variation in terms of the number of IPOs undertaken. In the United States, the 1970s and 2000s stand out as periods of relatively modest IPO activity, whereas the 1980s and particularly the 1990s saw a very high level of activity (see http://www.ipovitalsigns.com).[1]

It is thus not entirely straightforward to say that it has become more attractive to exploit the opportunities of the stock markets. Rather,

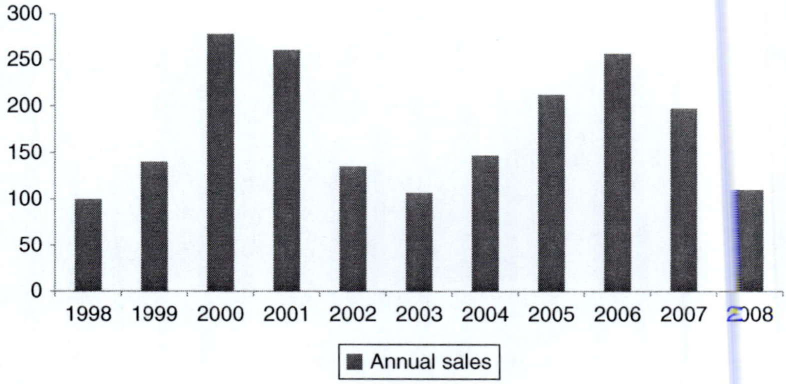

Figure 6.2 Sales development of corporate banking operations in one of the studied investment banks, 1998–2008 (indexed series 1998 = 100)

it would seem that this varies considerably over time, as implied also by the debate concerning the existence of merger waves (e.g. Gärtner and Halbheer, 2009). It seems clear that the stock markets did become increasingly important for corporate banking activities during the 1990s, whereas the 2000s has seen fewer IPOs and hence relatively less corporate banking activity. In Sweden, however, IPO activity quickly regained momentum (Figure 6.1). This is also reflected in the sales figures for corporate banking services in many Swedish investment banks (see Figure 6.2 for an example). While our material prevents us from making claims about the relative import of corporate banking practices as compared with other factors, it does suggest that these practices contribute to shape the stock markets by actively engaging with corporations and their shares.

Fluid hierarchical teams

In contrast with the other expert groups within investment banking, corporate banking is about project work performed within a fairly transparent authority structure. The senior banker, also referred to as the *director*, has formal responsibility for projects and is the person primarily involved in 'pitching' to clients (more about this later). In addition to the directors, there are three categories of employees in corporate banking. Newcomers start off as *analysts*, which means that they do a lot of 'leg-work' in preparing cases. Then, if successful at this, analysts may advance to become *associates*, and after a few more years, *associate directors*. These two categories are typically responsible for the daily activities in a project and for guiding their more junior colleagues. Finally, some of the associate directors gain the status of directors. The three subordinate levels provide the directors with detailed financial analyses of corporations and industries and prepare the cases that are to be presented to clients. Generally, a director will approve any document before it is presented to a client.

The project teams mix junior and senior bankers, but the actual make-up of the teams varies, for several reasons. First of all, it is not always desirable to maintain stable teams since corporate banking projects differ in character and thus require quite specific expertise; this might concern the particular solution being considered, or the industry in question. Second, projects also change character over time so that additional capacity and/or new forms of expertise become needed. Third, most employees in corporate banking are constantly 'overbooked', so that new projects will have to be squeezed into already busy schedules, making it difficult to maintain stable teams:

> The five directors heading the teams meet a few minutes every morning to discuss the current workload. There may be a couple of new projects that we need to find people for, for instance. This happens regularly. Typically, no one is really available, so we need to ask: who could take on some more work?
>
> (Director, Corporate Banking)

Despite the fluidity of the project teams, the bankers emphasize the collective character of their work. It is the team, rather than the individual banker that needs to have the necessary qualifications. This means that there is room for variation in terms of how skilled individual bankers are at such aspects as analysis, valuation, customer contacts. But it also means that bankers need to be team players:

> The team *has* to function well. Otherwise our job becomes unbearable since there is so much to do in such a short time. So many difficult questions... negotiations with the other party, *and* with our customers as well. If you would need to negotiate within the team as well – it wouldn't work.
>
> (Director, Corporate Banking)

Given that the make-up of a team can change several times over the course of a project, it becomes important to have co-workers that can easily fit into new constellations.

The secret services

At times, preparing corporate banking cases will require competences that are not typically found within the corporate banking department. Analysts working in the securities department, for instance, are held to command expertise concerning specific industries and their input may thus be important when assessing the consequences of a proposed acquisition, or when trying to set a reasonable share price for an IPO. However, bringing an analyst to work on a corporate banking case is problematic and requires careful arrangements. Information obtained from participation in corporate banking activities must not be allowed to influence the advice that analysts and brokers give to their customers. This is also a central legal principle that the regulatory bodies explicitly adhere to, including the Swedish FSA (see D'Agostino et al., 2007).

Since the corporate banking experts work with cases not yet publicly known, discussions with people working in the securities line of business is highly sensitive. Due to the character of corporate banking projects – mergers, acquisitions and so on – involvement typically means access to information that will affect stock market prices, 'price-sensitive information'. Until this information is made publicly known, it is 'inside information' and as such, it cannot be used as a basis for trading. Given current regulations and sanctions, it is in the interest of the firms active in investment banking to convince the market and the regulatory agencies that no illegal information is transferred between corporate banking and securities. The solution to this is the erection of 'Chinese walls' (firewalls) between corporate banking and other lines of business:

> [Name of investment bank] has guidelines and rules in order to ensure that the business areas within the Company operate independently of each other, so that the customer's interests are protected in a secure manner. In particular the Company will place emphasis on ensuring that satisfactory 'Chinese walls' exist between the corporate finance department and other departments, as well as between active portfolio management and ordinary brokering in the Company.
>
> (Excerpt from 'General terms of business for trading in financial securities')

These walls are not necessarily physical barriers, although the departments often are physically separated from each other. As Hayward and Boeker (1998:5) note, the term is 'a metaphor to describe a set of internal rules and procedures to prevent one department from obtaining information prejudicial to the clients of another'. There is also a temporal dimension to these barriers, since the information handled in a corporate banking project will change character during the project, such as when the project is publicly announced. For some time, then, analysts who have been involved in corporate banking projects are put in quarantine before being allowed to work in securities again. By allowing corporate banking and equities departments to co-exist within the same organization, these practical arrangements are a prerequisite for full-service investment banks to operate.

Still, however elaborate these arrangements are, the interaction between analysts and corporate banking has its problems, as suggested by this analyst who had recently assisted on an IPO case:

> The link between us analysts and Corporate Finance has indeed been sensitive historically. The whole story with Eliot Spitzer and the Global Settlement a few years back... You know: you are being positive because it will benefit the interest of the firm, or something like that. But then there is also the link that *can* exist, or the one that *should* exist. *If* we are involved in an IPO then we *must* have an analysis on that corporation, and it is of course highly unusual that we are extremely negative about the company we are introducing on the stock exchange, that is sort of in the nature of things...
>
> (Analyst)

Working in corporate banking

Although corporate bankers do not work with the extremely short time perspective of a trader, they still describe their working days as hectic. The business deals they are involved in are not decided on and closed within seconds, but the tempo is often high and their workload extremely stretching. When a client displays an interest in a case-scenario, an intense period of work follows. Thorough research will then be necessary in order to describe industry trends, analyse the key markets and the financial situation, examine legal conditions, identify problems and opportunities and credibly argue why a certain solution is the best one. A newcomer to corporate finance is expected to work extremely hard during these periods – days, nights, weekends:

> It is often quite hectic, you run from one meeting to another. It's always tight, in terms of time running out, meetings, and different projects running in parallel, so you have to be effective. You can't go around contemplating things; you have to get them done right away.
>
> (Director, Corporate Banking)

> A lot of the work is not very glamorous and fun. There is a lot of research, a lot of calculating, a lot of prospect writing. This is perhaps not so much fun if you've already worked a few years somewhere else and think you've moved up a notch.
>
> (Director, Corporate Banking)

Newcomers will also find themselves in such periods more often than not. Working 80–100 hours a week is regarded as normal during the first years, but long working hours and a 'flexible private life' is expected also later in your career. Even official job descriptions are quite outspoken about the difficulty of combining a job as an investment banker with an active social life:

> I try to keep the weekends clear. It takes a critical meeting on Monday to make me go to work during the weekend. Sometimes I go in and clear the table. It is situations of emergency all the time. My whole life is like one great drama. But this is also part of the fascination. In some respects I'm restless myself, and that's reflected in how I work, what kind of industry I've chosen. Sometimes restless, other times incredibly tenacious, persistent. If it's worth fighting for.
>
> (Director, Corporate Banking)

When the bankers describe their promotion prospects, however, the career goal is not about becoming managers (even if some managerial responsibilities do come with a promotion to director). Just like the other experts in investment banking, they primarily express ambitions to become really good and respected professionals (and earn money doing it):

> It is competence and specialist knowledge that counts. To be a good businessman, a really good negotiator and a respected adviser, that is what is most important – and also what is most rewarded.
>
> (Director, Corporate Banking)

While 'competence' could mean many things in the financial sector – from how one is dressed and posed to the ability to solve complex theoretical problems (Blomberg, 2004) – bankers emphasize that it is about process knowledge and about making things happen. A competent corporate banker is a person who has the ability to identify and successfully pitch cases to clients, and assist them in realizing the proposed scenarios. This ability is generally held to come with first-hand experience of corporate banking projects:

> Product and process knowledge is more important than if you are an expert on a particular industry, and that knowledge has to be acquired by working with these things. If you haven't worked with business deals, or IPOs, or new emissions before, then you kind of have to start over when you come to us.
>
> (Director, Corporate Banking)

> How does a timetable for an IPO look? How do you work it? What are the different stages in the process? This is not something you read somewhere or learn without doing it. It's good to have this type of knowledge in your backbone. To have a stable foundation.
>
> (Director, Corporate Banking)

These comments suggest that corporate bankers consider their trade to contain a fair amount of tacit knowledge, things that cannot easily be learned from books. But the importance attributed to 'on the job' training is not only about being shown the ropes of corporate banking. In addition to the educational function, bankers indicate that it is a broader socialization process:

> We don't deliberately indoctrinate people, but of course, it's advantageous to be able to shape people from the start, both in terms of values, working methods, diligence . . . When you're young, you're more prepared to accept that role and learn everything from scratch, accept the role at the bottom of the ladder.
>
> (Director, Corporate Banking)

The rewards for subjecting to this process are considerable. The norm for employee remuneration, also known as the 'comp ratio', is as high as 50 per cent of net revenue (Folkman et al., 2007). Of course, there is a considerable span internally among the bankers. Available figures suggest that newly employed analysts in the United States will earn between $65,000 and $80,000 per year, excluding bonuses. Figures for associate bankers with a few years experience range from $75,000 to $105,000 per year, also not counting annual bonuses.[2] The size of the annual bonuses differs across firms, over time and across regions. Although Swedish firms may not top the bonus list, bonuses have still been substantial. Over the ten-year period 1998–2007, the average size of the annual bonuses paid to the corporate bankers in one of the investment banks in our study was 138 per cent of their salary.

Corporate banking practices

Corporate bankers consider their job to require quite specific forms of expertise. Moreover, these requirements are held to be similar across corporate banking organizations, suggesting that it is indeed possible to speak about corporate bankers as an expert group:

> If you want to recruit someone who is functional from day 1, then you have to recruit from another corporate banking department. Then there are large similarities, both in terms of culture and the types of tasks and projects they work with.
>
> (Director, Corporate Banking)

We have identified five interrelated and sometimes overlapping functions and associated practices that corporate banking experts engage in. First, as mentioned above, bankers actively seek out potential clients and 'pitch' cases to them: they try to sell their ideas concerning what the corporations should do. Second, and related to this, corporate bankers spend considerable time on case analyses, work that both precedes and supersedes the delivery of a pitch. Third, once a client corporation has agreed to go ahead with a proposed business deal, corporate bankers act as mediators during its realization, which may include handling international liaison in international business deals. Fourth, corporate bankers help to reduce 'corporate anxiety' by providing legitimacy to strategic decisions. Fifth, and finally, corporate bankers assist in modifying the constitution of corporations so that their shares better reflect the underlying values. Below, we discuss each of these corporate banking functions and the practices linked to them in more detail.

'Pitching' advice to corporate elites

A central part of corporate banking is to offer advice to corporate executives regarding complex business decisions. This advice is primarily based on financial and market analyses and often contains recommendations about transactions to undertake as well as how these transactions can be financed. At times, corporate bankers also provide advice on matters that are more internal in character, such as suggesting how to restructure a corporation in order to improve profitability. One director described his work in the following way:

> You try to cultivate customer relations, we call it 'pitching', a form of marketing. What you actually do is present interesting new ideas for them. It could be acquisitions or to sell parts of a company. Or ideas for making adjustments in liabilities, for example repurchasing shares; if they are in need of capital it could involve the issue of new shares, and in other cases private placements. It can also be a question of splitting a firm, which actually could be seen as a trend right now; to focus the line of business in corporations.
>
> (Director, Corporate Banking)

A specific piece of advice to a corporation, a new idea, as the director puts it, is usually linked to several possible financial solutions, that is, ways of bringing the necessary capital into the firm to realize the idea. As can be seen from the quote, many of these solutions actively involve the stock markets: they may include issuing new shares or repurchasing existing ones. The different financial solutions have varying consequences both legally, in terms of costs, and in terms of the type and size of risk they entail. This means that it becomes necessary for the customer firm to carefully evaluate the consequences of the different solutions and choose one that fits their situation and strategy. Once again, then, expert advice becomes valuable.

For bankers, the process of selling their services is highly integrated with that of producing them. As with many other professional services (and services in general, for that matter), corporate financial services are not produced in their entirety until a potential client has agreed to buy them. However, the bankers are highly involved in what may be called pre-production work (Svedberg Nilsson and Winroth, 2005). This involvement appears to be slightly different than that of some other professional service providers, for instance, lawyers or accountants. Whereas the latter are usually contacted for a specific task or problem, the bankers actively contact potential customers themselves and also suggest solutions to what they consider to be possible inefficiencies. Consequently, the bankers not only supply the solutions but also define or suggest the 'problems' that top managers have. They are thus strongly and directly involved in the construction of the need for their services:

> We... ell... let's put it like this, when it comes to the actual deals, they [the bankers] can of course identify a number of different... they often have a certain amount of initiative there. They make

> suggestions. And that can be very good, because it can trigger *thoughts* in various directions.
>
> (CEO, recent acquisition deal)

The 'pitching' contact with prospective corporate clients is a very time-consuming activity that precedes the actual sale of a case, or idea. A rough estimate made by several directors is that they spend around 90 per cent of their time in meetings with possible future clients. The remaining 10 per cent would then appear to be what they spend on producing the actual services. This is in line with the basic characterization of corporate banking projects as teamwork in which more junior colleagues supply the analyses and perform the hands-on tasks. However, the selling procedure itself involves constructing an idea of what to sell and is therefore an important part of production.

The pitching process involves a gradually growing commitment of resources. Many pitches start with general conversations over the phone concerning changes in the industry and ideas for interesting financial solutions. If the potential client finds an idea exciting, it could lead to a more detailed discussion over lunch. If a top manager's interest in the discussion continues, a more thorough presentation will take place. For this, the director will involve the analysts and associates, who contribute more detailed analyses and presentation material. At the actual meeting, the director will probably also be assisted by an associate director.

In cases where a meeting is perceived as important for the final acceptance of an idea (which could be the first formal meeting or a meeting later on in the process), the bankers will invest considerable time in their analysis and presentation. This then becomes a crucial stage in their pitch, as it will determine whether their case will actually be purchased. If the pitched case is rejected, the bankers step down and continue their normal contact pattern, staying in touch with the top managers and trying to convince them that they have new interesting suggestions concerning the future of their corporation. The bankers are well aware that good personal relations are central to their business. To maintain access to the top managers, which enables them to arrange meetings, they need good relations. Since a lot of bankers from many banks try to keep in touch with the top managers and attempt to catch their attention and interest, this part of corporate banking work is highly competitive in character.[3]

Analysing opportunities for business deals

As suggested above, the pitching process is intimately connected to a process of analysis. The proactive role assumed by the bankers requires them to acquire detailed knowledge about individual corporations and their competitors, including such factors as their financial states, market positions and production capabilities. This knowledge is acquired in part through their close and continuous contacts with the top managers but also through the ongoing intelligence work and analyses carried out by their team of experts:

> Financial analysis is the foundation for what we do. Financial advice and financial analysis, questions concerning valuation, results, and balance sheets. But our advice is transaction specific, every transaction has its consequences, and you must always analyse them. Particularly when there are no market prices available on the things you are discussing. Then, we must perform our own, very careful valuation.
>
> (Director, Corporate Banking)

As a consequence of their research and analyses, bankers at times appear to be more knowledgeable about the corporations they advise than do the top managers working in them. Rather than a difference in the amount of knowledge, however, it is primarily a question of their knowledge being different from that of the top managers. The preoccupation with financial aspects of corporations makes corporate banking discourses different from intra-industry or intra-firm discourses on daily operations, current technologies and so on. This also means that bankers sometimes come up with proposals that strike their potential clients as both surprising and unthinkable.

If a pitched case is accepted, an intensive work period ensues. The depth and breadth of the analysis is extended, and a detailed scrutiny of the involved corporation(s) is carried out. At this point, the bankers' analysis not only serves to specify the likely financial consequences of the proposed deal, but also to identify possible extensions of the deal:

> If we are discussing an IPO, for instance. Then we may investigate whether it would be beneficial to do an additional acquisition prior to the IPO. If that would increase the company's attractiveness as an investment object. If there are synergies to exploit.
>
> (Director, Corporate Banking)

This underscores the dynamic character of corporate banking projects; a proposed IPO can turn into an acquisition project which will have considerable consequences on the expertise required in the project team. The interrelation between corporate banking practices is further pronounced when a project moves from the drawing board towards realization. Once again, new forms of expertise become important.

Acting as mediators in business deals

The bankers do not only assist their corporate clients with financial analyses. If a pitch is accepted, the bankers also actively assist their clients in realizing the proposed project. This means that they become mediators in a number of situations. First of all, their analysis of the deal may be of considerable interest to the managers of the other corporation in a merger or acquisition case. It can provide valuable information about the situation and the advantages that the deal offers, which can be used to gain support for the proposal internally. In deals involving other corporations, the bankers are also often involved in the actual negotiations with the other party:

> It becomes our job to coordinate the process. To some extent we also take part in it. Much of this is governed by formal requirements. We have to see to it that all the contracts are correct, verify the figures, etc. But we also help out during the negotiations, together with the lawyers, with us supplying assessments concerning the business side of things. Some issues are typically handled directly between the advisers.
>
> (Director, Corporate Banking)

Representatives of client organizations verify that bankers are often involved during negotiations, but offer some alternative characterizations of their involvement. One corporate VP in a client organization described the bankers' practical involvement:

> They [the bankers] were involved, or you could say that we *used* them in part as a contact surface. Many of the questions that always crop up in this context [an acquisition] are linked to … let's call it *negotiation tactics*. And in that area, the advisors handle a great number of issues
>
> (Corporate VP, legal affairs).

Another client reinforced the view of using the bankers in a tactic capacity:

> There are situations in which you don't want to 'front' yourself but you *allow* the investment bank to conduct some initial, preparatory

> work. This way you can sound out possible counterparts, without committing yourself.
>
> (CEO, recent spin-off deal)

Using bankers as mediators during the realization of a deal is also premised on the fact that they are superbly motivated to achieve results. The payment for their services is typically linked to the completion of the deal and set in relation to total deal value. According to independent financial services advisors Freeman & Co (1 October 2002), investment banking fees averaged 1.5 per cent of deal value in 2000.

Another type of mediation arises from the fact that corporate banking projects often have an international dimension. Attracting international investors during an IPO, identifying potential candidates for mergers or acquisitions abroad or working in a syndicated project with a foreign investment bank, all are examples of this. Even the relatively small investment banking operations active in Sweden typically have offices in a few other countries. Since the expert services mostly asked for in these foreign markets concern corporate banking, such as serving Scandinavian clients that are negotiating deals with foreign corporations, most of the employees are bankers. The offices are usually small and placed in financial centres like London and New York. Some banks also have offices located in regions that are considered particularly interesting. Due to their small size, the offices can be relocated without too much difficulty. As an illustration, one Swedish investment bank opened an office in San Francisco in the late 1990s, when the IT industry was booming. The office was closed in the beginning of the 2000s and instead new offices were opened in Latvia and Lithuania, since many Swedish client firms saw business opportunities in these countries.

These expatriate bankers primarily act as mediators between Scandinavian and foreign corporations. Foreign top managers may, for instance, be interested in exploiting their knowledge of the Scandinavian markets. However, to become credible, the bankers have to demonstrate that they represent an organization that is experienced in conducting transactions of this type in Scandinavia, such as acting as an underwriter in IPOs. Consequently, the Swedish operations create goodwill also in the other national markets. Scandinavian client firms, on the other hand, need support in navigating foreign business cultures. Discussions concerning financial solutions or mergers and acquisitions are often international, but they also have a local flavour. Local business culture needs to be taken into account, both when planning to combine previously independent organizations through mergers or acquisitions, and during negotiations concerning specific deals. The bankers located abroad regard their ability to handle cultural differences between Scandinavia and other regions as a crucial aspect when serving clients.

As suggested by the first quote (See page 120), the bankers also handle a number of other issues in addition to their various 'diplomatic' functions. Since they are familiar with the routines and practices involved in a specific type of business transaction, they typically handle administrative matters vis-à-vis authorities and legal instances. For some transactions, additional consultants may be needed, such as lawyers or technical consultants needed to perform investigations regarding past activities that may come to affect operations in the future (also known as due diligence processes). Usually, the bankers handle these contacts as well, since they must cooperate closely with all experts involved. Finally, many if not most corporate banking projects are syndicated, involving two or more investment banking organizations, so that temporary, boundary spanning working groups must be formed with representatives of all involved organizations.

It may seem surprising that external experts are so heavily involved in central strategic decisions and activities within corporations. To explain this, one banker characterized the use of corporate finance expertise as a form of outsourcing by the client corporations. A first rationale for such a move is linked to the amount of research that needs to be performed prior to and during transactions like a merger or acquisition. It would simply not be economically justifiable for a corporation, whose involvement in transactions of this kind is both irregular and relatively rare, to have all the necessary competence internally:

> We give advice on matters where there are no answers, or nothing black or white. That's the difficult part – what you charge for – the advice that is based on the experience that you have as an organisation.
>
> (Director, Corporate Banking)

This is also supported by representatives of client firms who argue that they cannot maintain expertise internally for the highly specialized tasks involved in generating prospects, evaluations and formal presentations. A second argument to pursue this 'outsourcing' strategy is that top executives view it as a way for them to legitimise their decisions. If anything goes wrong, they can at least point to the fact that they acted on advice provided by a well-known banker with considerable experience of this kind of transaction. Many investment banking organizations explicitly bring up the provision of reassurance as an argument when marketing their services.

Reducing corporate anxiety

The excerpt below is translated from the introduction to the website of a major investment banking operation in Sweden (accessed in 2008):

> In an ever-changing world, who can predict the future and know exactly what is going to happen?
>
> – Nobody!
>
> Therefore, it is becoming increasingly important to select one's investment bank wisely. An investment bank that knows how to connect people with ideas and capital.

If visitors to this site were unaware that investment banking involves the ancient business of forecasting the future, they are now enlightened. But since forecasting the future is not an exact science, it becomes important for corporations to team up with the right advisors. On the same note, but with added irony, Merrill Lynch aired the following commercial a few months before being acquired by Bank of America in September 2008

> (Opening scene showing a barn with flapping doors and stirring animals under a stormy sky.) Speaker voice: -In the midst of the storm, it's only natural to wonder where the future will lead.
>
> (Sudden change of scenery, sky clearing, string music added, animals becalmed.) Speaker voice: -To people who worry about the winds of change today, we'd like to remind you that no adversity lasts forever. And we'll be there. With the strength and resources you can count on. Because at Merrill Lynch, we're bullish on the future.
>
> (Description of a Merrill Lynch commercial produced by Jet Sets Visual Production, July 2008)

As implied in our brief history of investment banking in Chapter 2, the need for advice and visions for the future seems to have grown in the corporate world over recent decades. At least, the demand for expert advice to assist managers in strategic decisions concerning structuring and financing their businesses has grown. According to the bankers, top managers have increasingly realized the need for professional advice in strategic financial matters during recent decades. Not only is it legitimate to consult experts in the financial area today, such consultations have also become considered a necessity when faced with crucial strategic decisions. One associate director described the corporate banking offering as 'trust and relationships'. Still, one of our interviewees, a CEO of a corporation that had recently participated in a merger, was quite candid about his doubts concerning the role of investment banks:

> It would be interesting to analyze what role they really play these banks. Because that is something we think about ourselves: do we really need them? They are bloody expensive, you know! Could we solve this in another way? [...] In this case, the complexity of the deal contributed. And they push a bit. [...] Nonetheless, billions are poured over these advisors, expensive American banks like Morgan Stanley and Goldman Sachs and that lot. And we do it, too. But sometimes I wonder: do we really need them?
>
> (Corporate VP, publicly listed corporation)

While questioning the need for, and contribution of, corporate finance services from banks, this corporate vice president readily admitted that his corporation was a frequent customer. With even the agnostics being prepared to spend large sums on this type of service, it is not surprising that financial services was one of the fastest growing industries during the 1990s. Top managers of corporations also seem to have become increasingly attentive to the possibilities offered by exploiting the financial market. According to the bankers, traditional banks often financed new ventures a few decades ago. Over time, however, top managers have become increasingly positive towards the stock markets so that they now tend to view emissions on the stock market as a preferable form of financing corporate investments. This change is primarily attributed to a learning process on behalf of the top managers; from the bankers' perspective, top managers have gained a better general knowledge of financial strategy concerns and an awareness of the considerable amounts of capital flowing within the financial system. Hiring a well-known provider of corporate banking services to act as an underwriter when issuing shares is, for instance, considered to rub off on the corporation, increasing its chances of a successful issue (see also Podolny, 1993).

The increasing size and sophistication of the financial industry as a whole is also brought forward as an explanation for why demand has grown for corporate financial services. With the increased availability of information, the fear of mistakes is said to have increased. One financial director from a client organization used the term 'CYA' to describe the situation – 'everyone can Check Your Analysis, so you need to Cover Your Ass.' Calculations have become more public and the fear of mistakes based on bad judgements has become a sensitive issue. Consequently, asking for a 'second opinion' from one or two other banks is nowadays considered normal:

> It is a way of gaining security. The managers might already have made up their minds, but they still contact us, just to get to know that we see it as a good idea. 'Well, we hired the toughest of the investment banks' becomes a form of security, if something doesn't work out as planned.
>
> (Director, Corporate Banking)

Having a number of banks involved in just one transaction has obvious consequences for the demand for corporate banking services. Part of this market growth also seems to be linked to changes in how transactions are carried out in practice. In the following scenario, the international banks seem to have had a leading role:

> It is of course a question of legitimacy. But take a case like AstraZeneca. Such a merger takes a lot of advisers. First, there is a global investment bank involved. To accomplish the whole deal, they will also need advisers from Sweden, that is, experts from a Swedish investment bank. In addition, they might want a second opinion, another investment bank telling them that the deal is good and fair.
>
> (Director, Corporate Banking)

Not only are corporate managers seeking advice on central business ventures; they are also seeking advice on how to evaluate the advice. The role of investment banking organizations themselves in fuelling this type of client behaviour should not be underestimated. As our initial excerpt above illustrated (and many other advertisements and commercials as well), investment banks tend to stress the indeterminacy of the business world and the stability and reassurance they can help provide.

Finding hidden values or 'pimp my share'?

Irrespective of whether one chooses to interpret corporate banking practices as contributing productively to the dynamics of industries and financial markets, or as mainly performing a symbolic role of adding legitimacy to the activities of corporate elites, there are certain corporate banking projects that explicitly have a polishing purpose. Some of the advice given by corporate bankers is geared towards affecting the evaluation of a corporation's share without necessarily leading to any changes in how the industrial activities are being performed. An illustrative example was a pitch that one of the studied investment banks directed towards a large multinational corporation to 'render hidden values visible'.

The corporation in question, Betacorp, had pursued a strategy of vertical integration to increase production and distribution efficiency and had aggressively acquired a number of 'downstream operations' during a five-year period. This meant that Betacorp, besides its traditional base in production of raw materials, now had a sizeable production of semi-finished products and a growing number of wholly owned end product manufacturers spread across Europe. One of the corporate banking directors we interviewed, who had considerable experience of the industry, had followed these activities closely. In his opinion, the current price of the Betacorp share did not fully reflect the underlying value of the corporation's assets. Rather, it included a large rebate. Clearly, the stock market was not making a favourable evaluation of the vertical integration strategy:

> I knew their CEO had a strong vision and he had invested a lot of personal prestige in this vertical integration project. Still, if we simplify matters, they had three vertically positioned divisions, which we estimated to be worth roughly 20, 15 and 10, respectively. But the stock market refused to recognise this. So, the whole thing hovered at a stock market value of about 30 or so.
>
> (Director, Corporate Banking)

A pitch was prepared for separating the three business lines and divesting the newly acquired downstream operations. Such a deal, the pitch went, would provide an extreme payback to the owners in a very short period of time, while having relatively minor consequences from an industrial point of view. But the pitch was directed towards the chairman of the board, not the CEO. A few months later, a new CEO was appointed who very soon announced intentions to sell off one line of business. Within days, one of the major international investment banks announced a revised evaluation of the share, with a strong recommendation to buy:

> Morgan Stanley identifies strong potential in the Betacorp share. With [the change of CEO] Betacorp will enter a new phase, which will involve an adjustment of its operations. According to Morgan Stanley this means that the company will decide to focus its operations and also find a way to divest [one of its lines of business]. Morgan Stanley raises its target price from 17.3 to 20.3 per share.
>
> (Excerpt from press release, translated)

The excerpt suggests that the signals of an impending change in Betacorp alone led to a first change in valuation. According to the banker, the subsequent *actual* sale of the division led to further changes in valuation. Although the price tag for the division was not publicized, he suggested that the combined stock market valuations of Betacorp and the acquiring firm rose by approximately 20 per cent as a consequence of the deal.

This is but one example of how corporate banking projects may considerably affect perceptions of share value, without necessarily changing much of the underlying operations. In the case of Betacorp, the three business divisions remained more or less intact. What changed was the ownership of one of these divisions, not the way in which it conducted its business. Given that recommendations, such as the one from Morgan Stanley above, also have consequences for stock market trading, corporate banking projects not only affect perceptions of value but also affect actual values of shares.

The multiple roles of corporate bankers

The preceding five sections have illustrated that corporate bankers assume several different roles and engage in a wide variety of activities as part of their service provision to clients. These include, but need not be limited to, pitching practices (such as networking, generating and presenting ideas), analysis practices (conducting in-depth industry analyses, financial analyses of corporations, valuating assets), mediating practices (acting as a financial engineer, staging negotiations, acting as a go-between or cultural attaché, keeping updated on regulatory requirements), legitimating practices (providing seals of approval by underwriting or offering second opinions) and polishing practices (adjusting share content to current evaluation practices). Although there are some tools in the corporate banking toolbox that do not involve shares, such as syndicated loans and private placements, the shares of corporations and the stock markets are clearly central to many corporate banking projects. In an IPO project, corporate banking assists in making a corporation's shares publicly available for the first time. When conducting a new emission, corporate banking helps to sell new shares in already listed corporations thus altering the supply of this particular good on the stock market. In repurchasing projects, corporate banking assists in doing the opposite, reducing the number of shares in a corporation that is available on the stock market. During mergers and acquisitions, such as in the project described in the Section 'The multiple roles of corporate bankers', corporate banking contributes to significant changes in the 'contents' and valuations of specific shares by adding or divesting business areas or production units. In the Section 'Constructing share identities in corporate banking' , we once again use our descriptive model to characterize the share identities constructed in corporate banking.

Constructing share identities in corporate banking

What share identities do corporate bankers construct when engaging in their projects? Do these differ dramatically from the three distinct share identities constructed by traders, analysts and brokers? If so, in what ways? Table 6.1 summarizes the specifics of the share identities constructed by corporate bankers.

A dual identity: Stable, yet plastic

On the one hand, the share identity constructed by bankers resembles that of the analysts. Corporate bankers clearly construct shares as knowledge objects that can be constituted through proper analysis. They spend considerable efforts to establish the characteristics of the operations represented by particular shares; to identify possible changes

Table 6.1 Summary of the bankers' share identity characteristics

Constitutive associations	As *knowledge objects*: to analytical models and relevant information. As *products under construction*: to physical resources, intellectual property, etc.
What the share represents	Shares represent ownership in a corporation and its going concerns, which makes them a potential source of financing
Potential uses	Shares can be used to finance a client's operations and to realize values for owners of such operations
Temporal framing	(Mid- to) Long-term, linked to industry trends and prospects, and future-oriented, what it could become

to these operations; and, above all, to assess the possible consequences of such proposed changes for the value of the shares. Partly, this identity is constructed in collaboration with analysts, so that analysts become directly involved in corporate banking projects. On the other hand, bankers also assume a more pragmatic position vis-à-vis shares, such as during corporate restructurings. The pitching of proposals, and subsequent active participation in altering the make-up of the operations represented by a particular share, suggests that bankers regard shares as artefacts that can be actively shaped. In this incarnation, then, the share is more appropriately likened to a work piece or a blank that is given new or other features as a result of the bankers' efforts. Thus, bankers construct a dual share identity: shares are both fairly stable objects that can be accurately characterized by amassing knowledge about the going concerns that they represent, and fairly plastic objects that can be altered by modifying these going concerns.

The common denominator, then, is the view of shares as representative of going concerns. More specifically, the various practices that bankers engage suggest that shares both represent and signify ownership of a going concern, including its various resources. But there is a pragmatic corollary to this: due to their signification of ownership, shares represent a possible source of capital to current owners of a corporation (see the discussion on use, below).

Constitutive associations

The focus on going concerns can be clearly seen in the constitutive associations making up share identities in corporate banking. Both analysts and corporate bankers (re)construct share identities by associating shares with new pieces of information about the operations and about the market prospects for the products or services produced. However, the information handled by the bankers is classified as being 'price sensitive, inside information', that is, not yet publicly known information that is considered to be of importance for the valuation of the share. Regulatory frameworks thus differentiate between kinds of information that become associated with shares and seek to ensure that certain pieces of information only become associated with shares in a specific way.

Second, bankers actively shape shares not only by associating new pieces of information to them, but also by adding and/or removing more concrete parts from 'the contents' of shares. Adding a production unit through an acquisition is a good example. These activities, then, truly deserve the label 'inside'. The realization of these types of projects involve close cooperation with owners/managers of client organizations as well as various other experts, such as lawyers and other corporate bankers. The very ability of bankers to actively intervene in shares thus relies on the successful forging of associations. One important type of association often brought up in this connection is the personal relations between bankers and members of the business elite (Carosso, 1970; Eccles and Crane, 1988; Calomiris and Ramirez, 1996). Above, these relations were noted to be instrumental in giving the bankers access to their case corporations and mandate for seeking to realize proposed changes.

Bankers' use of shares

The strong link between shares and going concerns makes it possible to use them in order to finance operations. This can involve altering the relation between a share and the operations it represents, such as when emitting additional shares in a corporation to attract new capital. A special case is that of the IPO, which in many cases involves formulating for the very first time what the share is. Effectively, if not technically, then, IPOs could be said to represent the births of (publicly listed) shares. A second and related use of shares in corporate banking is in the realization of values for owners of corporations. As suggested in our account above, bankers can sometimes extract additional economic value from a given set of resources by modifying share content.

A durable but actively shaped identity

In terms of the temporal framing of shares, corporate banking practices contribute to construct relatively durable entities that require some effort to undo. The time frame for these entities is long term, grounded in historical developments, linked to intra-industry investment patterns and to projections concerning the prospects of the industries to which the corporations behind the shares belong. Moreover, the temporal framing is future-oriented: corporate banking projects involving shares are intimately linked to what these shares could be turned into, in a not-so-distant future. The stability of the share identity is largely dependent on industry developments; the occurrence of a major event may trigger proposals for restructurings. Still, shares do not change through some natural automatic; they must be made to change.

Conclusion: We need specifics

Beyond the share identities they construct, our account also suggests that bankers differ from other investment banking experts in terms of how their work is organized. Bankers work in projects. Although their clients may be the same over several such projects, and although the projects typically belong to one of relatively few categories (IPO, M&A, repurchasing, new emission and so on), each project is still unique. Both the constitution of the project team and the particular circumstances of the involved corporation(s) help to make it so. To further our understanding of how corporate banking practices contribute to the financial markets, a more detailed account of such a project would be valuable.

A closer look at a corporate banking project could also help us elaborate one of the main arguments in this book: that the expert groups in investment banking contribute jointly to the machinery of the financial markets. In corporate banking projects, analysts become involved in a much more direct way than as distant parts in the same machine. Generally, the question of how corporate banking practices relate to the practices of the other expert groups is a question of how the primary and secondary stock markets are linked. To be able to probe further into this relationship, it is necessary to study the process of how a share is born; how it is first put together, then sold on the primary market and subsequently introduced onto the secondary market for shares, a process in which the work of corporate bankers is often paramount. This will take us very close to how investment banking is both reproducing and changing financial markets. It will also allow us to shed light on one interesting difference between corporate banking and other areas of expertise, only hinted at above; the fact that bankers invent and modify the investment objects traded by traders, recommended by brokers, and analysed by analysts. In short, it would allow us to deepen our understanding of the contribution of bankers by examining their role as change agents in relation to shares.

In Chapter 7, we thus continue our account of corporate banking practices and their relations to the other expert groups by studying the very process of how a share is born. We do this by following the gradual realization of a project that engaged two major Scandinavian investment banking operations and resulted in the creation and public listing of a new share: Dolly Ltd. The account focuses on the role of corporate bankers, but also sheds light on the network of actors that contributes to constituting the financial sector.

7
The Birth of a Share

Having provided an overview of corporate banking practices, we now follow the gradual realization of a project that resulted in the birth of Dolly Ltd. Involving two major Scandinavian investment banks and combining a merger, a spin-off and an initial public offering (IPO), project Dolly is an unusually suitable case for tracing the activities of corporate banking. This case study, which offers a good fit with cursory descriptions of securities offerings processes (Wilhelm, 1999), allows us to follow at close range many of the practices identified in Chapter 6. Due to confidentiality issues, the identities of the involved corporations have been masked, as has the industry to which they belong. Drawing on this case and the insights from Chapter 6, we conclude by expanding our discussion on how corporate banking practices construct share identities. Let us enter into the nursery of the financial markets!

Project Dolly – The creation of Dolly Ltd

Project Dolly involved spinning off and merging two production units from Corporation Y (Johnsburg and Garland) and one unit from Corporation Z (Madison) to form a new independent corporation: Dolly Ltd. Given the strengths of the three production units, the corporation was to be dedicated to a particular product application and thus intended to be positioned in a market niche within the industry. The new corporation was subsequently sold by its previous owners, corporations Y and Z, and noted on the public stock exchange. Four years after the process started, a new publicly listed share had come into existence (see Figure 7.1 for an overview of the project). Throughout this process, the two parent corporations and the new spin-off received considerable

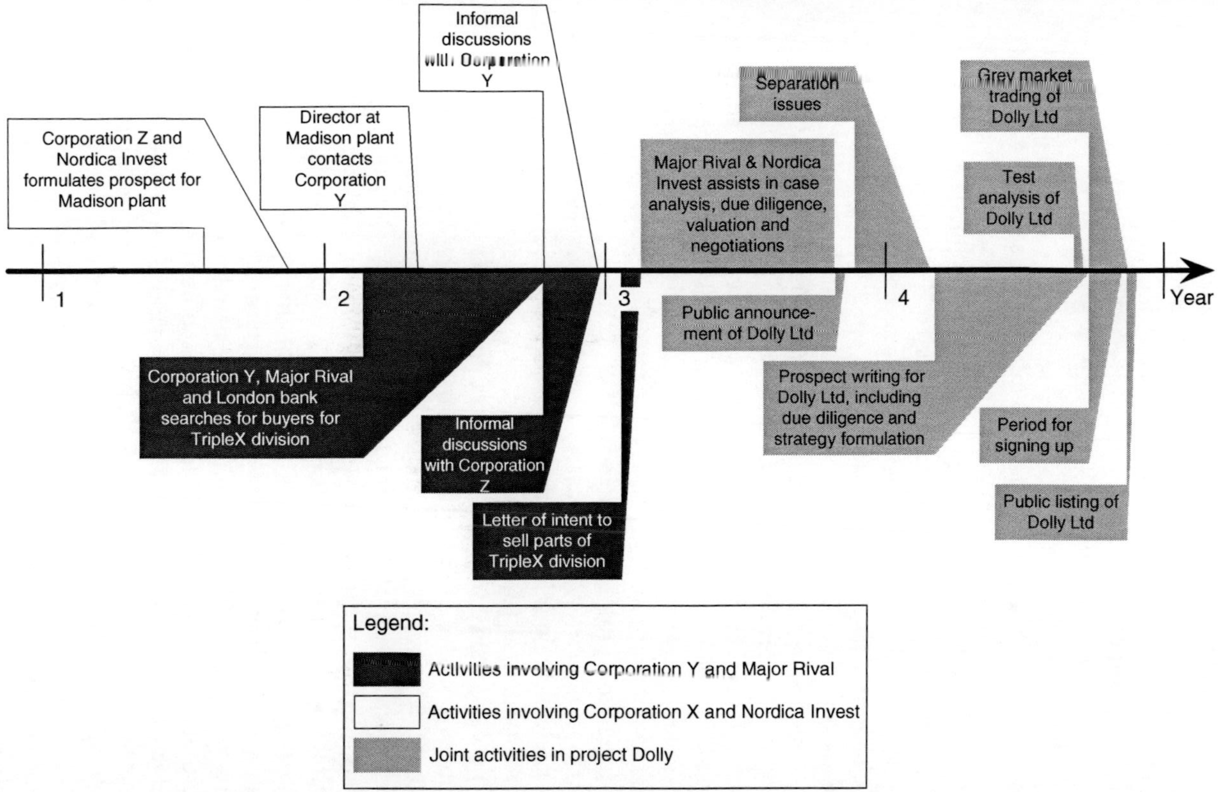

Figure 7.1 Overview of activities connected to project Dolly

assistance from two major Scandinavian-based investment banks, here called Nordica Invest and Major Rival. By following the project, we can thus trace the role of investment banks in the development of a share from its conception to its confirmation as a bona fide financial product and investment object.

Formulating the case

The bankers at Nordica Invest worked as advisors to Corporation Z during project Dolly, but they were not directly responsible for generating the case. Neither were their esteemed colleagues at Major Rival, the investment bank that advised Corporation Y. Still, both banks were deeply involved in related projects with their respective corporate client prior to project Dolly. Corporation Z had officially declared that their Madison production unit was 'for sale' two years before, and Nordica Invest had assisted in putting together a prospect for its sale. For Corporation Y, project Dolly was part of a larger effort to divest an entire line of business – a process in which Major Rival was heavily involved, together with at least one London-based investment bank. So, both investment banks played important roles in the process leading up to project Dolly.

In the autumn of year 1, Nordica Invest had helped Corporation Z put together a prospect for their Madison plant as a standalone operation (see Figure 7.1). The reason for this initiative was that Madison was a relatively poor fit with the new strategic direction established for Corporation Z. At least four venture capitalists showed interest in the prospect and visited the plant. However, due to a downturn in the market for one of Madison's major products towards the end of year 1, the profitability estimates in the prospect had to be adjusted downwards on several occasions. As the estimated profit decreased, so did the potential buyers' interest in the deal. By early spring of year 2, the bankers and Corporation Z were back at square one.

At this point, the managing director of the Madison plant informally contacted representatives of Corporation Y to see whether they had any interest in the Madison plant. He based this initiative on the idea that there were considerable synergies to be had from combining the Madison plant with Corporation Y's Garland plant. What he didn't know, but soon learned, was that Corporation Y was experiencing major profitability problems and was preparing to divest its entire 'TripleX' division to which Garland belonged. In fact, Corporation Y had already engaged Major Rival and a London-based investment bank to scout for potential buyers of the 'TripleX' division, which consisted of five production units and 12 wholly owned application specialists. So, even though there may have been potential synergies, Corporation Y were only mildly interested in acquiring another plant. They were looking to sell, not buy.

However, after a series of quite far-reaching discussions with potential buyers during the spring of year 2, Corporation Y began to realize that no single buyer was prepared to acquire the entire 'TripleX' division. Rather, the buyers were interested in acquiring one or two production units and some application specialists that fit into their own organizations:

> Our problem was that we wanted to achieve a joint solution, because this was a considerable grouping to divest. It was a big piece and we wanted to solve the problem once and for all. Unfortunately, the buyers made it pretty clear to us that they were not interested in the whole kit.
>
> (Former VP, 'TripleX' division)

A large European player soon stood out as the most interesting buyer, primarily because they were interested in acquiring the largest part of the 'TripleX' division. Exactly what was to be included in such a package deal was far from clear, however, and ten months of negotiations were required before a letter of intent could finally be signed. One of the top managers recalled the negotiations being 'extremely complicated and tiresome'. During these negotiations, it gradually became clear that the large European player would buy two production units and all application specialists. Based on this understanding, Major Rival was asked to search for alternative buyers for the remaining three production units and their sales organizations, including the Garland plant.

Beside the efforts made by Major Rival to find potential buyers, the managers within the 'TripleX' division who had been contacted by the director of the Madison plant six months previously now returned his call. This led to a series of informal and more or less secret meetings with a group of representatives from corporations Y and Z during November and December of year 2. During these meetings, the group identified a number of possible synergies that could be had by combining their plants, including savings from having one joint sales organization and from swapping products between the production plants to decrease switching costs and standstills in production. The basic idea that gradually took shape was to form a new company by combining the Garland and Johnsburg plants from Corporation Y with Madison from Corporation Z (see Figure 7.2).

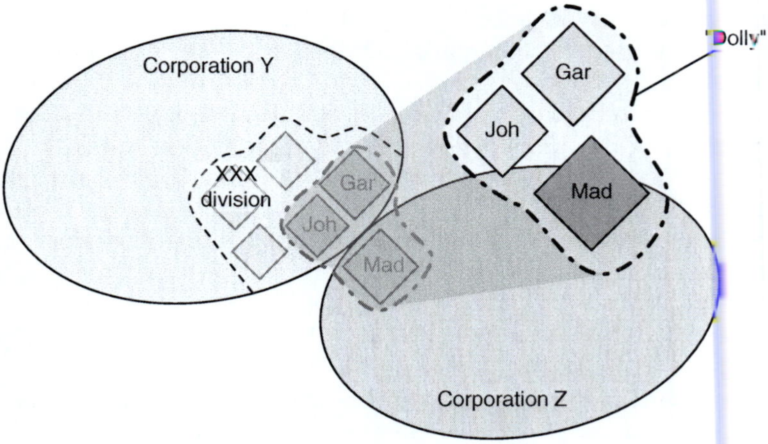

Figure 7.2 A new corporation taking shape: the basic idea of Dolly Ltd as envisioned in December, year 2

Neither Nordica Invest nor Major Rival were kept in the loop about these meetings. This is not surprising given that the group had no formal support from their respective top management. During late December, armed with their rough and ready proposal, the group approached the top managers. However, Corporation Y hesitated because their negotiations with the large European corporation concerning the 'TripleX' division were still ongoing. In the worst case, they would need to find alternative buyers for all plants and it was therefore in their interest to keep all options open. These negotiations were also consuming a lot of time and effort both from the managers and from their advisers at Major Rival. Thus, Corporation Y was looking to stall the deal with Corporation Z. By mid February year 3, a letter of intent concerning 'TripleX' was finally signed with the European buyer. This clarified the situation in the sense that neither Garland nor Johnsburg were part of the deal. It also freed up resources at Major Rival, whose corporate banking department hade been working intensively to close the European deal. In early March, Corporation Y formally gave the head of the 'TripleX' division instructions to resume the discussions with Corporation Z, this time reinforced with a support team consisting of both internal staff and advisors from Major Rival.

Breeding a new corporation

Despite the fact that representatives of the two corporations themselves had made the initial match, the bankers now became heavily involved in the project (see Figure 7.1). The original informal group was expanded to include representatives from both Nordica Invest and Major Rival. Representatives of the two corporations explained that there were at least two reasons for this. First of all, they literally needed a hand in pulling everything together. Second, it was a way of saying to each other 'we are serious about this, now':

> Nordica Invest and Major Rival were heavily involved in the negotiations and handled a considerable number of questions. They proposed negotiation designs, or should we say, valuation designs, primarily. This was a fundamental issue here. We had the business competence ourselves; the bankers' role was to assist us in sorting out how we could reach a comparable valuation of the three units.
>
> (Director of legal affairs, Corporation Z)

As a first step, the advisors were given the task of producing standardized descriptions of the three plants, based on information provided by the plant managers and the technical experts at the respective plants. These descriptions were to follow a template worked out jointly, and agreed upon, by both parties. The template included what product and application areas the plants were focused on, the state of the production facilities, current environmental permits, estimated investment needs, current sales organizations and so on. After an intensive period of work from mid March to mid April year 3, a revised and considerably more detailed proposal than the December, year 2 draft was presented to the boards of both corporations along with a request for an official go-ahead.

Both sides approved the proposal and by the end of April, project Dolly moved into a more acute stage. Focus shifted entirely to the content of the deal: what would actually be brought to the table by each side? In collaboration with two law firms, the advising investment banks set up 'data rooms' to which the corporations delivered agreed-upon material concerning their plants (see Table 7.1 for a sample of contents). The other party then sent expert committees from different areas, such as technical staff, accountants, marketers and lawyers to the other party's data room to go through the information.

The banker in charge of project Dolly at Nordica Invest explained the process in an e-mail to the project group in Corporation Z. He explained that the goal of the process was to "find factors that in one way or another are held to substantially affect the value of Corporation Y's Garland and Johnsburg plants." This would be achieved by having specialists responsible for particular areas – lawyers, accountants and

Table 7.1 The scope of the data room prepared for the Garland plant

Category	Description
1	Financial information
2	Customer information and contracts
3	Supplier information and contracts
4	Other contracts and engagements
5	Real estate properties
6	Ownership rights
7	Insurances
8	Information and control systems
9	Machines and equipment
10	Product safety information
11	Product quality information
12	Management and employees
13	Environment

selected experts from Corporation Z – document what they found in the data room and draw conclusions based on this. The experts were also instructed to identify any need for additional information beyond what was available in the data room.

During May, the expert groups visited the data rooms, made assessments and put queries to the other party. They also prepared responses to the queries they received from the corresponding expert group within the other corporation. In addition, a technical assessment of the status of the plants was commissioned from an external consultant. In this way, an impressive number of technical and administrative issues were dealt with in a fairly short period of time. A summary due diligence meeting was then arranged in mid June at the office of Major Rival. At this meeting, the project leaders from corporations Y and Z and their respective specialists were present, as well as the complete advisory teams from the two banks and the external technical consultants. Within each area, a summary report was prepared and any issues that needed further work were listed. For instance, it was agreed that a more careful estimate of the reinvestment needs in the three plants would be needed in order to reasonably assess the costs of continued operations.

The process continued throughout the summer and by August the character of the respective contributions had largely been established. However, one important issue was still to be settled before the deal could be closed: the price tags of the contributions. Once again, the process changed character, this time into more overt haggling over the value and price tags of the respective plants. This also meant that the top managers of the two corporations became actively involved in the project for the first time.

The initial positions assumed by the top managers on the basis of the assessments made during the summer were quite far apart. Corporation Y argued for a 65:35 valuation in their favour, while Corporation Z argued for a 50:50 deal. Nordica Invest and Major Rival played important roles in gradually reducing this gap. First of all, the advisors were instrumental in running the calculative centre that produced new figures. During August, the two advisory teams put together a general calculation model that both parties were prepared to accept. This model was gradually refined by reaching agreements on which factors to take into account and what assumptions to use for the calculations, including prices, interest rates, market prospects and investment needs:

> In this kind of process you need to use a method of going halves on issue after issue until you are down to a difference that you believe could be resolved in a final negotiation. Here, the advisors were very important. [...] I don't think we ever invented issues just to stall the process. No, they were real issues that had to be solved. You know: 'What about *this* issue, we need to look at that, as well!' And then you send the bankers off to work on that for a while. Because the bankers, they really want to get the deal together. Because they have a percentage on it, you know!
>
> (CEO, Corporation Z)

By working their way through a number of issues in this way, the advisors were able to bridge a considerable part of the gulf initially separating the two corporations' valuations. However, this process also exposed a fundamental difference between the bankers and their customers. This was most clearly expressed by the head of the 'TripleX' division:

> It's not just a question of looking at cash flows and the plants' future potential. I also want to look at the reality a number of years back. And then it was evident that the Madison plant had a worse track record than our plants, even though ... everything can be explained. But this somehow faded into the background.
>
> (Division Head, 'TripleX', Corporation Y)

This suggests that, by engaging the investment banks, the two counterparts also indirectly agreed to hand over some of the responsibility for defining the 'world of the deal'. Another member of the negotiation team from Corporation Y suggested that this was in fact one of the functions sought when using corporate banking advisors:

> If both parties work with a high quality advisor with a good reputation and these advisors reach a certain valuation level on the various parts that are to be included in the deal, then a lot is needed to claim a deal at a completely different level. They produced an interval that both parties accepted as a basis for negotiations. They put their name on the line and we had to accept or assume that their assessment was sensible.
>
> (Director, legal affairs, Corporation Y)

After a number of reiterations and a gradual reduction of the gap between the two corporations' positions, the final negotiation ensued. At this point, the advisors' roles seem to have been less clear-cut. All the technical issues that could help to bring the two parties closer to each other had been exhausted:

> We were close to ruining the deal over a quarter in the end. We were sitting there harping on the same strings hour after hour. Even the advisors were becoming irritated on each other. So finally, we sent all of them out of the room – the advisors, our own people, everyone. Then, we made one final effort and closed the deal.
>
> (CEO, Corporation Z)

> I recall it vividly. It was about a quarter of a percent. And I know I wanted that quarter badly. But at the same time, this was a major thing for us, and a small thing for them. So when we sat down just the two of us, I folded and we had a deal. In hindsight, I'm glad that I wasn't too stubborn.
>
> (Division Head, 'TripleX', Corporation Y)

A couple of days later, in October year 3, a joint press conference was arranged by corporations Y and Z to officially announce the forming of the new corporation:

> **Dolly Ltd – Corporation Z and Corporation Y to form a joint company for TripleX products**
>
> Corporation Z and Corporation Y have met a principal agreement to form a new jointly owned company consisting of the plants Madison (Corp. Z), Johnsburg and Garland (Corp. Y).... The intention is to list the shares in Dolly Ltd on the Stockholm Stock Exchange.
>
> (Excerpt from press release)

Turning Dolly Ltd into Dolly the public share

According to the publicly announced agreement between corporations Y and Z, Dolly Ltd was intended as a separate corporation, independent from its two founders. The founders planned to turn Dolly Ltd into a public corporation and sell their shares. Since the deal only included production units and sales organizations, a completely new head office had to be created. At the outset, then, there were few internal resources available for generating a prospect for the initial public offering of Dolly Ltd:

> A lot of my work initially went into creating conditions that would allow us to pass the stock market test. I mean, putting together an independent board, a complete management team, and also creating organizational and accounting routines needed for life as a public, listed corporation.
>
> (Chairman of the Board, Dolly Ltd)

Given this situation, it is not surprising that the two investment banks were asked to team up and work with the owners, the board and the gradually forming management team of Dolly Ltd to list Dolly on the stock exchange. In fact, during year 4 the investment banks were largely in charge of the prospect process. As the then newly appointed CFO of Dolly Ltd put it: 'They wielded the pen.' In late January, the two banks presented a preliminary time plan called 'The road to market listing' (Figure 7.3).

Figure 7.3 'The road to market listing': proposed time plan for stock market listing of Dolly Ltd by Nordica Invest and Major Rival, January year 4

The first issue that the two owners needed to address concerned the overall viability of the plan:

> It was necessary to test the idea, since the idea built on the fact that neither parent corporation would take over. You know, is this a viable company on the market? Is this something that can stand on its own two feet? That's a kind of competence that *we don't have*; to make that assessment.
>
> (Director, legal affairs, Corporation Y)

Hence the first part of the process was devoted to preparing material to support the owners' formal decision to go ahead and divest Dolly Ltd. 'We needed to know whether Dolly Ltd could be noted on the stock exchange or not', said the Chairman. But there were also more practical reasons for relying heavily on the two investment banks in the process. Representatives of both owners and Dolly Ltd suggest a perceived lack of internal competence and resources as a major reason:

> Investment banks have organisations that work extremely well for generating prospects, valuation materials, presentation materials, etc. For us, this would require a lot of work, and we had a corporation to run . . . two actually.
>
> (Director, legal affairs, Corporation Y)

There seems to have been two facets to the alleged competence or expertise of the investment banks. First, they knew the drill and could sort out many practical issues involved in producing a prospect that would speak to an audience of investors and analysts. This was underlined by a banker from Major Rival:

> They [Dolly Ltd and their owners] had to think about the market, you know. In their situation, I think it was necessary to use us. I mean, a completely new corporation with a small, not even fully staffed, head office producing a prospect . . . No, they needed our competence. To be one hundred percent sure about the requirements, not only formally from the stock exchange etc., but also in reality. What do they need to present based on what analysts and investors expect from them? Not only from a technical point of view, you know, follow the template, but also in real terms. What kind of information is needed and what it is that is important? There, we have experience that they will never have. And I also think our names added a certain seal of

> approval vis-à-vis investors and analysts, when they are to assess the corporation in their turn, based on the prospect.
>
> (Director, Major Rival)

The final comment by the banker in the quote above highlights a second aspect of engaging corporate banking expertise that we addressed in Chapter 6, that of producing legitimacy. In this particular case, with a newly formed corporation that both founders wanted to sell off, legitimacy is likely to have been especially important. Potential investors would wonder why the owners wanted to sell Dolly Ltd if it was a viable corporation. The bankers underscored this early in the process, emphasizing the need to construct a credible 'Investment story' for the corporation. In fact, they explicitly argued that their participation would be instrumental for Dolly Ltd earning the trust of the stock market:

> It is of central importance for investors that a well-reputed and independent investment bank underwrites the prospect.
>
> (Presentation: The road to stock market listing, Major Rival and Nordica Invest, 25 January year 4)

The January plan presented by the two investment banks (see Figure 7.3) contained a summary of the contents of the prospect-to-be, structured in five parts: (1) listing of Dolly Ltd; (2) description of Dolly Ltd and its operations; (3) financial information; (4) other formal matters; and (5) accounting information. A relatively detailed proposal concerning the division of labour during the process was also included:

- *Accountant* (audit of accounting figures in the prospect)
- *Jurists* (legal formalities)
- *Investment bank* (project management, investor relations, sales of shares/options, due diligence)
- *Investor Relations advisor* (market contacts with journalists and analysts, communication plan and media training)
- *Advertising agency* (graphic design, advertising campaign)
- *Printers* (print prospect and sign-up forms)
- *Euroclear* (shareholder registry)
- *The stock exchange* (market place and audit of corporation)
- *Financial Supervisory Authority* (registration and audit of prospect, insider regulations)
- *Patent and Registration Office* (registration of decisions, emissions, etc.).

This proposed division of labour put the investment banks in the driver's seat regarding project management. Conspicuously absent from the list was Dolly Ltd, reflecting its purported position as an object rather than a subject in the process. The ensuing activities, however, suggest that the banks exaggerated the passivity of Dolly Ltd.

Prospect writing

During the spring and summer of year 4, most of the project work was linked to the prospect. Among other things, it included solidifying the views of the rogue managers who came up with the initial idea of a new corporation in December, year 2: what were the synergies they had seen? How could they be translated into figures and presented in the prospect? What were reasonable descriptions of the production units, the markets and the future potential of the new corporation? By mid May, a first draft was presented to the Board of Dolly Ltd outlining the prospect structure. In terms of content, this version mainly dealt with formal matters and financial information. It was now evident that the process of creating the prospect was not only a question of putting on paper that which the industrial experts had already identified. As the bankers guided the owners and managers of Dolly Ltd along their schedule, real issues arose as well:

> We worked our way through the bankers' prospect template, draft after draft, and along the way a number of new issues cropped up. The most significant one, of course, concerned strategy. We had to define: What is the strategy of Dolly Ltd? Sure, they had had strategy discussions along the way, but I was new to the job and now we needed to move from vague ideas to an explicit strategy. So, we hired additional consultants, MegaStrat and Stella, to help us out.
>
> (CEO, Dolly Ltd)

The process of formulating a viable strategy ran in parallel to the prospect process during the summer. But, as hinted at by the CEO, a prospect is not only future oriented; another important function of a prospect is to work as a 'declaration of contents'. This made the prospect process heavily dependent on yet another parallel process that was underway during the spring and summer of year 4, the so-called *due diligence* process:

> Due diligence amounts to establishing: *what* does this corporation that is now being noted on the stock exchange contain? So you

> could say it is a sub process to writing the prospect, although a very comprehensive one. We needed to be able to say: What we are now offering looks like this and this. And then I'm not only talking figures, that is one aspect of it, but there are others: what kind of staff do we have; what's the history of the plants; what legal issues are there; what risks are there, etc. You go through what is there, and perhaps more importantly what isn't there.
>
> (CFO, Dolly Ltd)

The due diligence process was comprehensive. To make the process manageable it was divided into three major parts: commercial, legal and accounting due diligence. The areas covered in the process included legal aspects, organization, financial information, product information, market situation, competition, taxation issues, insurance situation, outstanding securities, patents and brands, wages and benefits, computer safety, existing contracts and legal disputes. The broad scope of the process required that a number of consultants had to be engaged to deal with specific issues, such as technical status, potential environmental problems and auditing of previous accounts:

> A law firm had the main responsibility for the due diligence process. Then we had an environmental assessment made of the Madison plant site since there had been other industrial activities there historically and we lacked complete knowledge of them. And we had an industry consultant do a technical assessment of all three plants, partly to assess future reinvestment needs and partly to benchmark against other plants in the industry when formulating our strategic direction.
>
> (CFO, Dolly Ltd)

By September, the due diligence process was coming to an end. The strategy process had also led to concrete results, adding another piece to the prospect puzzle. Prospect drafts had by then been discussed at every board meeting from May to September as the official description of Dolly Ltd and its future potential gradually took shape. The final prospect was approved by the board and made public in October.

Behaving as a public corporation

In parallel to finalizing the prospect, the investment banks also sought to prepare Dolly Ltd for life as a public corporation assisted by an Investor Relations advisor. Primarily, these activities were directed towards the management team who would soon be heading a public corporation. The activities included media training and trial meetings with analysts, and also the creation of templates for official communications such as quarterly reports and company presentations:

> They [the bankers] tried to teach us how to behave as a listed corporation. With seminars and exercises. Nowadays I think this is obligatory for corporations applying to be listed, but at the time it was voluntary. We had seminars and traditional lectures by experts. But we also did some acting. They presented different types of situations to us, an interview, a press conference, etc. And they filmed us in these situations. To learn what you can and cannot do and say. You can't say whatever you want. A plant director can't say: I believe in a very good result this year! There are rules you need to follow.
>
> (CFO, Dolly Ltd)

Closely related to the media training were also a number of activities specifically focused on investor relations. These activities were linked to the planning of a roadshow for marketing the Dolly Ltd share to potential investors, which was organized by the investment banks, with their international subsidiaries contributing suggestions on suitable locations. Since this would involve company presentations, a number of routines were created for this, as well as a template for presenting the corporation:

> What you are supposed to talk about. Like competitors, markets, our products, well, you know, production. All these things. We designed that presentation in connection to the first roadshow that the bankers put together. They still organize much of our investor contacts, you could say, since we don't have a large IR department. But now it's not just the two of them, but maybe eight or ten.
>
> (CFO, Dolly Ltd)

During September, both investment banks also brought in analysts monitoring the industry in which Dolly Ltd was active, to meet with the CEO and CFO:

> We sort of guided them through ... What do the shareholders want to know? What will they be asking you? Because they didn't have ... [The CFO] came straight from a position in a German 'DoubleY' division and [the CEO] had been head of Minor Molecules within Corporation Z. None of them had had active, daily contacts

> with analysts. We tried to teach them what this contact is like; give them some idea of it. Because analysts ... Investors can be quite tough sometimes. Their questions can be quite pushy, you know. So we introduced the kind of questions shareholders are interested in. The questions you *have* to address in a presentation. You *have* to address: What is the industry structure like? How does demand growth look? What are your market positions? What will you do with your money? What are your investment needs?
>
> (Analyst, Major Rival)

As described in Chapter 6, involving analysts in corporate banking projects within an investment bank is a delicate matter. Both analysts that became involved in project Dolly were very clear about their role in the process; they were engaged to 'prime' the management team:

> We were never in on the sensitive discussions; our corporate banking people handled those. We were there ... of course we learned about their business. That's obvious, since we got to discuss things with them, but I'm not supposed to ... the company had like ... they met a lot of other investors and made presentations, as well. So I think that went down in a fair fashion.
>
> (Analyst, Major Rival)

The analysts were also asked to do a preliminary analysis and valuation of the new corporation as an investment object:

> I was asked what I thought could be a reasonable trading price for the share, and so was the analyst from [Major Rival]. I think it was interesting for the board to hear what we believed this corporation would be valued at, you know, given these results which had been audited and so on. I mean, as voices from the field. As I recall, we were both quite positive. But it wasn't a beauty contest or anything, between us and [Major Rival], we didn't compete to be the most optimistic, or anything like that. One question was whether or not we believed the corporation could be valued above equity capital. Yeees, I think there is a relatively good chance of that, sort of.
>
> (Analyst, Nordica Invest)

Once the prospect was finalized, the two analysts also performed a regular, initial analysis of the new share. Both analyses came out in favour of Dolly Ltd and concluded with strong recommendations to purchase.

In parallel to this, and still prior to the official listing on the stock exchange, the two investment banks also engaged their equities departments to operate as market makers. Thus, the banks maintained a 'grey market' for the share during a few weeks prior to the actual listing. Finally, in early November, Dolly Ltd was noted on the stock exchange. A new public share had been born.

Links and consequences beyond project Dolly

Although not very tangible, the most obvious effect of project Dolly for the financial markets was the introduction of a new share, a new potential exchange and investment object. In this respect, the corporate banking activities clearly link to other activities within investment banks, providing important input to traders, analysts and brokers alike. A corporate banking director described the relation between 'Equities' and 'Corporate Finance' as a successful combination:

> In 'Equities' they do transactions with shares. So what they need is new material to sell on the market. In that way we live in a successful symbiosis. We provide them with the new 'products'.
>
> (Director)

Even if this is a simplified description of the relationship, it does convey the practical link between the activities undertaken by corporate banking and the work in equities. In the case of IPOs, like Dolly, the link between the activities within the two departments coincides with the link between the primary and secondary markets for shares. The character of the link also reinforces an image of 'making money to make money', in that the investment banks derive revenues both from creating the shares and from trading them on the stock exchanges.

If we regard project Dolly as an individual corporate banking project, its link to trading does not seem very significant. The new share would indeed constitute a possible trading opportunity for traders, but it would hardly change their world. On an aggregate level, however, the activities of the bankers in projects like Dolly are arguably important for the traders. Without them, it is unlikely that the increase in the number of publicly listed shares on stock exchanges around the world would have been as great. This type of link between primary and secondary markets was also something that we noted in our brief account of the history of investment banking (Chapter 2). But there was also a more direct link between investment banking and trading in project Dolly: prior to the official listing of Dolly Ltd, the traders provided a grey market for the share. In this respect, the corporate banking project clearly generated work for the traders.

Similar links were found between project Dolly and the brokers. Since the two original owners were intent on divesting entirely, selling Dolly Ltd on the primary market for shares represented a considerable undertaking: the brokers needed to find new owners to all of the shares in Dolly Ltd. Here, the two owners chose different approaches. Corporation Y sold off all of its shares to the primary market. To manage this, two types of sales efforts were made. First, a standardized offer to sign up for shares was made in connection to the publication of the prospect. Second, the brokers working in institutional sales were engaged to attract larger investors into making more sizeable investments. The latter efforts were intimately linked to the international roadshow undertaken during October year 4. Corporation Z chose a slightly different approach for divesting its shares. Besides relying on the brokers' efforts to attract investors on the primary market, they also sold off a large part of their shares on the secondary market during the six months following the public listing of the share. In both cases, of course, brokers were responsible.

The links to analysts, finally, were more prominent in the case: First of all, the two corporate banking departments were actively tinkering with the contents of three shares that analysts were trying to make sense of and value: corporations Y and Z, and Dolly Ltd. Second, the corporate banking project also made use of analysts to 'test' the construction of Dolly Ltd as a share underway. Hence, two analysts were asked to pass through the Chinese walls and help emulate life outside for the management team of Dolly Ltd. Third, and most interestingly, the listing of Dolly Ltd on the stock exchange also seems to have affected the analysts' work in a more fundamental way:

> When Dolly Ltd was created with a focus on these specific niches in the market, we analysts also became a lot more attentive to them. The *division* to which the Madison plant used to belong had a turnover five times as large as Dolly. Just that part. Corporation Z as a whole has maybe 20 times the turnover. So you don't pay attention to these niches when analysing Z, because they are so marginal. But for Dolly, a niche can account for 25% of the turnover, so it becomes important. And there are only three production plants, so we can even discuss profitability at the level of individual plants. So, with the creation of Dolly, we had to generate new market images, well I did at least. But I can't imagine anyone sitting with large spreadsheets with

> information about these markets *before* Dolly was created. I seriously doubt that, haha.
>
> (Analyst, Nordica Invest)

Even though Dolly Ltd looked like a marginal player within its industry, its introduction prompted the stock analysts to revise their image of that industry and the markets it serves. This suggests a more complex web of associations between corporate banking and equities than that of producing exchange objects alone. Under certain circumstances, the construction of a new share (identity) in corporate banking can lead to changes to the way in which analysts construct their share identities. Potentially, then, corporate banking practices may influence analysis practices, subsequent recommendations, and brokering efforts far beyond the specific project.

The share as a product under construction

At first, the preoccupation with the construction of share identities seems to lose part of its initial zing and analytic leverage when applied to a corporate banking project like Dolly, since some of the activities undertaken therein are very literally about share construction. In project Dolly we saw how two corporate banking teams assisted in, first, turning three production units, an international sales organization and a new head office into a corporation, and then in launching shares in this corporation as an investment object on the stock market. Clearly, this can be understood as a case of new product development for the stock markets. To say that such activities are about constructing share identity borders on the obvious. Still, there are important differences in *how* the bankers construct share identities compared to the other experts. The detailed account of project Dolly allows us to expand and further develop the general characterization of these differences presented at the end of Chapter 6.

First of all, project Dolly underscores the claim made in Chapter 5 that bankers link the identities of shares closely to the corporations 'behind' them. More specifically, the going concern 'behind the share' is central to the bankers. As representations of corporations, shares offer business opportunities for bankers, although not in the same sense as they do for traders, brokers or analysts. As in project Dolly, corporate bankers do not generally engage directly in buying or selling shares. Their role is rather to match potential buyers and sellers on the primary markets for shares (which underscores their historical role discussed in Chapter 2).

Project Dolly underscores that their engagements with shares differ both in terms of the size of the deals and the specific activities they undertake. The deals that bankers engage in are large and often include actively putting together the exchange object in question. For instance, bankers may engage in brokering a production unit, a division, a business unit or an entire corporation. This variation suggests that bankers do not necessarily accept the current boundaries established for a particular share. What the share represents is considered adjustable. Rather than selling 2 per cent of the shares in a corporation, then, bankers are more likely to try to sell 2 per cent *of each share* in that corporation, for example, a particular production unit.

This leads us to a central aspect of how corporate banking engages with shares, an aspect that we hinted at towards the end of Chapter 6. We could say that bankers operate a sort of tuning-service for shares directed towards shareowners. By actively tinkering with the corporation represented by a share, bankers claim to be attempting to realize economic values. As part of this work, the contents of shares are subject to considerable attention. While bankers share this attention to contents with analysts, there are important differences in just how they attend to share content. The bankers' attention to share content comes across not only as epistemic but also as *ontic* (Law, 2004), this is, they are explicitly concerned not only with analysing shares as knowledge objects but also with engaging directly with them. Many of their activities are geared towards changing the insides of shares by adding or removing content. In short, bankers *intervene* in shares by engaging with the objects represented by them (confer Mol, 2002; Ashmore, 2005).

Project Dolly illustrated that the bankers' interventions may involve a variety of entities. Given our claim that shares represent corporations to bankers, it is hardly surprising that attention was directed towards entities that could be considered important for the corporation itself, such as its production facilities. Another such entity that was given considerable attention in connection with the public listing of Dolly Ltd was the top management team. The efforts to train the top managers in investor relations, such as how to officially present the corporation and how to respond to questions from analysts and investors, can be seen as part of a process to socialize the share. These officials would represent the corporation and hence the share in various future settings, and it was considered important that they did this in a particular way. Through these efforts, the corporate bankers promoted a particular version of Dolly Ltd, a version compatible with the template for a publicly listed corporation, emphasizing the share identity of the corporation over other possible identities.

The share identity constructed in corporate banking

The bankers' efforts to add, remove or alter share content provides a view of the constitutive associations of shares recognized and employed in corporate banking. In their analyses, bankers forge the familiar associations between shares and pieces of information that we saw the analysts do in Chapter 4. When moving on to active intervention, however, two particular types of associations stand out as central for determining what is, and what is not, part of a share in a specific corporation: employment and ownership. The importance of employment as a constitutive association is partly illustrated by the attention given to top management. More generally, this type of association is used to link one particular class of entities to a share: human beings. Although these associations were acknowledged in project Dolly (see the quote from the CFO on p.15), they are given particular attention in projects involving corporations in industries classified as knowledge intensive, such as biotech and pharma (see Winroth, 2004). Ownership is the primary form of constitutive association for linking all other classes of entities to a share, such as production facilities, patents and sales offices. (In some cases, other forms of constitutive associations may be used that do not signify ownership, such as long-term contracts and strategic alliances with partner firms.) Given the character of the industry in which Dolly operated, process-based with substantial investments in production facilities, the main thrust of the identity construction in project Dolly concerned ownership relations. Establishing such associations could be said to clarify what it is you own if you own a share in a corporation (see Figure 7.4).

Both these types of association differ in form from the ones forged during analyses, in that they are based on some kind of contract. Although contractual associations are by no means irreversible, the contractual form arguably adds durability to the association. This can be most clearly seen in the case of ownership: whether or not ownership of an entity is distributed across several owners, there can only be a total of 100 per cent at each point in time.[1] Ownership associations are thus excluding in character. No such limits are attached to the associations forged as part of analysis. As a whole, it would seem that the character of the associations forged by bankers contributes to making their share identities less ephemeral in character.

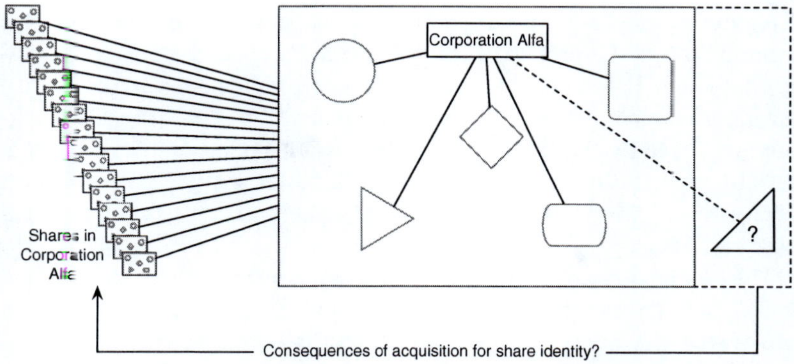

Figure 7.4 Schematic illustration of how corporate banking may reconstitute a corporation's share identity by forging an ownership association to a novel entity

But the added durability of the contractual form also makes these associations problematic. This is particularly evident in the case of ownership which was nicely illustrated by the *due diligence* processes in project Dolly. Ownership of assets typically implies certain liabilities in addition to whatever benefits they offer. Before forging an ownership association that would subsume a specific entity under another, such as the Madison plant under Dolly Ltd, considerable efforts are thus made to assess exactly what would become associated through such a move. Did the Madison plant come with environmental liabilities? What future reinvestments were needed in the Madison plant? And so on. This type of activity on behalf of the bankers and their expert consultants is once again more similar to what analysts engage in as they seek to characterize the insides of a particular share. It is an epistemic practice – a matter of associating pieces of information with specific entities.

The similarity is further pronounced by how the outcomes of the activities are put to use. In both cases, these efforts purport to serve as a basis for decisions about changes in ownership, as a basis for qualifying exchange objects (Callon et al., 2002). For analysts, the exchange objects being qualified are shares; for the bankers, they can be entire corporations, divisions or individual production units. Irrespective of which, the construction of an exchange object seems to be closely linked to epistemic practices that serve to temporarily stabilize the characteristics of the object. The import of this work for an exchange to take place was clearly illustrated in the negotiations leading up to the formation of Dolly Ltd, where the valuation issue was considered crucial given the lack of market prices (see p. 137–140). These practices come across as a regime for handling the uncertainty associated with the exchange of unique objects (Karpik, 2010). With no readily available price to attach to the object, its qualities are scrutinized to provide support for a price estimate. As noted by one of the participants in the process, the methods employed by the bankers to do this are not neutral, but emphasize certain aspects (in this case future cash flows, market potential and reinvestment needs) at the expense of others (in this case historical performance).

The qualification of exchange objects brings us to the issue of how corporate bankers use shares. As we noted in Chapter 6, the most obvious use of shares is as a source of financial resources for the client organization. IPOs and new issues of shares are ways of bringing new capital into a going concern. Strictly speaking, however, this is a use of shares that owners and managers of corporations engage in, although bankers do assist them. As a financial solution, shares are thus tools in the corporate banking toolbox, along with syndicated loans and bonds. Project Dolly illustrated that bankers also actively use shares when restructuring corporations and industries. As part of this type of activity, the corporations represented by the shares are modified and hence their share identities also become products under construction, closely linked to changes in ownership.

In this process, there are also more intricate interrelations between the share identity constructed through analysis and the one shaped through active intervention. Depending on the character of the former, the relative import of particular types of association varies across shares. In Dolly Ltd, ownership of production facilities and machinery was given more attention than the employment of skilled staff, whereas in an R&D or service-intensive corporation. it may well be the other way around. Hence, the share identities constructed through analysis may have considerable consequences for how bankers subsequently attempt to intervene in shares. But project Dolly also illustrated that the influence may go in the opposite direction, so that the construction of a new share may influence how analysts construct future share identities. Hence, the forging of novel constitutive associations in an investment banking project may influence the constitutive associations forged as part of other experts' share identities.

As a final observation, project Dolly illustrated that a large number of external actors routinely participate in corporate banking practices as partners or suppliers, including legal firms, technical consultants, accountants and experts on investor relations. Corporate banking was thus performed not through a dyadic relation with a client corporation, but through the enactment of an action net engaging a variety of specialized actors. One important reason for this complex organization concerns compliance. On several occasions during project Dolly, reference was made to rules and regulations that the involved investment banks and their clients had to consider, including formal requirements on prospects, requirements placed on publicly noted firms, rules concerning the disclosure of information from such firms, amongst other factors. Many activities in the project were geared towards establishing correspondences between Dolly Ltd and these rules, and towards explicating the existence of such correspondences. Requirements to comply with rules and regulations are not only visible in corporate banking projects, but can be said to increasingly influence investment banking organizations at large. This has consequences for the internal organization of investment banks as will become evident when we now turn our attention from the practices of the four expert groups to those who seek to manage their work.

8

Behind the Scenes – Management, Risk and Compliance

> We are a very flat organization. Here in Sweden we have the CEO and his top management group and then heads of the experts.
>
> (Chief Compliance Officer)

> Well, managing an investment bank is not really like management in other places. We try to manoeuvre primarily by soft and hard regulations, where the soft ones are about fostering a culture where individuals learn to create their own space.
>
> (CFO)

In previous chapters, representatives of the four expert groups have often described themselves as entrepreneurs, suggesting that their work is like having 'a business of their own, within the business'. The image they convey is one of competent professionals being given considerable leeway concerning how to plan and conduct their work. The focus is said to be on delivering (financial) results rather than on following specific procedures. They also suggest that this state of affairs is conducive to high performance in situations where you need to respond quickly and flexibly to external changes and adjust to the specific needs of your clients. As part of this characterization, managerial activity is regularly downplayed, for example: 'as long as we deliver, they do not interfere'. This description of investment banking practices is hardly unique for our study and has led some observers to characterize investment banks as 'self-designing organizations', emphasizing the entrepreneurial facet of the experts' work (e.g. Eccles and Crane, 1988).

Should we accept this view of investment banking experts as relatively independent entrepreneurs who are left to conduct their business at their own discretion? Arguably, the world of investment banking has changed since the study by Eccles and Crane of US investment banks in the 1980s. Stricter regulations and more far-reaching methods for monitoring market activities have been introduced in the wake of globalized trading patterns, rapid growth in transactions and diversification in financial instruments. Investment banking organizations are expected to align their operations with these regulations; to carefully assess the risks they are exposed to; to control the use of inside information and so on. Whether they do so or not is continuously monitored by both public and private organizations, such as the Financial Supervisory Authority. As a result, the performance of each expert is meticulously monitored. Potentially, then, these efforts at domesticating the financial markets have resulted in practical constraints on the principle of self-design, irrespective of whether they have influenced the experts' narratives about their work or not. It is thus reasonable to question how far investment banking experts have been transformed into docile cogs in the machinery of finance, controlled by rules, regulations and control systems.

The purpose of this chapter is to examine the efforts made to manage the experts working in investment banking. When turning our attention to these issues, we were struck by the apparent tension between two managerial principles being applied in parallel. On the one hand, many managerial initiatives served to pave the way for and motivate the experts to perform well in terms of generating profits, not least through generous bonus offers. On the other hand, an increasing number of initiatives seemed geared towards controlling their behaviour in quite specific ways, thus limiting their freedom to act, such as through controlling risks. In short, the organizations appeared to apply both the throttle and the brake at the same time.

At the 'Middle Office'

Investment banks are often presented as having a *front office*, a *middle office* and a *back office*. *Front office* is used to denote activities within the various business lines (securities, corporate banking, asset management and so on) that involve contacts between the experts and their clients. *Middle office* refers to top management and central functions such as legal services, risk management and compliance. This is where you find the Chief Executive Officer (CEO), the Chief Financial Officer (CFO), the Chief Risk Officer (CRO), the Chief Compliance Officer (CCO) and the Head of Legal Affairs. The board takes overall responsibility and answers to the internal audit. *Back office* refers to the various functions that

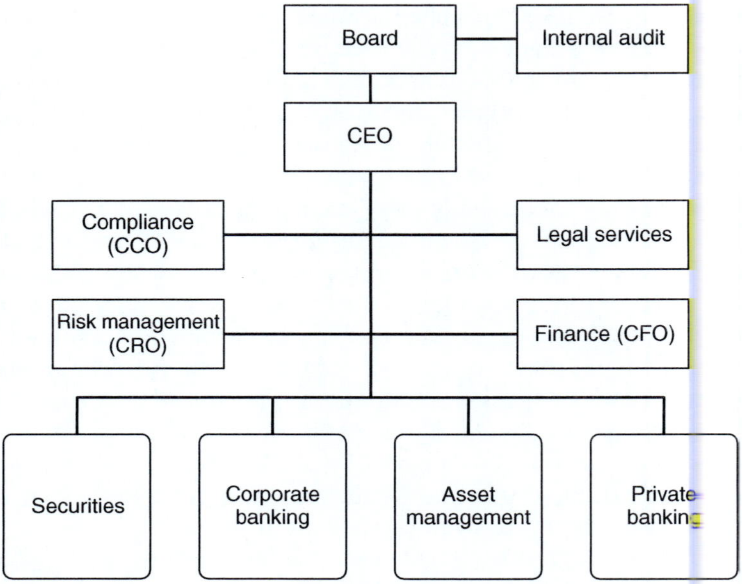

Figure 8.1 Organization chart for one of the studied investment banks

handle trading administration and technological support, and can be found in all business lines and departments. (See Figure 8.1 for an example of an organization chart.)

Top management is responsible for developing the overall strategy. Some investment banks in our study explicitly sought to position themselves as offering a complete line of financial services, whereas others sought a top position in one or two of the business lines. These strategic considerations sometimes directly influenced decisions concerning resource allocation within the banks, such as whether or not to hire additional experts to a business line or invest in specific information technologies. The top managers are also responsible for the day-to-day work conducted within their respective departments, which typically includes a group working at the head office and a number of employees working at the bank's foreign offices. Finally, top management is responsible for distributing the financial risk of the firm. The activities within the various business lines are linked to different kinds of risk, each with their own set limits, but the overall risk exposure of the bank also has to be monitored and kept in line with the owners 'risk appetite'. In addition, the risk exposure has to be aligned with the rather extensive legal framework provided by international and national regulations.

The attention given to regulatory and risk-related matters during recent years has placed risk management and compliance in focus. The risk management function is led by the CRO and involves analysing the market and credit risk consequences of the traders' activities, such as changes in their portfolios of shares and other investments. Every day, the risk managers need to ensure that the traders' overall risk exposure does not threaten the firm if the market takes an unfavourable turn. The compliance function is led by the CCO and is responsible for ensuring that the experts follow internal policies and regulations explicated by the Financial Supervisory Authority. Since there is considerable public attention to issues concerning the use of inside information and illegal trading, the compliance function is seen as important for safeguarding external trust in the bank. The legal department, finally, has an advisory role and is responsible for updating those departments or expert groups involved when there are changes in national or international regulations.

Offering a stage for performance

How then do the managers intervene in the work of the experts? As suggested by the quote from one CFO at the beginning of the chapter, the managers combine 'soft and hard regulations'. The starting point for their efforts seems to be a view of the experts as the key resource for investment banking. Providing these professionals with a suitable organizational platform to work from is consequently seen as a (the) central task for the managers. Largely, this is what the soft side of their managerial efforts is about.

The organizational platform they seek to create consists of both the technological infrastructure needed for work and the social setting within which it is performed. The managers emphasize the need to establish an atmosphere that allows the experts to take advantage of one another's competences. As in many other professional organizations, learning the specific practices, standards and signifiers of the profession is put forward as central in order to perform well (Friedson, 1973; Abbott, 1991). Some observers have described the trading and sales desks as 'arenas for learning' (Hasselström, 2003). Newcomers are initially expected to follow more experienced experts to familiarize themselves with both the technical and task-related environments and gain an understanding of the key factors involved. More autonomy and responsibility then follow with experience and results:

> I was totally fresh when I came here, but you learn from where you sit. Most of what I know I have learned from colleagues sitting next

to me. You get most of your impressions, influences – and deterrent lessons – from the guys working right beside you.

(Broker)

Even though the experts are expected to contribute from day one, the ambition is to create a setting in which they can continue to develop. To this end, the top managers claim they give the experts responsibility, but also considerable degrees of freedom to develop their own work. 'We want to create a tolerant culture', one CFO explained, suggesting that there were few or no 'fences' restricting what the experts could do as long as they focused on the core business: the Nordic market. Other managers describe the experts as entrepreneurs who 'learn by doing' and the investment banks as being a suitable place for engaging in these entrepreneurial activities. Expressions like 'breeding talent' and 'making them flourish' are used to describe the managers' efforts to softly guide the experts towards high performance:

There is something here that supports the individual, the system sort of breeds individuals. We have the network and the security to provide the experts with support and inspiration. It becomes sort of a 'university'.

(Chief Financial Officer)

The managers thus seek to develop the experts' performances by letting them practice their trade. Given our own backgrounds, we quickly realized that this was a very different type of 'university' compared to what we were used to. When we started to visit the investment banks, the level of service offered to the experts struck us. Their 'university' came across as very convenient, practical and comfortable, albeit a bit chaotic at times. It offered up-to-date computers, decent coffee machines, fresh fruit and even a chef serving breakfast and lunch. Indeed, some of the experts explicitly commented on the level of service they received:

It is like franchising in our business. Back office just keeps us in order. And they have some control function too. To see that notes are in order, written properly, that the chef serves us good food. Kristina [secretary] tousles our hair and assures that we just generally feel good. We are really spoilt – I think it is wonderful place to work.

(Broker)

One expert exemplified how they were being spoiled with a story about how his firm got all the experts red roses to give to their wives/girlfriends or husbands/boyfriends at Valentine's Day. Smiling, he added that few would have thought of it otherwise. To the managers, this type of service is part of a bigger picture in which the experts are believed to deliver better results if they feel that they are cared for. This view is reinforced by the fact that the individual experts are well aware of their own contributions to firm performance. Some of them are simply very profitable to the firm. So, they expect to be pampered:

> The stars are demanding, even a bit spoiled. It is like – I am too precious for my PC not to work. All details have to be in order. 40 copies of the material have to be on the desk and the client has to be booked – the support is not allowed to fail in any way. Very expensive persons come to a system, where they expect everything else just to work.
>
> (Chief Financial Officer)

This work of setting the stage for the experts is also something that the heads of the various professional groups talk about: trying to support a creative environment where the experts feel comfortable and enjoy their work:

> I am responsible for eight Institutional brokers in Stockholm. We have to perform well. My job is about co-ordinating and motivating, the brokers have to enjoy work, have the drive to develop business. Overall we need to give the customers what they want.
>
> (Head of Institutional Sales)

The trading managers have similar comments, emphasizing that their work is about fostering team spirit among a number of talented individualists:

> The personal chemistry within the group is crucial, when you work so close together. We have a fun guy who really loves shares, but he is not performing that well. He creates a good atmosphere though, so I keep him. We need a good atmosphere, so I try to create that – establish a frank and open climate.
>
> (Head of Trading)

Motivating the individual experts to perform well is not regarded as very problematic. It seems that investment banking attracts people who expect to receive monetary rewards for good results and are willing to work hard to get them. Maybe as a consequence of this, managerial issues are seldom discussed in terms of control. When asking an analyst about control measures, she seemed rather astonished and explained, smiling:

> Control!? I do not think there is much control here. But I guess Fredrik [Head of Analysts] would be rather surprised if we did not deliver cases or if nobody said anything.
>
> (Analyst)

The heads of the various expert groups often explain that they do not act as a stereotypical manager (whatever that might entail). They claim not to steer the experts, but rather to act as team coaches encouraging them to perform well. By putting together dynamic groups, they seek to encourage the experts to take advantage of their colleagues' knowledge, develop their own approaches for exploiting market opportunities, and deliver good results. Besides the managers' belief that their efforts have a direct positive influence on firm performance, they also suggest that they are motivated by strategic considerations. It is vital, or so they claim, not only to cultivate the employees but also to attract new talents. Creating and maintaining a reputation of being a good employer becomes an important part of corporate branding.

Although the experts are given considerable leeway, the managers still monitor their activities closely. Part of the learning environment is also the acknowledging and celebrating of success to encourage others. The best performers are set up as examples to follow. Finally, even if the experts are free to develop their own approaches, the reward system is extremely clear on what counts as good performance: economic results. And these are more or less continuously monitored for each individual expert.

Evidence in numbers

If the 'soft side' of management is described as encouraging the experts to develop their business talents, the hard side is related to figures. Calculating the (economic) contributions of individuals and groups is a central preoccupation within investment banking and there are a number of common practices across the organizations. These practices develop over time, not least through the exploitation of opportunities offered by new information technologies. Since the experts' activities vary, so do the monitoring procedures. Still, the continuous efforts to monitor the experts' performances and the level of detail in these measurements would seem to bring investment banking very close to the notion of a panoptic governance regime (Foucault, 1991). There is a strong desire to measure performance in numbers and a strong belief in the possibility of translating the performance of diverse and complex practices into financial figures. In this sense, managers in investment banking can be viewed as major supporters of the idea of 'governing by numbers' (Miller, 2001).

A first type of monitoring practice is the measuring of economic results. Taking the traders as an example, their contribution is measured in terms of the monetary results of the transactions they execute. Their performance is evaluated on daily basis; the results of their trading activities are calculated overnight and presented the next morning. However, the traders are also evaluated in a longer time frame. All traders make considerable losses during some days, the key is to 'earn more than you lose' over a longer period. Specifically, it is their performance during a full year that constitutes the basis for calculating the individual bonus.

A second type of monitoring practice, used throughout all securities departments, is the recording of telephone conversations. All calls are recorded, making it possible to count and evaluate the calling activity of each expert. This is considered particularly important for evaluating the brokers. In their case, the number of calls made is compiled and related to the number of transactions triggered, allowing the managers to evaluate both the level of activity and the effectiveness of the broker in triggering transactions. Another important benefit of having the telephone calls recorded is the ability to resolve ambiguities around the particularities of specific deals. Occasionally, the experts and their clients will disagree on what they agreed on, such as the volume or price of a security in a specific deal. The recordings can then be used to settle these matters.

This hints at a more general reason for recording the experts' calls: transparency. Since the experts cannot trade using inside information, it becomes important to be able to prove whether they have or haven't. Recording their conversations becomes a way of ensuring that their activities can be traced and scrutinized in retrospect. Indeed, many of the experts see this as a safety measure also for themselves, since it allows them to prove their innocence if accused of engaging in dubious activities. (The familiarity with recorded conversations was evident also during our interviews. The securities experts were perfectly comfortable with us taping the interviews, and some even explicitly said they preferred having the conversation taped.) Of course, the recording of telephone conversations does not resolve all problems with respect to unlawful behaviour. It is not always easy to determine whether confidential subjects have been discussed. In a Swedish court case concerning inside trading a few years back, the defendants were accused of having had coded conversations about confidential matters. Although this was difficult to prove, the possibility of relaying coded messages concerning quite complex subject matters was taken seriously.

A third monitoring practice is internal cross-evaluations between the experts. These evaluations are still in use in some banks, but seem to have been more fashionable during the 1990s. The motive behind this type of monitoring is related to the character of the experts' work. Even if the individual traders, brokers and analysts need each other to conduct their work, there are no stable teams working together. The experts act relatively independently of each other; cooperation with others is dictated by the specific task-related circumstances rather than by personal relations. Still, it is easier to perform well if others do so too. In order to highlight this aspect of the experts' work, all experts are regularly asked to evaluate each other in terms of service provision and contribution of interesting ideas. This information is then compiled and fed back to the individual experts, making it possible for them to adjust their behaviour and so increase their contribution to colleagues. The managers also use these cross-evaluations as input when discussing individual performance and development.

A fourth type of monitoring practice is that of ranking or comparing competing investment banking organizations. The rankings that became popular in the 1990s gave analysts a prominent role when determining the expertise of the securities departments. Several business magazines conducted yearly evaluations where clients ranked the most interesting analysts across industries and sectors.[1] Usually the rankings listed the top three or top five analysts in each specific sector, such as pharmaceuticals or telecom. The star analysts became public figures, their names and faces published in connection with the ranking lists. Consequently, it became important for investment banks to have highly ranked analysts as they brought star quality. During the first decade of the twenty-first century, these rankings have gradually lost in importance, according to our interviewees. In part, this is attributed to the recent turbulence in the financial markets. Moreover, the rankings have also changed character so that they are less focused on the individual experts.

In parallel with the public rankings of analysts in the 1990s, there were also specialized companies offering rankings to investment banking customers to 'calibrate the relative market position and service quality of financial services providers'. On the Scandinavian

Table 8.1 Cross Nordic Equity 2010, top five ranking of stock brokering

	Rank	Mean value	Name of bank
Ranking by large institutions			
Industry mean value 3.5	1	3.8	Handelsbanken
	2	3.7	SEB Enskilda
	3	3.6	ABG Sundal Collier
	3	3.6	Carnegie
	3	3.6	Deutsche Bank
Ranking by small institutions			
Industry mean value 3.7	1	3.9	Handelsbanken
	1	3.9	SEB Enskilda
	3	3.8	Carnegie
	4	3.7	Danske Markets Equities/ESN
	5	3.6	ABG Sundal Collier
Ranking by all interviewees			
Industry mean value 3.6	1	3.9	Handelsbanken
	2	3.8	SEB Enskilda
	3	3.7	Carnegie
	4	3.6	ABG Sundal Collier
	4	3.6	Danske Markets Equities/ESN

Source: Adapted from www.prospera.se/reports/ranking-lists, accessed 11 November 2010.

market, TNS SIFO Prospera established themselves as the major supplier of rankings for the Nordic financial industry.[2] Globally, firms like Greenwich Associates offer similar services.[3] Prospera offers a number of rankings, based on both regular syndicated and tailor-made surveys. Table 8.1, above, offers one example of a regular ranking, the Cross Nordic Equity stockbroker ranking for 2010. This ranking presents the most appreciated stock brokering firms on the Nordic Exchanges based on telephone interviews with 61 large and small institutional investors. The ranking is calculated using a 'weighted average of 14 criteria covering a stockbroker's general features, analytical competence, sales & sales traders' performance'.

Even though the rankings made by Prospera are less public than those made by the business magazines, they are given more attention within the industry. Many of the organizations offering financial services are themselves customers of Prospera, and their annual reports seldom fail to mention that they have received a high ranking:

> Rankings are important when you work with foreign institutional investors. They sit in London or New York and distribute their various

> transactions on several investment banks. For their own sake they prefer to limit the number of firms they use for these transactions. So the ranking becomes a prime competition parameter.
>
> (CFO)

The many evaluations do not seem to disturb the experts, who seem used to the idea of having their professional performance assessed. One reason for this could be that they are working in a highly competitive environment. Most investment banks clearly express the view that they expect their experts to deliver top-quality service to their clients and top results for their employers. In this dimension, there seems to be considerably less tolerance towards alternative strategies:

> The first house I was working in, were in those days outstanding – always the highest ranked. There, you were fostered to become the best, or leave.
>
> (Analyst)

The experts are usually aware of these expectations and that a considerable workload will be required of them already when they start out in the industry. If someone does not fulfil these expectations, he or she often leaves voluntarily. The competitive atmosphere does not seem to be indulgent with those whose performance is not up to par. On the other hand, the managers rarely have problems with low motivation among the employees. Also, it seems that investment banking attracts people who are very interested in monetary rewards. The managers suggest that the experts quickly and easily adjust and adapt to most measures as long as they lead them in the direction of increased profit:

> It is easy to steer business-oriented individuals – just give them a good bonus system. It is the other side of the coin that is harder, aspects that you cannot relate to profit.
>
> (CFO)

Another reason why the experts appear easy to steer is related to their career paths. Working in an investment bank – especially a prestigious one – could be the height of their career, particularly in terms of monetary benefits. Even for those who start their career in an investment bank, these years will probably be the most financially rewarding in their lives. However, these years could be rather few. The intensity of work at 'the sale side' of the markets, that is investment banking, makes most experts continue their career at sites where the pace of work is slower. This often means moving to the 'buy side', such as working for an institutional investor. There is no 'up-or-out' system as in many other professional firms. There are no 'ups'; the next step in the experts' career is instead to start working for another organization where they cannot expect to receive the same level of financial rewards. Thus, the individual goals of the experts converge with that of the investment bank – profitability.

Rewarding performance through the bonus

Bonuses are used in many industries to motivate certain groups of employees. In investment banking, bonuses are typically given not only to top managers and board members but also to the various experts working in the firm. In fact, some investment banks include all their employees in the bonus system. Although the bonuses are generally thought of as individual performance rewards, this is not always easily accomplished for all expert groups. Most firms try to reward the various business lines in relation to the results they achieve. This makes it possible for the individual experts to directly affect their income. For traders, this is fairly straightforward since the economic consequences of their transactions are monitored in detail. However, some firms still split part of the bonus among all traders to encourage the team. For the other expert groups, the bonus is often related to the performance of the group as a whole to encourage cooperation and discourage extremely egocentric behaviour. The bonus for the top managers and board members is usually based on the overall result of the firm.

The bonus systems vary between countries and between firms. National attitudes towards bonuses, as well as explicit regulations, have influenced their development in each country. However, as financial markets have become increasingly international, so have the investment banking experts. Thus, there seems to be an international isomorphic pressure making bonus systems more similar across firms and countries. The best experts are generally open to moving to other firms and countries. Several of our interviewees had worked in other countries for some time. As a consequence, the bonuses offered by the banks cannot diverge too much from what their international competitors offer. The bonus levels also have some relation to the general income level and cost of living so that investment banks in financial centres like New York, London and Frankfurt typically offer higher gross rewards than others.

Within securities, all bonuses depend on the trading results. Brokers, analysts and back office staff are all rewarded when trading is successful. Brokers and analysts receive a higher bonus because they are considered to contribute directly to the clients' orders and thus to the bank's revenues. Since it is difficult to establish the contribution of each individual broker or analyst, many firms give the heads of these expert groups some degree of freedom in distributing the rewards among the experts. Within corporate banking, the bonus is typically distributed among the experts based on their project participation and the profitability of these projects.

The overall amount of the bonus paid depends on the firms' financial results, although a variety of measures are used to determine just how to distribute the rewards among the experts. During profitable years, the bonus often makes up a considerable share of the experts' annual salaries. Table 8.2 illustrates the magnitude of these monetary incentives within investment banking by relating annual bonuses to fixed salaries and annual profits in a Swedish investment bank since 2000. The bank in question had offices in all Nordic capitals and an additional five foreign offices during these years.

The table shows that the bonus paid to employees varies considerably over the years. The average employee in this bank received anywhere between €25,000 and €200,000 as the annual bonus during this ten-year period. In five of the ten years, the bank paid its employees more in bonus than in salaries. The total bonuses paid during the period were 10 per cent greater than the salaries paid. In relation to the annual net profit of the firm, the bonus typically represents 130–140 per cent. Since some countries do not require firms to separately report the bonuses

Table 8.2 Salaries, bonuses and annual profits of one Swedish investment bank, 2000–2009 (in € million)

Year	2000	2001	2002	2003	2004	2005	2006	2007	2008	2009
Salaries	43.3	58.5	64.2	56.2	57.1	58.2	66.2	83.0	92.8	70.8
Bonus (% of profit)	151.4 (139)	78.4 (137)	27.7 (110)	28.7 (136)	52.4 (132)	90.9 (136)	126.5 (137)	125.0 (208)	23.9 (–)	17.7 (130)
Annual net profit	109.0	57.2	25.0	21.1	39.6	66.7	92.3	60.1	–222.0	13.5
Average no. employed (of whom women)	765 (262)	924 (308)	941 (324)	793 (248)	791 (239)	747 (220)	775 (230)	1.035 (402)	815 (246)	703 (216)

paid to employees international comparisons are difficult to make. When comparing the relation between the total compensation paid and the annual net result of the Swedish investment bank with that of an American competitor, we found the levels comparable.

Risk and compliance management applying the brake?

Above we suggested (pp.159–162) that investment banking managers primarily seek to foster a productive setting in which the experts can excel. One could liken it to bringing an expensive race car to a perfect track for an attempt at the world record. The performance of the experts is fuelled by a system of monetary rewards that responds to both performance improvements and performance drops (although maybe not as quickly and forcefully in the latter case). However, this image disregards the fact that investment banking has been subject to considerable regulatory efforts during the past 20 years. This has resulted in a host of new functions within investment banking; most importantly, risk and compliance management have expanded considerably. These functions are positioned as mediators between a number of external parties and the investment banking experts. As such, they are set up to directly influence the expert practices. These changes within the industry become apparent when we compare our account to that of Eccles and Crane (1988), where risk management figures only marginally.

Risk management: Setting up defences from the sidelines

The risk control managers are responsible for the risk control system used by the investment bank. This means that they try to identify, assess and monitor the various risks to which the investment bank is exposed at each point in time. This includes assessing the market and credit risks that the traders are taking, and gauging whether these risks are in line with the risk appetite of the board. The overall approach to risk management has been subject to some changes over the course of our study. The objective of the risk management function in the early 'naughties' was primarily said to be the elimination of unnecessary operational risks. As a contrast, the investment banks currently emphasize compliance with legal requirements to safeguard the functioning of the financial system and protect individual investors. In response to the financial crisis, the investment banks in our study made considerable efforts to strengthen their risk control procedures during 2009, including changing policies and instructions, considerable investments in electronic risk-monitoring systems, and hiring additional risk managers.

The character of investment banking exposes investment banks to considerable financial risks, that is, to probabilities of incurring losses.[4] Risk managers distinguish between three types of risk, which are also recognized in the regulatory frameworks: credit risk, market risk and operational risk.[5] As far as stock trading is concerned, the most important risk is market risk, although operational risks are always present. Since investment banks handle vast numbers of transactions every day, even minor mistakes can have costly consequences. The back office function thus needs to check and compare every order to the data from Euroclear (the provider of settlement services for bond, equity, fund and derivative transactions). Many of these routines were once conducted manually, but are now automated and performed by the IT systems, which consequently are one source of operational risk. In terms of market risk, one risk manager expressed the challenge in the following way:

> Our customers control most of our trading activities. The fundamental logic is that the customer wants to be relieved from some particular risk. Then the trader says – ok we will buy that risk from you – and then he tries to do a good deal on the risk-reward relation. To be perceived as a serious house, and to be able to do good business, we have to be able to take quite large positions. But, and this is THE question, how large positions should the individual trader be allowed to take?
>
> (Risk Manager)

To handle operational, market and other risks, the risk managers are responsible for setting up a risk control system, sometimes described as a three-line defence system (for an example, see Figure 8.2). In such a system, the first line consists of the individual risk owners (a share trader taking a position for the investment bank), a designated product risk controller (the securities risk manager), and the manager for that specific business area (the head of securities). The risk owner is responsible for the risk s/he takes in a specific deal and cannot legitimately blame somebody else or the system. Although their responsibility does not extend to actual losses, they may well be fired for trading beyond their limits and thus threatening the financial balance of the firm. The head of securities is responsible for keeping the department's total risk exposure aligned with the bank's risk policies. The risk manager assists in guiding and controlling the individual traders. Since these activities are part of everyday practice, this is often what the experts refer to when they talk about 'risk management'.

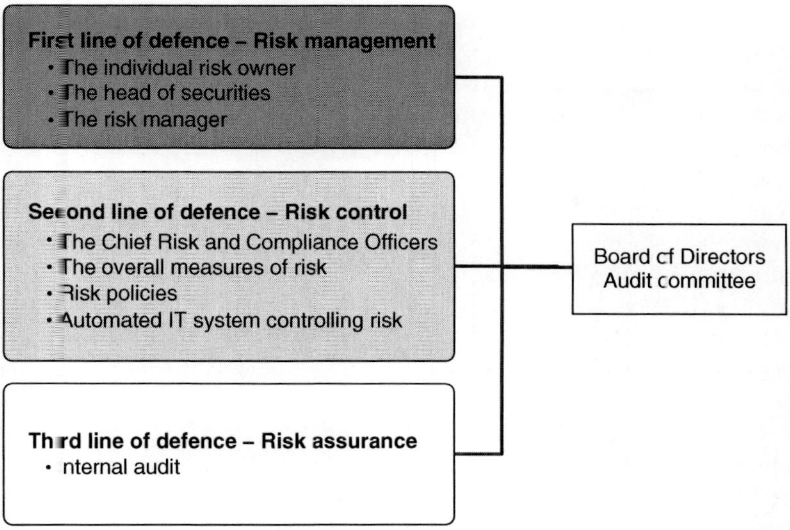

Figure 8.2 The three-line defence model for internal risk control at one of the studied investment banks

The second line of defence is referred to as 'risk control' and consists of the banks' central risk manager groups. These groups are led by the CRO and consist of central risk managers for each of the three major types of risks (market risk, credit risk, operational risk). In addition to these central groups located at the head office, each national office has at least one national risk manager responsible for all types of risks at that office. This second line of defence is concerned with the architectural aspects of risk rather than individual or group responsibilities and conduct. They define the different types of risk, determine how to measure them, design risk reports and formulate risk policies. The risk managers continuously assess whether the risks that the bank is exposed to are measured properly and whether there are risks that escape the current system. Operational risk is of special interest in this respect:

> For market and credit risk we have several well-researched and well-functioning models that we apply. Operational risk is a fuzzier concept, newer and harder to get a grip on. Currently we have a special team dedicated to operational risk and how we should deal with it.
>
> (Risk Manager)

The second line of defence is also built into the trading system itself. In the best of all worlds, this more or less automated IT system monitors and ensures that the risks produced by the activities undertaken within the bank are within the overall limits set by the bank's risk policies and risk architecture. For instance, if a trader tries to take a position (i.e. buy a certain number of shares at a certain price on behalf of the bank) that would produce a risk beyond his/her risk limit, the system would prevent the trade from being executed. If a trader requests to do something that exceeds his/her current limit or lies outside of current routines, the system will automatically send an alarm to the risk control manager. The objective of this line of defence is to automate as much as possible – to limit the operational risks by circumventing the human factor.

The third line of defence, finally, consists of the internal audit. This line of defence is often referred to as 'risk assurance' and can be seen as the prolonged arm of the board checking that top management and risk managers are assuming their responsibilities. This is to some extent part of the more general audit procedure, but there is an element in the auditing process that specifically focuses on the bank's risk control.

As part of risk management, there is a clear hierarchy within the bank consisting of several 'boxes' of formally accepted risk limits. The board sets the limit for the bank's total risk exposure, as defined and measured by the risk managers, and within the limits given by laws and regulations. Within this box of total risk, you can envisage a smaller box that is the authority of the CRO. Within this box there are national risk limits for each office, and within these boxes, each business area has its own box. Within the risk box for securities in Sweden, to take one example, each trader represents a box, with an individual limit set by the head of trading in Sweden and the securities risk controller. There are also policies concerning how much risk you are allowed to assume in each type of security, for example, a limit on a specific stock or on all liquid stocks.

As long as the traders' total risk exposures are within the limits of the trading box and are aligned with the policies and instructions developed by the risk managers, everything is fine. But if a specific deal results in risks that exceed those accepted for the trading risk box, the trader and the head of trading have to apply for an exception at the bank's Credit and Risk Committee (CRC). This will typically result in negotiations between the trader, the head of trading and the CRC, which in the end will allow the deal or not.

The risk managers are the architects, developers and maintenance crew for this defence system, but they also act as communicators between top management and risk-takers. They have daily contacts with traders, analysts and brokers. At the Stockholm office of one of the investment banks in our study, three risk managers are physically located in the middle of the large trading room. There they help, guide and control the activities. This physical placement allows them to answer questions from traders as they arise. The risk managers also stress that it helps them develop a feeling for areas and subjects that the experts perceive to be difficult. Such matters are reported to the central risk managers and sometimes result in new instructions, policy documents and educational efforts. In short, risk managers try to translate the board's appetite for risk into policies, instructions and limits that the traders can understand. In addition, they seek to translate the customer needs indicated by the traders' requests to assume positions, that is, buy securities, into messages that the board can understand. In this respect, risk managers have a typical middle management function:

> If a trader says – 'We need to do 10 000 futures in this.' – it is my task to translate that request into risk, or rather to ask, what is the worst thing that can happen if we do this? A really black bad day, how much can we lose on this? Then I go to the board and explain: The traders want to do this, if everything goes against us, we will lose this, are we prepared to take this risk?
>
> (Risk Manager)

This mediating role is also reflected in the risk managers' perception of themselves as 'selling' the risk system to the experts and managers. Maintaining a working line of communication between the operative staff (traders and brokers) and top management is held to be essential for the system to work. If this communication breaks down, the traders will start to look for loopholes, seeking out actions 'below the radar'. According to most risk managers, they will also find such alternatives, no matter how formalized the system is. Hence, a lot of effort is put on ensuring compliance:

> We have to weed out the bad behaviours and bad attitudes. We need a 100 percent risk-proof culture and in good times that doesn't come by itself.
>
> (Risk Manager)

The compliance function

The compliance function focuses on the acceptance of, and adaptation to, both external rules and regulations and internal policies. The compliance managers are responsible for ensuring that the experts comply with these directives in their daily activities. Like risk management, compliance has become increasingly topical during the past decade. This is a consequence of both increasingly encompassing and detailed external regulations and stricter internal policies. Many of these rules concern the use of inside information. Consequently, a considerable part of compliance control is geared towards monitoring whether the experts take unlawful advantage of their close connection to the market and the information they receive:

> The major difference between us [compliance managers] and them [risk managers] is that risk always has a primary owner in terms of a trader, a banker, or someone. And they have control systems. When it comes to compliance we work independently of risk ownership, trying to control the compliance risk; to assess if we have routines and processes that are aligned with the external regulations.
>
> (Compliance Officer)

The primary task of the compliance officers is ensuring that all employees are aware of the rules and regulations that apply to their particular practices. To this end, they arrange mandatory seminars to inform of regulatory changes for the various expert groups. The experts are required to participate and acknowledge the problems and possibilities that are related to the new regulatory situation. Since the external rules typically are non-negotiable, the employees are expected to express their commitment to work in accordance with them by formally signing a document. The top managers typically place considerable emphasis on the need to achieve a high level of compliance within the organization, not only for gaining the trust of clients, but also from civil society as such. If someone tries to 'bend the rules', the consequences are said to be both direct and severe:

> People who break the rules are just sent away. We fired a person in command last year, someone who was doing business on his own account. You have to be clear and determined when cases like this arise. Like 'this is the way it goes if you do not follow the rules'
>
> (CFO)

Having the experts act according to the rules concerning inside information is put forward as crucial for maintaining public confidence in the investment banks. Secret negotiations that, were they known, would affect the market price of a share, such as concerning a merger or acquisition are part of everyday activity. Consequently, considerable efforts are made to ensure a correct handling of this type of information among the experts. The 'Chinese Walls' discussed in Chapters 2, 4 and 6 are one well-known facet of this. Keeping the corporate bankers physically separated from the other experts is one way of preventing information from falling into the wrong hands. In addition, the compliance function also continuously monitors the experts' private trading activities. The experts are not allowed to take advantage of rumours or information not publicly known for their own personal benefit. To reduce the experts' possibility of doing so, they are not allowed to trade too often and required to report all changes to their private investment portfolios to their compliance officer.

Many banks have installed automated investment management systems that include control functions sending alarms to the compliance officers if certain parameters are not in order. This is known as pre-trade compliance and involves checking whether the bank has some kind of insider knowledge about this share or security, for instance due to an ongoing assignment, customer relationship or upcoming analysis. If this is the case, compliance will say no to the requested trade. Within the automated system some individual employees are also unable to do certain types of deals: analysts cannot trade shares within their own sectors, bankers cannot trade in securities that are related to corporate banking projects they are working on, and so on. In less sensitive cases, requests are automatically checked against one or several 'stop-lists' that the compliance function keeps. For instance, if somebody working in the back office wants to buy or sell a specific share, and the person in question is not on the stop-list for this share, that specific deal can proceed.

Within the compliance function one also finds the bank's IT system used for market surveillance. This is similar to the systems used by the stock exchanges. If the compliance officer has reason to believe that any of the bank's customers, or someone else, is dealing on insider information, the bank is legally obliged to report this to the Financial Supervisory Authority. If they fail to do so, the bank might be prosecuted and sentenced to pay fines. Most of the reported suspicions emanate from the traders and brokers. In addition, there is an automated system which supervises trading activity and sends alarms if the bank's customers trade among themselves, place large orders just before the exchange closes (to influence closing prices illegitimately) or do anything else peculiar via the bank.

There are quite a number of regulations that apply to investment banking, including national Swedish legislation, directives from the European Community and the rules of the US Federal Trading Commission.[6] Keeping track of the relevant regulations can be rather complex:

> If I identify a new regulation or something we missed that we need to attend to, I put forward the issue and what I think we need to do about it to top management. Then management might consult with the legal experts and come up with a solution, some kind of new routine, on what to do. Then, in the best of worlds, I'm supposed to take over and implement it.
>
> (Chief Compliance Officer)

In addition to the regulations that concern compliance directly, there are also additional legal restrictions to take into account, including accounting rules, taxation laws and labour market regulations. These issues are handled by the legal department, which also supports the compliance function in complex legal matters.

Control versus creating business

While risk and compliance managers put considerable weight on achieving conformity to routines and procedures, they also acknowledge a trade-off between detailed and rudimentary risk monitoring and control. To be able to measure dynamic and complex risk-taking on a detailed level, the system needs to comprise several theoretical definitions of risk, make strong assumptions about the character of operations and include monitoring devices capable of capturing the defined risks. But the more complex the system, risk managers argue, the less well it works when somebody is doing something that does not fit the model:

> When we talk to traders we try to explain the risk model as consisting of five moving parts: price... which you could hedge... volatility, interest rate, future dividends, and time. But even this borders on being too complex. So we simplify further, and this is a good example of the practically useful stuff: We've made a 2-dimensional model focusing on the two most important parameters: price and volatility. We draw that diagram and illustrate to the traders where they should

> be . . how they must compensate increased risk in one dimension in terms of the other.
>
> (CRO)

This view has its corollary among traders who perceive the prospect of a very specific system with a myriad of risk limits as moving focus away from actual trading. If every trade has to be within a specific limit, they argue, engaging in trading would become very stiff-legged and bureaucratic, and on many occasions outright impossible. Thus traders prefer a system with a few robust parameters, which they can keep in mind while trading:

> There is a classic conflict within finance, between the entrepreneurially driven and the rule-lovers. It is within the regulations, how one relates to ethics and risk, but also in the attitude towards risk assumed by the Financial Supervisory Authority. This regulatory system tends to inhibit our friends the entrepreneurs.
>
> (CEO)

But what constitutes a good balance between control and innovative trading? This varies considerably over time and also between investment banks. During our first interviews in 2005, the scales clearly favoured innovative trading as compared to the more recent interviews conducted in 2009. There is also considerable variation between individuals, and the merits of either position appear to be contestable. For now, increased control appears to be gaining ground, but the work of controlling for risks and achieving compliance with set routines appears to be a task with no obvious end-point in sight.

Behind the scenes, or another front stage?

Our account above provides a relatively glossy view of management in investment banking as preoccupied with safeguarding the position that business is conducted in the most efficient and prudent way possible; investment banking comes across as being rational and efficient. This stands in relief to our accounts of what the expert groups actually do in and outside the trading room; accounts filled with social trade-offs, organizational problems, hopes and fears. In particular, the account of risk and compliance management resembles what has been described as the myths of management (Mintzberg, 1973; Kotter, 1996). Managing investment banking experts is an analytical, well-structured and rational process; previous problems of excessive risk-taking have been solved by implementing efficient risk control systems; continuous efforts are made to further improve this already efficient system; the chances of bad calls, excessive risk-taking and illegal trading are minimized. All is well.

The credibility of this image is disturbed by the fact that the managers are so good at describing their conduct, strategies and systems in this manner. Their story is simply too good. One of the primary tasks of these managers is to do exactly what they have done in our interviews: to describe the management of investment banking positively to various stakeholders. This suggests that the risk and compliance management function not only takes place back stage but also constitutes another front stage for investment banking practice. Successfully engaging in investment banking requires both efficient operations and legitimacy in the eyes of owners, customers, stock exchanges, regulatory and supervisory authorities, media and others. Thus, management is not only about coordinating practices towards efficiency but also about generating legitimacy by accounting for these practices. If the supervisory authorities require extensive risk management control systems, the production of such systems can be regarded as a primary function on a front stage involving that actor. The actual control of traders, brokers, analysts and bankers might then be of secondary interest. This suggests that investment banking can be described as a loosely coupled (Weick, 1979) or even de-coupled system (Meyer and Rowan, 1977) in which different actors, activities and artefacts play important roles on different stages.

Our empirical material lends some support to this interpretation. There are two major management tools used to influence the practices of the front office experts: the bonus system and the risk control system. The bonus system appears to encourage the individual experts to take risks in order to reap short-term benefits:

> When I explained to a trader what the long-term costs could be of buying the risks he wanted, his counter-argument was how much we would charge the customer for the deal and thus earn in the short run. When I emphasized the long-term costs, his reply was that by then he would probably work for another bank. He wanted his bonus now and saw no reason to take long-term responsibility. That's how bad the bonus system can work. On the other hand we need to attract the stars, and that's done with bonuses.
>
> (Chief Risk Officer)

The risk control system, on the other hand, is explicitly set up to limit risk-taking. If investment banking were a logically coherent rational system, we would expect these systems to be coordinated. But they are not:

> We don't have anything to do with the bonus systems. We would really like to have some kind of influence but that is decided by a separate remuneration committee in which no risk managers are included... it's a bit odd when you come to think of it.
>
> (Chief Risk Officer)

In investment banking, generous bonuses are offered to attract and motivate individuals to work hard and generate short-term profits, while extensive risk control systems are set up to ensure that the same individuals at least *seem* to be controlled in the eyes of those requiring it. Thus both systems make the bank more attractive. The bonuses attract the stars and encourage them to be creative risk buyers. The risk control and compliance systems make the bank look good in the eyes of regulators, supervisory authorities, business media and others, but do not necessarily interfere with the practices of the experts. The traders, brokers and bankers hardly ever mention the control systems and, when prompted, they all suggest that management control of their work is not an issue.

Collaboration with and without frictions

What kind of consequences do the managerial activities have for the organizing of investment banking? The fact that the risk managers seek to make their methods as simple as possible could be interpreted as a serious attempt to increase genuine compliance. But it could also be interpreted as an expression of investment banking having to seek support on two different stages with conflicting requirements, preventing the implementation of a tight control system. Regardless of how serious the managers are in their attempts to control the experts, achieving such coordination might be more problematic than the managers suggest. This tension, we argue, is replayed in the use of distinctly different coordination methods by the front office experts and the risk managers: boundary objects versus methods standardization.

Whereas the front office experts are receptive to the multiple identities of shares, risk managers are much less eclectic. In contrast to analysts, who offer their analyses of specific shares to other experts more or less as topics for conversation, accepting and expecting there to be other views, risk managers are less flexible concerning how others respond to their work. Compared with the brokers' recommendations and conversations with their clients, the contrast is even more visible. Risk managers are concerned with the spread of their way of approaching the knowledge object, which essentially involves translating shares and other financial products into the currency of risk. Other actors within the investment bank are encouraged to do the same, and, in this respect, the shares cannot function as boundary objects between risk managers and other occupational groups. This can be seen in the efforts to establish procedures for handling risk, including the introduction of various limits as safety valves in the trading system used by the traders. The risk managers seek to establish fences for the financial entrepreneurs to respect and accept. The boundary object is translated into the one quality to consider – that of a risk container. The decentralization accentuated in the front office is here contrasted with formal rules to control and thus hamper initiative and exploration. This means that the characteristics of the boundary object are no longer allowed to differ, but are locked into a model of standardization with a fixed significance.

We suggest that these activities on behalf of the risk managers are examples of *methods standardization* as discussed by Star and Griesemer (1989). By educating, promoting and imposing their methods for measuring and calculating risk, and requiring others to adjust their actions accordingly, risk managers (try to) interfere directly with trading practice. The use of terms such as *compliance* and *alignment* to discuss the results of these efforts further underscores the ambition to standardize methods; such terms are completely nonsensical when coordination is achieved via boundary objects.

While most management activities appear to support the flexible work of the experts, there are also frictions between managerial initiatives and expertise practice. How, then, does this influence the organizing of investment banking practices?

9
Organizing Investment Banking

How is investment banking organized? In this chapter, we directly address the first of our two major research questions. As shown in previous chapters, specialized expert groups contribute to jointly perform investment banking. As suggested in Chapter 1, the outcome of this joint performance – investment banking – needs to be both innovative and coordinated. Our account of investment banking, as well as previous studies, thus leads us to address a series of traditional issues in organizational analysis. Is it possible for investment banking to be spontaneous, innovative, coordinated, as well as controlled? If so, how? What constitutes the 'self-designing' process that Eccles and Crane (1988) claim to be characteristic of investment banking? What constitutes the activities of *bricolage* that Engelen et al. (2010) argue is necessary for 'improvised financial innovation'? How is investment banking organized to enable the 'creative adoptions' described by Beunza and Stark (2005)? And how is this type of organizing coupled with the explicit attempts by management to coordinate and control?

Our analysis will focus on three aspects of investment banking organization:

(1) The share as a boundary object.[1] Does the share as a boundary object and organizing device offer a solution to the problem of organizing both for control and creativity? If it does, how does this organizing device differ from other such devices and logics? This is the main focus of the chapter.
(2) The risk control systems. How do the risk control managers' attempts at controlling the practices of the expert groups work? How can we explain these attempts and the consequences they have for investment banking?

(3) The bonus systems. How do the liberal bonuses in investment banking affect the expert groups' practices? Do they coordinate and control the experts' activities? Do they foster creativity and improvised innovation?

A brief recollection of where we are

Chapters 3–7 showed that the expert groups within securities and corporate banking all enact shares as central objects in their everyday work. They all agree on the centrality of issuing and trading shares. The different experts seem to have few problems enacting their specific versions of shares despite the fact that these are qualitatively very different from each other. Viewing the share as a boundary object was one of the starting points for our study. Since the empirical account indicates that the expert groups enact different share identities, while at the same time being able to interact with each other smoothly on matters related to shares, there is empirical support for such a view. In Table 9.1 we summarize the characteristics of the share identities constructed by the four expert groups using our four descriptive dimensions of share identity.

Table 9.1 summarizes more than the enacted share identities. Enactment (of shares and other entities alike) requires action (as in en-*act*). Since the enacted share identity within each group is qualitatively different from the others, it follows that the expert practices are qualitatively different. The different share identities constructed by the experts can be seen as *results* of them engaging in qualitatively different practices. Since the expert practices are partly geared towards, and evolve around, the share, the share can be viewed as co-producing, constituting or performing both the various share identities and the expert practices. Thus Table 9.1 implies that the expert groups under study engage in distinct and qualitatively different practices. But, even if the constructed share identities are informative regarding the expert groups' practices, we have yet to address how the share, as a boundary object, helps to produce these practices. This will be the main issue in the following sections.

Fluidity and friction in investment banking

What do our findings say about the specialization and coordination of work within and between the various expert groups? If the share identity is highly flexible, can it still provide some kind of order to investment banking, can it allow for, or even foster, creativity and innovation?

Table 9.1 Summary of the enacted share identities

Dimension of share identity	**Traders**	**Analysts**	**Brokers**	**Bankers**
Constitutive associations	Potentially to 'everything', filtered by the trader and the (emotional) interaction between traders	To 'data', valuation models, investors, managers, and (business) media	To analyses of corporations and sectors, and to clients' investment portfolios and policies	To analyses of corporations and sectors, and to contracts signifying e.g. ownership and employment
What the share represents	Does not represent anything 'in itself' beyond a trading opportunity	Represents an investment object with a materially heteroge-neous body	Represents one among several investment opportunities offered to clients	Represents a corporation under construction and a business opportunity for bankers
How the share can be used	A commodity that can be traded for short-term gains	A singularized good constructed to attract investors	To motivate clients to transact and hence generate brokerage	A possible source of capital to finance a client's enterprises
Temporal framing of the share	Momentary. Each transaction is a new situation	Medium- to long-term. Historical events affect the future of the share, which changes only gradually	Variable. Day-to-day adjustments, quarterly updates, and long-term projections	Mid- to long-term. Due to contractual associations as well as industry investment trends

Fluidity – Due to simultaneous multiplicity

Many accounts of boundary objects describe them as objects travelling between different locations or sites (Trompette and Vinck 2009; Zeiss and Groenewegen, 2009). The sites could be different physical spaces, different geographical places, different formal organizations, different teams, different professional groups, different fields like 'science' and 'politics' and so on. In contrast, our results indicate that the share does not need to travel, or at least, that it only needs to travel very short distances to attain enough flexibility to be enacted differently by different groups. There are many situations in which the expert practices become linked to each other: brokers are invited to make use of the analysts' insights during their daily sales efforts; bankers employ analysts during their IPO projects; traders are given the task to trade on behalf of a broker's client. In these situations, traders, brokers, analysts and bankers work close to and with one another, but still perform different practices that transform the share into qualitatively different entities. They enact these different share identities, not only when working with experts within their own group, but also when interacting with experts from other groups. As a boundary object, the share is thus plastic enough to adapt to the needs and constraints of several occupational groups, while being robust enough to maintain identity *across sites* (Star and Griesemer, 1989). But it is also *simultaneously* and *in the very same site* able to have multiple identities. This simultaneous multiplicity of the share can be observed in a number of situations, illustrated by these three examples.

When a broker needs to know the price of a share s/he can look at the price movements on any of the many screens in the trading room. But since the prices are changing, the broker might seek a more informed opinion on future prices by consulting with a trader or an analyst. When doing so, the broker will adopt a temporal frame that is relevant for his/her task at hand, possibly being influenced by a clients' current situation. Asking a trader, the broker will receive an answer implying a very short time horizon, maybe comprising a few seconds, minutes or at most an hour or two. If the broker asks an analyst, the time horizon will be much longer. Of course the broker could ask both a trader and an analyst. Thus, in this situation, three different temporal framings of the share can be enacted, without anyone questioning the frames enacted by the others. The share coordinates the conversation, allowing multiple temporal framings to coexist.

The trading room is the main site, and the daily morning meeting is the main occasion, for the face-to-face interaction between analysts, brokers and to some extent traders When the analysts present their views on selected shares (see Chapter 4), they enact a share identity with a 'full' body, being relatively stable. The brokers listen and ask questions about the share, enacting it as a resource for motivating specific clients to make specific investments. Thus in the interaction between analysts and brokers, two share identities are simultaneously enacted. Sometimes the brokers are very attentive to the presentation, sometimes less so. Sometimes there are arguments and opinions exchanged concerning the value of, and possible changes in the value of, a share. But there are seldom any major controversies regarding what constitutes the share as such. In the trading room during the morning meetings, the interaction between analysts, brokers and traders is coordinated via the share as a boundary object. The discussions in the trading room can thus be viewed as creating productive friction where different practices and specialized, distributed knowledge meet, possibly resulting in innovative actions in partly new and always changing situations (Beunza and Stark, 2005). The result of this interaction is also used during the rest of the day: the brokers use it in their conversations with clients; the analysts use it in prioritizing what to analyse and what to inform about during the following days.

A third example of situations of simultaneous enactment of multiple share identities is the schedule of seminars and roadshows arranged in investment banking. Here, both brokers and analysts interact with investors and corporate managers. The corporate managers help the analysts enact their characteristic full-bodied share identity, while the investors help the brokers enact a singularized share related to their particular circumstances. Even though there are discussions and sometimes arguments going in different directions concerning what specific value a share has, there are hardly any conflicts regarding what the share represents, what it is used for, or within what temporal frame it should be valued. Again, we can view the interaction as productive friction increasing the probability of finding new solutions and innovative adaptations. Different opinions coexist regarding what value a share has or what value development can be expected, but the conversations rarely end in conflicts regarding share identities. At the same time, at least two qualitatively different share identities are enacted during these meetings.

Based on the above, our first main conclusion concerns the share as a boundary object and as an organizational device. Shares are flexible to such an extent that they can be ascribed different identities *simultaneously, in the same site*. Thus, we would argue that shares have an even higher flexible capacity than what has been observed for boundary objects in other accounts (e.g. Star and Griesemer, 1989; Trompette and Vinck, 2009; Zeiss and Groenewegen, 2009). Beunza and Stark (2005:91) suggest that 'entrepreneurship is the ability to keep multiple evaluative principles at play and to exploit the resulting ambiguity...'. Based on the above, we suggest that the share contributes in important ways to generating and maintaining such innovation-enhancing multiplicity within investment banking (possibly in tandem with other boundary objects in investment banking). Our account of the interaction between members of different expert groups who enact different share identities is also consistent with the conceptualization of financial innovation as a Lévi-Straussian *bricolage* (Engelen et al., 2010). The experts can be said to pick and choose, translating components of the other available share identities into their own identity constructions. But there is also an important difference between our account of investment banking and the argument made by Engelen et al.:

> ...there never was a system or systems, only a ramshackle series of chain connections between heterogeneous objects found, constructed and imagined by a multiplicity of individuals and groups whose conduct was only temporarily aligned.
>
> (Engelen et al., 2010:55)

We have focused on one heterogeneous object that seems to allow and foster improvisation. But in the case of investment banking, we *do* see a system as well, and our expert groups and individuals align more than temporarily. This system is what we refer to as the investment banking machinery, in which the alignment of experts is possible due to a repeated enactment of shares as boundary objects.[2] These observations lead us to the first main conclusion regarding the organizing of investment banking: The share as a boundary object and organizing device stimulates multiplicity, ambiguity and improvisation *in an orderly and systematic manner*. As a boundary object, then, the share produces fluidity in investment banking.

Problematic friction – Due to different uses and temporal frames

But all interaction between the experts is not fluid. There are situations in which friction becomes problematic. One such example involves the bankers. Since the bankers are not physically co-located with the experts in securities, they are of special interest. Based on the main theme of boundary object accounts, such a more distant location should not be problematic (Trompette and Vinck, 2009). Since the shares' journey between corporate banking and securities is relatively longer than between the expert groups within securities, we would expect even fewer difficulties from enacting multiple, qualitatively different share identities.

Even if the bankers' enactment of new or changed shares is important for the other groups (see Chapters 6 and 7), there are situations in which the simultaneous enactment of different share identities does become problematic. The analysts enact a rather stable share; it has associations both with advanced analytical valuation models and with the material resources and the history of the corporation behind the share, all of which serves to stabilize the share as an investment object (see Chapter 4). The traders then take these investment objects for granted, and use them as commodities for making deals (Chapter 3). The bankers, on the other hand, do not accept the investment objects as given. Instead, they try to find arguments and reasons for changing them. Any change that the bankers can sell to corporate managers and to investors will make some of the analysts' constitutive associations (in terms of calculus recommendations, materiality and sociality) obsolete. In the strict sense this is also true for the share identities of brokers and traders, but these experts do not put any major effort into stabilizing singularized shares; for example, the traders use shares as commodities with a much shorter temporal frame. The analysts, on the other hand, put considerable efforts into building and stabilizing their share, at the same time as the bankers try to change it. This tension has practical consequences. The analysts do help the bankers with their expertise, but regard this work as disturbing their own practice of analysing shares and sectors. As noted in Chapter 4, the analysts have difficulties explaining why they view this help to bankers as disturbing.

One explanation could be that it threatens to 'marginalize' them and their contribution, in the sense discussed by Star and Griesemer (1989:411). Potentially, analysts could be seen as having multiple memberships, being both corporate bankers and analysts, which would force them to 'oscillate' between two social worlds (ibid.). But analysts do not appear to view themselves as members of the banker group even when working on corporate banking projects. They have a strong identity as analysts and their enactment of shares is based on analyst practices. This results in their enactment of share identities that conflict with, and are threatened by, the share identities enacted by the bankers. The traders and brokers, on the other hand, enact shares that are much less stable. The brokers' share is variable both due to changes in market prices and due to clients' financial situations and strategies. The traders' share is qualified momentarily; each moment is unique and the emptiness of the share makes it change along with whatever external developments there are. As a result, their versions of shares do not collide with the more long-term identities enacted by bankers and analysts.

Here we may have touched upon a limit to how flexible the share can be. Due to conflicts between the bankers' and the analysts' constitutive associations, uses and temporal framings, the share cannot be several things simultaneously in the same site. But even if we have some empirical indications that the share as a boundary object does have some limits in terms of how flexible it can be, our main conclusion remains intact: The share as a boundary object works as a highly flexible coordinating device. This device not only tolerates heterogeneity but also generates improvisation and innovation. The productive friction between the simultaneously enacted and interacting multiple realities of investment banking makes new solutions and flexible adaptations possible.

Heterarchy – Combining bureaucracy and community

If we view each expert group as a community of practice (Wenger, 1998, 2000), it is hardly surprising to find each such group enacting a specific share identity. The group members interact with one another and with similar other actors and artefacts during most of their working days. This interaction is often face-to-face, or face-to-similar artefact. The traders are interpreting and discussing price movements and news on their screens; the analysts work together or in solitude with their DCF-models, to take two examples. The repetitive interaction within a group makes the members 'grow old together', and potentially creates what Schutz calls 'genuine we-relations' (1964:21–33; Schutz, 1967:163–167). Via their interaction, their subjectivities can be interlinked and high levels of inter-subjectivity attained. This enables each expert group to enact a more homogeneous reality, relative to those of the other expert groups. When experts from different expert groups interact, even face-to-face, they bring with them their respective share identities. But they need not calibrate these different share identities to be able to interact. On the contrary, the debates and discussions triggered by differences in share identities can be seen as creative or innovative friction. Thus the share as a boundary object coordinates the different expert practices, while allowing for heterogeneity in the very here and now. No need for travels between sites to enact multiple worlds in investment banking.

The coexistence of multiple worlds can be translated into viewing investment banking as a heterarchic form of organizing (Stark, 2001, 2009; Beunza and Stark, 2005). It comprises coordinated action, but at the same time heterogeneous practices and distributed knowledge. In terms of management, coordination and control, different practices are allowed to coexist, to live their different lives, involving flexible reactions, friction and creative acts. When a trader sees an opportunity to make a quick profit, s/he is affected but not strictly limited by what the brokers are recommending to their clients; when an analyst changes a recommendation, s/he can choose to take into consideration how brokers use such recommendations and what is currently happening on the trading markets. If investment banking was organized around a stricter, more explicit coordination and control mechanism, this might not be the case. Indeed, with such a more strict organizational ambition, the current state of affairs is likely to be conceived as an example of a sub-optimized bureaucracy, or as an adhocracy out of control. What we see is neither. We see an organizational form that resembles very much what others have described as *heterarchy*.[3]

Heterarchy highlights non-hierarchic, ambivalent, multi-perspective but still orderly systems. We propose that the share, as a boundary object, enables and sustains investment banking as a multi-professional, multi-perspective and multi-practice system, that is, a heterarchy. According to Beunza and Stark (2005), heterarchies are characterized by minimal hierarchy and organizational heterogeneity:

> Heterarchies, however, are not simply non-bureaucratic. Heterarchies interweave a multiplicity of organizing principles. [...] A robust, lateral collaboration flattens hierarchy without flattening diversity. [...] The challenge is to create a sufficiently common culture...
>
> (Beunza and Stark, 2005:90)

In our interpretation, the concept of heterarchy applied to investment banking *does* incorporate one of the two most fundamental parts of a bureaucratic logic: specialization through division of labour (Weber, 1947 [1922]) or differentiation (Lawrence and Lorsch, 1967). The diverse practices of the experts within securities and corporate banking could be viewed as the result of a functional division of labour (Eccles and Crane, 1988). But the other fundamental part of bureaucracy the coordination or integration of the units via hierarchical control (Weber, 1947 [1922]; Lawrence and Lorsch, 1967) is missing, or at least minimal. How then is a heterarchy coordinated? Or more specifically: how is investment banking coordinated? Several authors have touched upon this, without developing a systematic answer. In the quote above, Beunza and Stark argue, 'the challenge is to create a sufficiently common culture', but they do not elaborate on the production of such a 'culture'. Eccles and Crane (1988) describe investment banking as 'self-designing organizations', but do not analyse this process further. Engelen et al. (2010) reason in terms of *bricolage* and 'series of chain connections' in their analysis of financial innovations, but do not elaborate on what that entails for the organizing of investment banking.

Our study suggests that heterarchies can be coordinated via boundary objects, or more specifically, that the heterarchic machinery of investment banking is coordinated by shares (and presumably other securities) working as boundary objects. The investment banking practices are diverse, or specialized, to use a concept from the bureaucratic logic; the groups, or communities, to borrow a concept from a non-bureaucratic logic, interact without reducing their diversity, creating friction that generates flexible adaptations and innovations. The share is enacted by all groups, but with distinct and different identities co-producing the organized heterogeneity. Heterarchy is the organizational form and boundary objects (shares) the primary coordinating device making investment banking possible. This is our main conclusion regarding how investment banking is organized.

The practical paradox of investment banking – Innovative and controlled

Our observations concerning heterarchy and coordination via boundary objects still leave us with questions regarding management, motivation and control. Investment banking may be heterarchic, but it is also highly and increasingly regulated. That is, it is coordinated and controlled by explicit rules created and enforced by both 'internal' actors such as risk control and compliance managers, and 'external' actors such as the national financial supervisory authorities (see Chapters 2 and 8). These rules, regulations and directives conflict with the heterarchic notion of minimal hierarchy (Sjöstrand, 1985; Stark, 1999). To account for how investment banking is organized, we thus need to introduce at least one more group of actors into the analysis: the risk control managers.

Efforts to control risk

As noted in Chapter 8, risk control managers in investment banking do not enact a specific share identity. Shares do not really work as a boundary object when it comes to risk control management. Risk control managers do not qualify shares as having an identity distinct from other financial instruments. Indeed, they treat shares the same way they treat investment banking at large. Instead of enacting a distinct share identity, the risk control managers view shares as one of many containers of risk.

Following the argument made by Millo and MacKenzie (2007), investment banking *is* risk management, at least from the perspective of how investment banking relieves clients of financial risks by buying them. But these are not the risks with which risk control managers are directly involved. The risk control managers are concerned with the risks involved in the investment banking business itself, the risks taken by the bank, not the risks taken by its customers. Of course these risks are related; of the three main types of risks that the risk control managers and their systems handle (credit risk, market risk and operational risk), the credit and market risks emanate from the same positions that the clients have taken.[4] But the total risk of investment banking is very different, and is due to the banks' positions, technologies, routines, practices and so on.

The risk managers' main concern is the current and future total risk of all the investment banking activities. Although they use similar calculative models and technologies as the experts in securities for measuring and valuing various risks, the risk control managers' models do not distinguish between risks related to shares, bonds, other instruments or even corporate banking projects. With the help of their models, they not only assess the banks' total risk at each moment and in the forecasted future, but they also try to *control* the potential near future risk. The main object(ive) for the risk control managers is not the potential gains from investing in a share, or the potential earnings of a specific trade, or to find out whether a share is under- or over-valued by the market, or whether there are any possibilities to restructure firms to enable the birth of new shares. The main objects that are enacted by the risk managers are various types of risk. Risk management does not include the enactment of a qualified share identity; the risk managers are occupied with risks, not shares.

A second boundary object?

Drawing on the analysis of risk management by Millo and MacKenzie (2007; 2009), we could argue that 'risk' (or rather, 'a risk model') works as a boundary object in risk control management. This boundary object is enacted not only by risk control managers but also by compliance managers, members of the bank's risk committee and by other bank managers (see Chapter 8). Outside the bank, it is enacted by surveillance authorities and at least sometimes by business media (when reporting on financial setbacks and 'scandals'). Viewing risk as a boundary object in this context would allow us to investigate how qualitatively different risk identities are enacted by various groups (for a similar analysis, see Millo and MacKenzie, 2007). But for our analysis of the organizing of investment banking, a more interesting observation is that, within securities and corporate banking, risk does *not* appear to be an important boundary object. The practices of the various investment banking experts do involve risks, but the handling of the banks' current and future risk is not enacted as an object(ive) by the members of these groups.

Millo and MacKenzie (2007) propose that the underlying model that the risk control managers use to calculate risk works as a boundary object, at least to some extent controlling the traders' practices. Our data point in another direction. When analysing the experts' enactments of share identities, risk is not very prominent; traders talk a lot about risks, but these are usually the risks that clients want to sell. The risk control managers themselves suggest that their models are too complex and too rigid to be used by the traders. This is why they try to develop other, less precise and more flexible models to be used by the traders (see Chapter 8). Thus, there are at least two different risk models enacted by the risk control managers, one for their own use, and one developed for the traders. Our account of the traders' practices indicates that they use neither, apart from those aspects of the risk model that are incorporated into the electronic trading system. But even then, both the risk control managers and the traders testify that there are good reasons, incentives and opportunities for sidestepping the system to make creative, new unique deals in the market. Taken together, this implies that neither risks nor shares work as boundary objects between the expert groups and the risk control managers. Neither the risk models nor the shares travel between their respective worlds.

The experts do not try to control the risk control managers. As long as they have enough leeway to practice their own trade, which our study indicates they have, they are not concerned with the banks' risk control at all. The risk control managers, on the other hand, explicitly try to control the expert groups. But they do not do this by enacting the share as a boundary object. Of course, relying on boundary objects is not the only or even the most common way to manage, coordinate and control. We suggest that the various control technologies employed by the risk control managers, including formulating rules and informing and educating the experts, can be viewed as attempts to coordinate and control by 'standardization of methods' (Star and Griesemer, 1989:392, 404). This approach to co-ordination, 'emphasizing how, and not what or why' (ibid.:407), lacks much of the flexibility of coordination via boundary objects, and thus meets resistance from the experts. The efforts of the risk managers are built into the trading technology, they comprise formal rules that the traders are expected to follow, and they are expressed in simple calculative models that the traders are supposed to use. Regardless of which, their attempts to control by standardizing methods do not seem to be very successful at coordinating investment banking.[5]

The idea of standardization of methods as a coordination device has a long history. Weber (1947 [1922]:328–341) argued that formal-legal authority and bureaucracy was the most precise form of control (compared to control by traditional or charismatic authority), suggesting that such other forms of control were gradually being replaced in a process of historical rationalization driven by economic, political and religious factors. Weber was also very clear that regardless of the type of coordination employed, it needed to be based on legitimate authority, meaning that the actors involved must share a belief in the legitimacy of the authority at hand (ibid.:124–130). In the case of the risk control managers' attempts to control investment banking by 'standardization of methods', or 'formal-legal bureaucracy', the invasive character of this type of coordination might just be too much to be legitimate in the eyes of the investment banking experts. Instead of complying, they resist by ignoring.

As a boundary object, the share coordinates investment banking, but not in a very precise way. It enables experts from different communities of practice to interact and help each other, thus making it possible to organize investment banking according to both bureaucratic logic – with specialized expert groups – and according to a more communal logic – with experts performing complex tasks in a less structured, more flexible and even creative way. Weber did not elaborate much on what kind of coordinating devices traditional authority comprises, but boundary objects can certainly be understood as such a device. Our analysis suggests that the primary coordination device within, as well as between, communities of practice might very well be the boundary object.

Performativity and the multiple worlds of investment banking

According to Star and Griesemer (1989), boundary objects can be both communicative and performative devices. As communicative devices, they maximize the autonomy of the social worlds involved and the communication between them. As performative devices, they bring with them communication infrastructures; even if a boundary object is enacted differently within the different worlds, it still has distinct performative consequences within these various worlds (Fujimura, 1992). In our account of investment banking practices, we have shown that all expert groups enact distinct but different share identities. Our analysis indicates that the share contributes to perform these different social worlds while at the same time being performed by them. This is the very core of understanding the share as a coordinating device within the heterarchy of investment banking: (1) the share carries with it specific instructions or infrastructure that is enacted by the various experts, (2) the share allows for very different conduct within each expert group and (3) the share fosters flexible adaptation and innovation when the different groups interact.

The fact that the infrastructure that the share carries with it is not usually visible is central to its coordinating role. Or to be more precise, the share is not thought of as a coordinating or controlling device by the interacting experts. In contrast to formal rules or explicit agreements and instructions, the performativity of the share is rarely noticed. It is an object largely taken for granted, both due to its embeddedness in the discourses of the experts, their expert knowledge and their subjective meanings, and in the various material infrastructures that support their practices. This coordinating role of the share is also supported by its long historical development as a boundary object (see Chapter 2). In this sense, a Weberian account of historical rationalization might not be all that misplaced in understanding the share as a boundary object within investment banking. The current growth of risk control within investment banking could be viewed as part of the rationalization of society at large and of finance in particular.

Why the share works so well, and the risk models don't

The growth of risk and compliance management in investment banking could be seen as the most recent chapter in a Weberian historic process of rationalization. This process can be traced much farther back in time than the current rapid growth of risk and compliance management, or the rapid growth in trading volumes and trading instruments over the past three decades. In Chapter 2, we accounted for the historical emergence of the share as we know it today. Nowadays, shares are enacted in many and qualitatively different guises, but this has not always been the case. The share has developed from being a highly contested and marginal object to become one of the most fundamental objects in the financial sector. But the share has had many and sometimes contradictory functions from its inception: these include a method to finance government debts and business enterprises, a contract regulating an investment, a promissory note of dividends, an instrument to trade, a component in a combined basket or structured product. Various actors such as bank owners, kings, political leaders, entrepreneurs, stockjobbers, institutional investors, media, investment bankers and others, all have had their stakes and interests in enacting and developing the share. Throughout its history, different actors have used the share in different ways. It has not been successfully 'stabilized' by one actor managing to get everybody on board (cf. Callon, 1986), but rather, a wide range of actors has more or less simultaneously enacted the share for different purposes. Despite this *distributed* or *ecological* history of enactment and development, and maybe because of it, the share is taken for granted – as a stabilized object – by many different actors. This makes it especially fit as a coordinating device in a multi-communal heterarchic organization like contemporary investment banking. As such it is able to perform both as a communicative and interactive device connecting several different expert groups and providing invisible infrastructures for the practices within these groups.

This historical backdrop concerning the distributed and heterogeneous uses of shares can also add to our understanding of the risk control managers' attempts to control the conduct of the experts. In line with Millo and MacKenzie (2007), we could view the risk management technology, or at least the simplified risk assessment model that the risk control managers try to impose on the traders, as a boundary object. Compared with the share, this risk managemement model is a late arrival in investment banking. While shares have been around for several hundreds of years, risk (in the form of risk management models within investment banking) is much more recent. Millo and MacKenzie (2007, 2009) trace current risk models to the early 1970s, and our own empirical material indicates that the risk control managers are still trying to develop a model that can and will be used by the traders. This points to a second difference: the simplified risk management model is to a large extent developed by one specific group of actors with a specific object(ive) in mind. The risk control managers try to develop methods to control, rather than develop, the flexible and innovative investment banking practices. This makes the process of translating risk models into a 'stabilized' boundary object much more problematic. Investment banking experts already enact their different share identities as well as their different social worlds, and they do so successfully. In other words, there is a working infrastructure in place. And as Star (2007) notes: 'Infrastructure does not grow de novo; it wrestles with the inertia of installed base and inherits strengths and limitations from that base. Optical fibres run along old railroad lines; new systems are designed for backward-compatibility.' The bureaucratic risk control system championed by the risk control managers does not seem to be compatible with the existing heterarchic infrastructure of investment banking. Here our analysis of the share as a boundary object merges the ecological micro-sociology of Star and Griesemer (1989), the ANT-treatment of artefacts (Latour, 1992, 1994) and the Weberian treatment of authority (Weber, 1947 [1922]). The share as a boundary object does seem to have a lot of power, both by carrying with it an invisible infrastructure, and by being a strong ally to the experts trying to resist bureaucratic control through standardization of methods.

Summarizing the analysis of the relation between attempts at risk control and the 'fluid' practices of investment banking experts, we can conclude that: (1) The risk models developed by risk control managers are not enacted as a boundary object by the members of the expert groups. (2) Attempts at risk control are an example of methods standardization, which is an important coordination device within bureaucracies where it is usually coupled with hierarchical relations, but which fits poorly with the heterarchic logic of investment banking. (3) Investment banking thus comprises two conflicting organizational forms and two conflicting coordination devices. But does this conflict make investment banking a little less 'possible'? Or does it enhance the possibilities of investment banking? We end this chapter by discussing whether the current attempts at risk control are helpful or problematic for investment banking.

Managing investment banking – Control and bonuses

The heterarchic logic, supported by the share as a boundary object, affords division of labour between the expert groups and coordinates their diverse practices into an orderly but still flexible and innovative system. The bureaucratic and hierarchic logic involves the risk control managers' attempts to control the expert practices via 'standardization of methods' (in collaboration with others like compliance managers and surveillance authorities). But since our analysis indicates that the risk control managers' attempts are not very successful, a further elaboration on managerial efforts is in place.

Risk control management – Failure or solution?

Enacting the share as a boundary object in a process of heterarchic coordination could be said to make contemporary investment banking possible. Regardless of whether this heterarchy is designed or not, we have suggested that it is a key factor that enables organized and innovative investment banking. From a management perspective, then, top-down control of risk becomes a much more elaborate matter than to develop and implement robust risk control systems. The risk control systems do not fit very well with the heterarchic logic, but rather work against it, competing with an already existing coordinating device – the share as a boundary object carrying with it an invisible infrastructure. Moreover, our empirical material indicates that these risk control systems do not have any paramount effects on the practices of the expert groups within investment banking. This can be interpreted either as a failure to control investment banking, or as a smart way of protecting a heterarchy from external pressures of regulations and thus the prospect of a less profitable business.

From the perspective of the risk control and compliance managers, but perhaps foremost from other actors who do not stand to benefit from an extremely profitable financial sector, failure is a reasonable interpretation. Given the consequences of speculative bubbles, financial setbacks, bank failures and so on, the lack of successful and strict risk control in investment banking is a failure from a policy, societal and stakeholder perspective. But the lack of formal control over investment banking practices is not necessarily a failure from the perspective of investment banking managers and institutional investors. Throughout its history, the financial sector has been one of the most governmentally supported (see Chapter 2). Major banks and financial institutions have been held to be too important for the economy and society at large to be allowed to fail. The fate of the world's largest economies is intimately entangled with that of the sector, such as via loans to finance their national debts. Even when banks and institutions are allowed to fail, most high-profile characters within investment banking come out well off, despite the fact that such events might involve personal tragedies for a few of them (Engelen et al., 2010:51–52). Compared with the dire consequences that financial crises may have for the man in the street, the experts and managers in investment banking are relatively fortunate. From a management perspective, then, there is no fundamental problem in failing to control the risks involved in investment banking.

So why make such massive investments in risk control technologies? This is not necessarily problematic from a business perspective. Since governments, authorities and other 'external' actors could make investment banking much less prosperous via extensive regulations and stricter surveillance, the industry needs legitimacy. Support from governments and authorities, and also from business media and the general public, is a prerequisite for investment banking to thrive. Thus, the risk control and compliance managers and their more and more elaborate and costly systems can be seen as a way to buffer the practices of investment banking from explicit and implicit demands of control. According to Power (2007), the general discourse on 'risk' has since the mid 1990s evolved from treating risk as something that might be calculated, to something that is highly possible to manage and control. But Power's analysis also shows that the rapid increase and spread of risk control technologies can very well produce a false sense of security, leading to even riskier practices, and that the risk technologies thus fill more of a ritual than a substantial role (Power, 1997, 2004, 2007; Svedberg Helgesson, 2011 [forthcoming]).

From this perspective, the suggestion that the risk management technologies developed during the last three decades work as a boundary object within the financial sector makes sense (Millo and MacKenzie, 2007). Risk control is a boundary object, but *not within* investment banking. It is a boundary object *between* investment banking and surveillance and legislative authorities. Thus, one more important conclusion in this chapter is that what might be seen as a managerial control problem from a hierarchical, formal-legal perspective, could just as well be seen as a ritual and symbolic solution from a heterarchical perspective.

Another method of standardization – That works!

Before we can summarize our findings regarding the organizing of investment banking, we need to address one more issue – the bonuses. As noted in Chapter 8, bonuses are a major part of the total income for investment banking experts. The individual and group bonuses make up a powerful incentive system, based on measurable performance and resulting in measurable remuneration. Eccles and Crane (1988:163–177) describe the 'bonus determination process' as highly subjective, although their account shows how much time and effort top management spends on determining both group and individual bonuses. While bonus determination certainly involves subjective aspects, we would emphasize the formalized character of the process over the subjective one. The bonuses comprise a standardized system, typically decided upon by top management via a formal remuneration committee. Despite some efforts to replace individual bonuses with group bonuses, there is still a strong focus on the individual and on hard data as a basis for bonus. As suggested in Chapter 8, the bonus system could be viewed as the fuel that makes the race car run fast. To dole out generous bonuses based on short-term financial performance would then be like stepping on the gas, making the engine (the experts), as well as the car (investment banking), run faster.

The bonus systems can be seen as yet another example of standardization of methods within a bureaucratic logic, just like the risk control systems. The difference is that this standardized method seems to work just fine together with the heterarchic logic of investment banking. One intuitive explanation is of course that nobody would say no to extensive bonuses. A relativist version of this explanation is that investment banking experts work out of greed, and hence do not object to hard work as long as they get really rich from it. But if these bonuses also affect the experts' work, making them work much more and much harder, we should not automatically assume that they are appreciated.

Viewing the bonuses as a standardized method within a heterarchy, and comparing it with another such method within the same heterarchy, allows us to elaborate on their role. The bonus systems differ from the risk control systems in two important ways. First, they are not as clear an example of top-down authority as they seem. Even if the bonus system is standardized and follows formal rules, it still incorporates a component of negotiation. The bonuses are not only based on the economic performances of individuals or groups but are also distributed as a percentage of the experts' individual salaries. These salaries are the results of negotiations between management and the experts. If you are a successful expert, you have a strong case. To be an attractive employer in investment banking, you need to offer high bonuses. This is a part of corporate branding, and is not something top management has full control over.

The major difference between the bonus systems and the risk control systems, however, concerns the control they are designed to achieve. Bonus systems are designed to attract experts and make them work hard to produce economic results, but they are quite neutral in terms of *how* the experts do this. Thus, they do not keep the experts from doing what they would otherwise do; they simply ensure that they do it a bit more. If the bonus system is not 100 per cent neutral to what experts do, it clearly favours innovative initiatives that can generate profit. This is not by producing ambiguity and multiplicity, in the way the share does as a boundary object, but by fuelling increased activity. Since bonuses are paid according to short-term performance measures, they do not foster long-term development; rather they foster short-term innovations to create business and bonuses immediately. The risk control system, on the other hand, is an attempt at doing more than just controlling the speed. It is designed to steer the experts away from doing some of the business they want to do, enabled and fostered by their heterarchic organization. Thus the bonus system can be seen as a hierarchical gas pedal that supports the heterarchy of investment banking. The risk control system, on the other hand is not only a hierarchical brake pedal but also a sort of steering wheel that is used by management to try to redirect the heterarchy.

The major problem with these control systems is that they are used simultaneously but independently. By pushing the gas pedal all the way down (extensive bonuses), investment banking managers are able to run the machinery of investment banking at high speed. But running at high speed increases the risk of accidents, among other things by making it difficult to turn if the road does. To avoid the latter problem, the experts are allowed to stake out the way (via heterarchic coordination). Sometimes, however, others are not entirely happy with where the experts take them. So, a brake of sorts is introduced in the form of risk management systems. The problem is that this device is applied in parallel to the gas. To increase the possibility of directing investment banking, it might be better to ease up on the gas instead of slamming on the brakes and turning the wheel at top speed. The metaphor has obvious limitations, but offers an interpretation of the many setbacks and crises that can be observed in the history of investment banking. It also has some clear practical/normative implications concerning the management of investment banking, particularly in the light of the fact that the efficacy of risk control management efforts can be questioned. Maybe attempting to control investment banking via risk control while maintaining the powerful bonuses is the wrong method?

Organizing investment banking

In this chapter, we have focused the organizing of investment banking. We have analysed the interactions between members of different occupational groups, as well as between these groups and their management and management's risk control systems. We have sought to explain what makes investment banking possible by looking at the organizational processes taking place therein. Our main conclusions are summarized below.

(1) The share works as an organizing device in investment banking, a boundary object, which allows the different expert groups to support each other while maintaining their own qualitatively different knowledge, interests and practices. The share, enacted as a boundary object, makes investment banking both an orderly coordinated system and an action net characterized by simultaneous multiplicity, ambiguity and innovation. The share works well as a boundary object due among other things to its long and diverse history. It has

numerous recognized uses and can be enacted without too much effort. At the same time, it carries with it an invisible infrastructure that prompts actors to engage in certain practices. Hence, it coordinates without being seen as a coordination device.

(2) Investment banking is organized as a heterarchy. This heterarchy allows for heterogeneity and multiplicity, similar to the functional division of labour within a bureaucratic logic. But this heterogeneity is not coordinated by hierarchic or formal-legal control. Instead, it is primarily coordinated via boundary objects (shares and other securities). We would even argue that boundary objects constitute the primary coordinating devices in heterarchies. They perform orderly and fluid heterarchies, and by producing multiplicity, ambiguity and productive friction, they foster flexible adoption and innovative solutions.

(3) Management of heterarchy is not easily coupled with strict control and coordination by methods of standardization. But costly investments in risk control technologies might have other less obvious functions than coordination and control of investment banking. If the risk control technologies are enacted as a boundary object between risk control managers and important external actors, then they do have an important role in making investment banking possible. In such a more ritual capacity, they protect the investment banking heterarchy from external control, allowing investment banking to prosper and grow, through profitable, innovative and risky business.

(4) The bonus systems are another example of attempts to coordinate investment banking through standardization of methods and bureaucratic management. But compared with the risk control systems, the bonuses seem to work fine. Partly, we suggest, this is due to the fact that they are less ambitious in regards to precision. Bonuses work like a gas pedal, while the risk control system is designed to work both as a brake pedal and a steering wheel, trying to direct the experts away from doing what they want and are able to do. A normative conclusion from this analysis would be that if we want to make investment banking less risky and less prone to create financial setbacks, we might go further by being gentle on the gas, than by slamming the brakes and trying to turn at high speeds.

10
Enacting Stock Markets

How do investment banking practices contribute to shaping stock markets and, by extension, the financial markets at large? To answer this question, we go beyond the inter- and intra-professional interactions discussed in Chapter 9 to discuss how the expert practices of investment banking and the construction of share identities affect other actors. Eccles and Crane (1988:53) stress that investment banks are 'managed from the outside in'; that they are organized to handle the external network of investors, corporations and competitors that forms as a consequence of the intermediating functions performed by the expert groups. While we acknowledge the porous boundaries of investment banking organizations and their close links to these groups of actors, we emphasize how investment banking practices drive, rather than are driven by, such external constituents (Folkman et al., 2007).

Our first step is to (re-)construct an 'ecological' action net illustrating how investment banking practices related to shares interlink to form an invisible infrastructure that shapes stock markets. An important characteristic of this action net is the prevalence of cycles of mutually reinforcing practices that engage the financial markets and lend investment banking an autopoietic streak. The action net also highlights how investment banking practices intervene throughout the 'careers' of shares, from their birth in IPOs or new issues, to their death through mergers or acquisitions. In so doing, investment banking practices come across as 'stock marketing', and blur the distinction between efforts to shape markets, on the one hand, and efforts to market in markets, on the other. The action net of investment banking includes and relies on stock markets, but is also (part of) the machinery that produces them.

Second, in addition to this general contribution, the experts also contribute to shaping stock markets specifically through the share identities

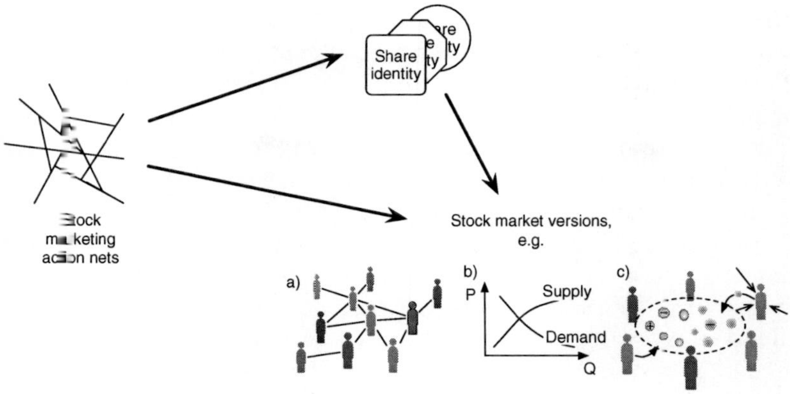

Figure 10.1 The action net of investment banking and the multiple share identities produced therein contribute to produce multiple versions of the stock markets

they construct. These identities have consequences for the qualification of shares as exchange objects in markets (Callon et al., 2002); hence they become devices for coordinating economic exchanges. Through their respective expert practices, and through the share identities they produce, the investment banking experts contribute to producing stock market versions within which their respective shares can be exchanged. (See Figure 10.1 above.)

These observations have consequences for our understanding of the financial markets, which is the third and final topic addressed. Investment banking does not produce one set of stock markets, but several overlapping stock market versions. There is thus little support for the existence of a singular and uniform 'Market'. Nonetheless, 'the Market' remains an influential figure in public discourse. This implies that much of the messiness and multiplicity of investment banking practice has been successfully filtered out to produce an image of the market as a uniform and singular phenomenon. We discuss what allows this reductionism and what consequences it may have for the financial markets, as well as for investment banking.

The partially autopoietic action net of stock marketing

Does investment banking simply perform an intermediating role on the financial markets? Can the existence of investment banks be summed up by the microeconomic notion of 'asymmetric information' and their function be described as a set of practices that lubricates 'frictions in transaction technologies' on the financial markets (Freixas and Rochet, 2008)? The image of the (financial) Market as a force or being that individual actors cannot control certainly contributes to such a narrative. This narrative also conveniently deflects charges of responsibility for any negative consequences that may arise as a result of investment banking practices (see Shankar et al., 2006).

However, our account of the expert practices of investment banking has led us to a very different view of their role for the financial markets. To us, investment banking appears much more as a prime mover than a passive lubricant. In contrast to other observers, who advance a cultural/ideological explanation for the import of investment banking (Ho, 2009), we base our argument very literally on what investment banking experts *do*. More specifically, our basis is observations of mutually reinforcing links and feedback loops between the expert practices in our account. Across the expert groups, we see several examples of how the practices performed by one group contribute to create conditions which trigger other experts (within the group as well as outside) to engage in specific practices. These engagements, in turn, create conditions which trigger new activities on behalf of the first expert group, and round the loop again. To some extent, then, investment banking is a nexus of practices that reproduces itself, in other words, an action net with autopoietic characteristics (Maturana and Varela, 1980).

While investment banking practices to some extent self-reproduce, it is important to stress that they are part of an action net that is not closed on itself. In some cases, the need for external inputs is less obvious and investment banking comes across as a 'players' piano'. This is the case with activity cycles involving proprietary trading; for example, prop trading affects market prices, information about changes in market prices triggers prop trading, and so on. But even these loops in the action net of investment banking work *via* financial markets. Indeed, these loops are an important reason for portraying financial markets as 'cambist', that is, as containing their own raison d'être (Knorr Cetina and Bruegger, 2002a; Knorr Cetina, 2006). As noted by Knorr Cetina (2006), exchanges on financial markets do not concern products that have use value to some end consumer, but are instead fuelled by a logic of investment and speculation. This logic, we argue, is to a large extent performed through the observed loops of self-reinforcing investment banking practices.

A central vehicle for the involvement of investment banking experts in stock markets is the process of qualification and re-qualification of shares that they engage in. The proposition that products and services must be qualified in order to be exchanged on markets (Callon et al., 2002; Karpik, 2010) is well supported in our empirical material. Shares are subject to repeated re-qualifications in the form of analysts' recommendations, brokers' investment advice, traders' price quotes and (less frequently) bankers' proposed restructurings. By offering new suggestions on how to qualify a share, the experts stage, and provide input to, other actors' investment and trading decisions. Although all expert groups engage in the qualification of shares, their efforts are not jointly coordinated. Instead, each group engages in quite distinct qualification processes on the basis of the share identities they construct, respectively. At a given point in time, a share may thus be qualified as an interesting trading object, a correctly priced share, and an investment that should be divested. The different constitutive associations that each group of experts uses to construct their share identities support the production of multiple qualifications of shares as goods.

Each such re-qualification contributes to destabilize the stock markets. A modified recommendation concerning a specific share based on a new analysis may, for instance, suggest that the share in question is not correctly priced on the market. This triggers activity on behalf of other expert groups to restabilize the market(s), such as brokering or trading activity. By operating *via* the financial markets, such activities allow (and motivate) other actors to become involved in the action net, such as investors or other traders. The consequences of these activities (e.g. changes in market prices and investment portfolios) will provide reasons for further activities, which might be renewed analysis or divestment of a position (see Figure 10.2). This suggests that investment banking organizations gain stability (secure continued business) by routinely destabilizing the financial markets. Analysts and bankers destabilize

Figure 10.2 Analysis to trade to analysis loop, illustrating a practice cycle in the investment banking action net

shares either by associating them with new pieces of information or new methods of analysis (analysts), or by altering their constitutive associations (bankers).

The autopoietic streak in investment banking practice provides one key for interpreting the 'ecological' action net of investment banking that we have constructed in our account (see Figure 10.3 for a graphic illustration). The existence of multiple self-reinforcing practice cycles in this action net strengthens our view of investment banking as a driving force in the ongoing construction of the financial markets. These multiple cycles indicate that investment banking practices act on and respond to the financial markets in several different ways, and that they also can set off developments quite independently from other actors. They also hint at the frequency with which investment banking engages with the financial markets. This is further underscored by the bonus-based remuneration system discussed in the previous chapter, which adds a powerful incentive for the experts to be proactive, such as by engaging in speculation.

The self-reproducing practice cycles that can be identified vary in length from very direct intra-expert loops, via relatively short loops such as that between analysis and trade shown in Figure 10.2, to more convoluted cycles involving all four expert groups. One example of such a more complex loop is this: a trader trades for the house, which leads to changes in share prices, which affects the attractiveness of a given share as qualified through analysis, which is used by brokers to suggest de-/re-investment to clients, which triggers an order to buy or sell, which is placed on the market by a trader, which leads to a transaction on the stock exchange, which affects the price of the share, which leads traders to trade for the house. In general, loops that revolve around trading are likely to be frequently recurring, while loops that involve corporate banking projects are more rare.

In the following subsections, we identify how the central practices in which each expert group engages trigger responses from within the expert group and from the other expert groups in the 'ecological' action net depicted in Figure 10.3. This allows us to provide a very hands-on answer to our second research question: how investment banking matters to the financial markets.

Stock trading

Two frequently repeated actions dominate in stock trading: (1) entering the secondary stock markets by placing orders to buy and sell on the

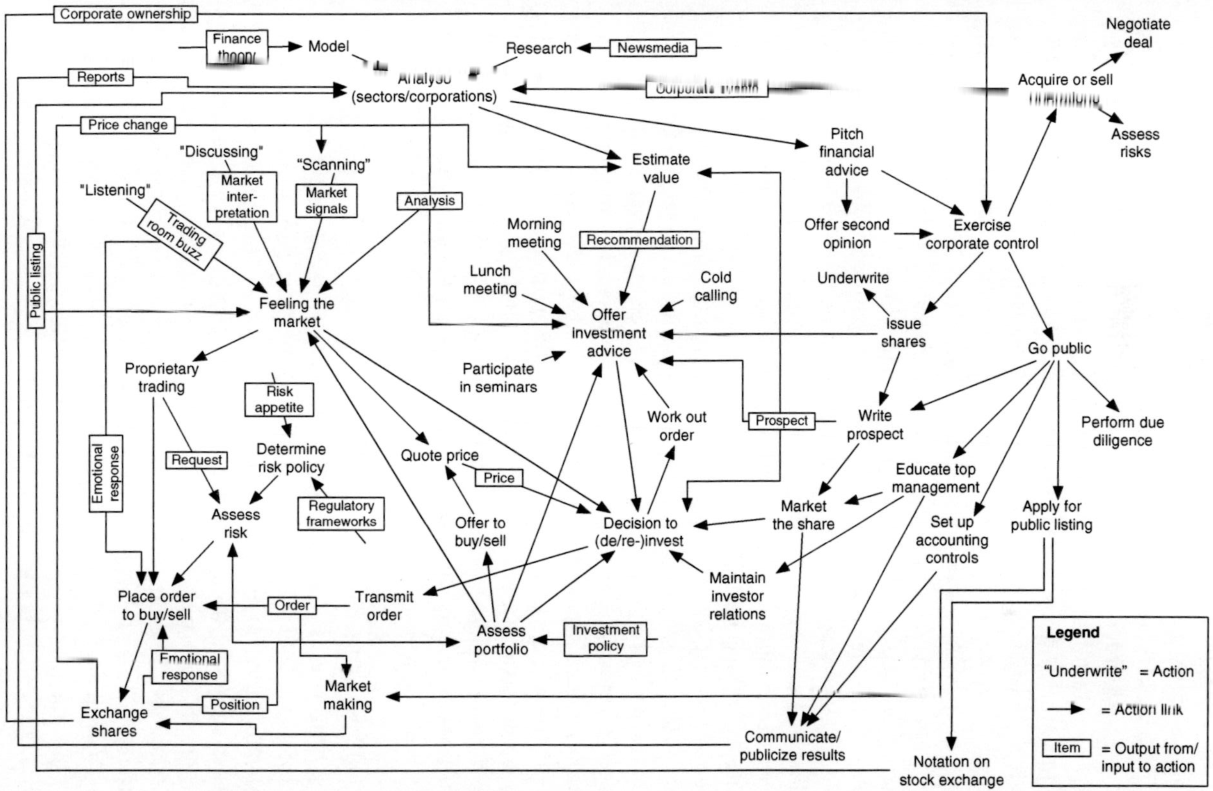

Figure 10.3 The 'ecological' action net of investment banking

stock exchange and (2) 'feeling the market', through monitoring various indicators, listening to the trading room buzz, discussing events and developments with other traders. Some orders to buy and sell are triggered by brokers who turn the investment decisions taken by investors into trading orders. Others are generated by the traders themselves, either as a result of a decision to take a position for the house, or as an emotional response to some event, such as a successful trade. If the order is proprietary, it will trigger a risk assessment which has to be performed before the order can be executed. Since large institutional investors may have their own trading operations, there may be some overlap in terms of activities here. Orders to buy or sell shares are then matched at the stock exchange, and exchanges are executed, leading to changes in prices and positions. Such changes can trigger activity on behalf of others and can lead to further trading during the day, so that trading activity begets trading activity. Here, the bonus system plays an obvious role in motivating continued trading. Proprietary traders are employed to speculate for the firm, to generate profit by using their expertise, which is then turned into personal bonuses. This has consequences for the way in which traders re-qualify shares. Re-qualification is usually presented as a consequence of changes in demand and supply, or new information becoming available. However, in Chapter 3 we saw that traders also try to manipulate situations to their own advantage as part of their speculative activities. Such speculative re-qualification of shares may have very little to do with new information. Since traders, in addition to actual trading, quote share prices to brokers whose clients are interested in buying or selling, their re-qualifications also constitute input to brokering activities.

Stock brokering

Stock brokering is about getting investors to engage in transactions on the stock markets by providing them with advice and information on interesting investment opportunities. Brokers try to trigger orders to buy and sell stocks on the secondary markets by offering investment advice to their clients. For this, they make use of the re-qualification information they receive from analysts during morning meetings and via their written analyses and recommendations. As we noted in Chapter 5, brokers then make their own specific qualification of investment objects by adapting them to the investment portfolios and policies of their clients. The orders to buy and sell that they receive are transmitted to the inhouse traders, who 'push the button' on behalf of the brokers. Brokers engage in a number of activities that allow them to cultivate relations with clients, including arranging and participating in lunch meetings and seminars with investors and experts. They also cultivate relations with corporate managers who seek to interest investors in their shares. Brokers keep themselves informed about and assess their clients' portfolios and investment policies through direct contacts and daily telephone calls. They are typically proactive, for instance, providing information about IPOs and new introductions on the stock market. But brokers also receive direct offers from clients, which may require them to ask a trader to quote a price. If the position a client wants to sell is large enough, the current market price is not necessarily valid since brokers will have to work the position out in the market during the course of a trading day. This will require pitching the share in question to prospective investors, so that brokering activity begets brokering activity. Three actions serve to link stock brokering and stock trading: (1) transmitting orders (from brokers to traders), (2) quoting prices (by traders for brokers) and (3) assessing investment portfolios (which change as a consequence of executed trades).

Stock analysis

As we noted in Chapters 4 and 5, there are considerable overlaps between analysis and brokering in the area of offering investment advice. Both involve cultivating relations with investors through participation in meetings and seminars and through direct contacts. The second major cluster of analyst activities – analysis and value estimation – is the engine for their re-qualification of shares and provides input to brokering in the form of written reports and recommendations. Analysts also engage in direct discussions with (primarily institutional) investors concerning their analyses and estimates. The links to trading are less pronounced, although traders may include analysts among their sources when 'scanning the world'. Conversely, the results of trading provide input to analysts' qualifications of shares, specifically to their value assessments, such as price changes on the stock markets. In general, the inputs used in analysis indicate that this practice regularly enacts links to a variety of both primary and secondary sources outside the investment banking organization, such as news media and journalists, industry experts, corporate communications (reports, press releases), direct contacts with top managers and so on. At times, analysis is also triggered by IPO or emission projects organized by the corporate bankers, providing a link to the fourth expert category.

Corporate banking

At the heart of corporate banking is the pitching of financial advice to corporate top management and owners, with the explicit ambition of becoming part of their exercise of corporate control. These actions are based on sector and company analyses and value estimates, thus overlapping with the action net for stock (market) analysis. There are three major action clusters of corporate control that involve and have consequences for shares: (1) acquiring and selling 'corporate parts' (altering share content), (2) issuing shares, and (3) initial public offerings of shares in corporations. Engaging in these activities typically means forging links to other experts, such as legal advisors and technical consultants for conducting due diligence, or accountants for setting up financial control systems. Negotiating with buyers or sellers of specific operations (corporations as well as institutional investors) creates further links. Interacting with stock exchanges and financial supervisory authorities that place requirements on public corporations are also important for these activities. Finally, due to the uncertainty and complexity of the issues involved, other corporate banking organizations may be enrolled to provide second opinions on a project, so that corporate banking activity begets corporate banking activity.

In terms of consequences, corporate banking activities trigger a multitude of activities involving other experts in the action net. (1) Public listing allows shares in corporations to be traded on the stock markets; it transforms them from indicators of ownership only into publicly tradable goods. Traders may also become involved prior to the public listing to provide market-making services, also known as 'grey market trading'. The public listing, in turn, makes the shares interesting to analyse. (2) Mergers and acquisitions are corporate events that provide important input to sector and company analyses. (3) Public offerings that are underwritten in corporate banking constitute input to the provision of investment advice, and typically require active brokering on the primary market. (4) IPO projects include setting up infrastructures for public corporations (such as accounting controls) which affects how they present themselves to analysts and investors. (5) Educating corporate managers in such things as how to develop and maintain investor relations and how to publicize results, may influence investors' decisions to invest in their shares. These links are an important reason for the various attempts made to regulate the flows between the action nets. Moreover, the buying and selling of shares on the stock exchanges determines, at least in part, the power balance in exercising corporate control and thus creates a feedback loop into corporate banking.

An action net for stock marketing

The 'ecological' action net of investment banking described above and illustrated in Figure 10.3 contains a large number of self-reinforcing and possibly self-reproducing activity cycles. This observation provides empirical support for the argument made by Engelen et al. (2010:55) that 'finance feeds finance in numerous (connected) long chains'. These cycles do not constitute a closed system, but can also be triggered by, or trigger, activities undertaken by investors, corporations, regulators, stock exchanges, news media and so on. Despite this, it seems clear that the interplay between practices that stabilize and destabilize markets, undertaken by investment banking experts, constitute an important engine within the wider financial system. One important consequence of their repeated and heterogeneous re-qualification of shares is to destabilize the stock markets and create trading and other business opportunities. While volatile markets might be a source of concern to the average investor, they primarily represent profit opportunities for professional traders (Abolafia, 1996). In addition, they provide good arguments for convincing investors to hire expert advisors.

Beyond the observation of self-reinforcing activity cycles, the action net also reflects the fact that investment banking experts insert themselves in, and contribute to configuring, a number of critical situations in the buying and selling of shares. If we regard shares as products with 'careers' (Kopytoff, 1986), it is possible to distinguish between different moments in their lives, such as their birth (through IPO or new issue) and initial sale on the primary markets, their subsequent sales on the secondary markets and possibly their death (for example, through a merger or acquisition). Investment banking experts are involved in all of these situations, from conception to trading via analysis and brokering. Seen in this light, it seems more appropriate to label this action net 'stock marketing' rather than 'investment banking'. Investment banking can thus be understood as a nexus of activities that markets shares (and other securities). As suggested in the marketing literature, this process involves both being 'market driven' – adjusting your offering to customer demands – and 'driving markets' – altering market conditions to make your offering more attractive (Jaworski et al., 2000).

The plasticity of the share, which was put forward as central for coordinating investment banking organizations in Chapter 9, is important here as well. At each moment in the career of a share, it must be qualified as a good (Callon et al., 2002). This involves temporarily stabilizing its characteristics to allow comparisons with other similar goods (shares and other securities). In the event of a favourable outcome of such a comparison, market exchange may follow. As discussed in Chapter 9 these qualifications are local and temporary; there is no need to strictly coordinate their results for economic exchange to be possible (see also Dubuisson-Quellier, 2010). The multiple share identities constructed by investment banking experts thus contribute to make several types of exchanges of shares possible: constructed in accordance with rules and regulations, and with the seal of approval of one (or more) investment bank(s), shares can be exchanged for capital on the primary markets; constructed as complex knowledge objects, they can be evaluated and exchanged as long-term investments; coupled with the qualification of the customers, such complex knowledge objects can be exchanged as building blocks in investment portfolios; constructed as entities with little or no content, shares can be exchanged as commodities; constructed as objects of intervention, they can be exchanged strategically to alter industrial structures. Through the partially overlapping action nets enacted by the expert groups, a seller seeking to realize one type of exchange may successfully negotiate a deal with a buyer seeking to realize another type of exchange, underscoring the fact that no absolute consensus on the object of exchange is required for exchange to be possible.

Contributing to the shaping of stock markets

What kinds of markets does this stock marketing action net contribute to producing? Above, we argued that the share identities constructed by the experts contributed to shares being repeatedly re-qualified in several ways, thus both affording and encouraging a number of different exchanges of shares. In addition to this, the existence of self-reinforcing activity cycles emphasizes that the very actions the experts engage in themselves contribute to producing what we recognize as the stock markets (confer Alderson and Cox, 1948). In this respect, there is no clear distinction between efforts that explicitly aim to shape markets and efforts that simply aim to 'market in markets'; both contribute to producing markets. Our account of the ecological action net thus provides a partial image of the invisible infrastructure that constructs stock markets. It highlights some of the work necessary to enable those seemingly atomized transactions that take place on the stock markets throughout the world. The action net of investment banking we have constructed comes across as a production-machinery that contributes to continuously reproducing the financial markets, or more specifically the stock markets. However, due to the expert groups' enactments of relatively distinct social worlds, their practices do not result in a single, unified version of the stock markets. Rather, they enact qualitatively different versions of the stock markets depending on how they construct their exchange objects, that is, depending on their construction of share identities.

Stock markets enacted by traders

In Chapter 3, we argued that traders construct shares as monolithic entities – commodities – that can be compared with other such objects. This identity construction supports their enactment of stock markets as force fields that shift shares around in terms of ownership and price, but leave them intact (see Figure 10.4). Lacking recognizable content and internal dynamics, the shares in these markets are shifted about by forces external to them. These forces are manifested in the orders to buy or sell specific amounts of specific shares at specific prices that traders place. When placing these orders, the traders factor in a wide variety of events, for example: the head of the US Federal Reserve makes a statement; there is a political development in the Middle East; new

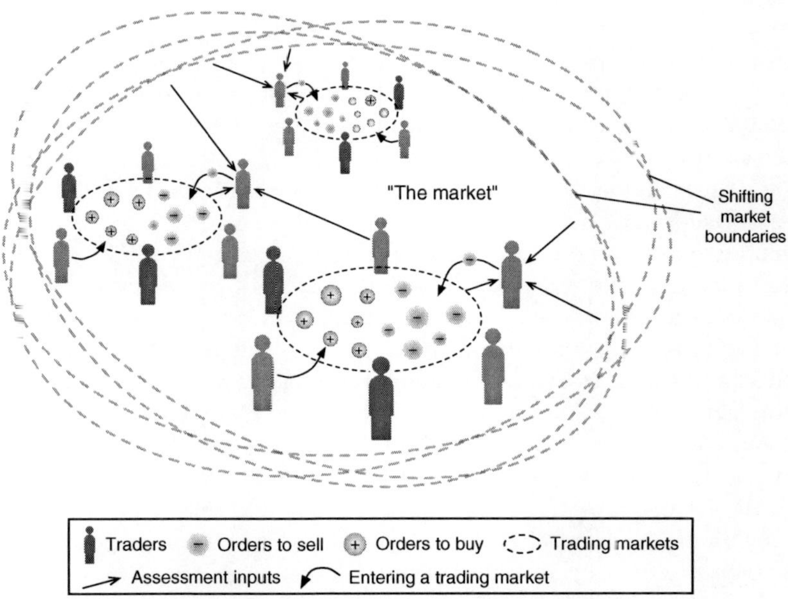

Figure 10.4 Traders continuously re-enact 'the market'. By placing orders to buy and sell specific shares, they enact nested trading markets therein

statistics show greater than expected economic growth in South East Asia. Events such as these thus become part of a specific trading market when traders place orders to buy or sell based on their more or less continuous scanning of various information sources during the day. But this means that the specific trading markets have no independent existence; they are nested within and always conditioned by 'the market'. At any point in time, this 'creature' is made up of a very large number of events and information flows. Its boundaries are never clear-cut; they are constantly being adjusted to accommodate new pieces of information. This is the realm of the expression 'everything matters'. As should be clear, however, new information will have no effect on the market unless it triggers actions on behalf of the traders (some of which may be highly automated responses). It thus seems more appropriate to use the expression 'anything can matter' to characterize trading markets.

But even this notion may require some tempering. Knorr Cetina (2006) highlights the import of *scopic systems* for the organizing of trading markets, that is, systems that generate and disseminate standardized images of the market in question. The instant access to standardized market images on screen doubtless contributes to formatting the trading situation. For stock traders, the relevant trading markets are typically found on the same stock exchange. However, our empirical material clearly suggests that the traders' activities are not exclusively responses to the reflected, represented reality of market information systems. The formatting effects that these systems have are complemented by the activities of brokers, analysts and bankers, triggering trading activity. Direct interactions with other traders also remain important, whether these traders are present in 'your' trading room or reached via telephone. Finally, apart from the assessment of current forces in the market, which has a rationalistic touch to it, traders also seem to understand their own actions as emotionally cued, depending on the relative success or failure of previous actions. All these observations suggest that traders enact a less standardized and systemic scoping process that counters the emergence of a 'global inter-subjectivity' (Knorr Cetina, 2006:555).

But the traders' actions also differ depending on whether they are engaged in proprietary trading or customer-driven market making. In the former case, traders engage in buying and selling on behalf of their employer. Any piece of information can trigger a sudden burst of activity, the placing of orders to buy or sell. Together with the self-reproducing loops discussed above, this type of arrangement renders the trading markets a self-perpetuating character (Knorr Cetina and Bruegger, 2002a). During customer-driven market making, on the other hand, new orders are triggered by specific customers wishing to buy or sell. These triggers are mediated through brokers and channelled to the traders. Here, then, alternative purposes besides trading for the sake of trading may affect the trading market. This suggests that trading markets are not purely cambist, although the bulk of trading volume growth is likely to be attributable to cambist trading. In addition, our reconstruction of the ecological action net in investment banking highlight the fact that these activities are still largely influenced by investment banking practices (analyses, brokering, banking).

Markets for investments enacted by analysts

Turning to the markets enacted by the analysts, these differ considerably from the situation depicted in Figure 10.4. To analysts, there is no dramatic contrast between a global creature with constantly changing boundaries and a neatly contained force field shifting about monolithic shares. But, just as for traders, the analysts' construction of the share has import. Indeed, the differences between the markets enacted by traders and analysts reflect the differences in their respective construction of the shares.

For the analysts, the share is the very engine when enacting stock markets. As discussed above, they construct the shares as investment objects representing a going concern and its environment, the particularities of which give rise to expectations about future pay-offs relative to alternative investments. Guided by their valuation models, the analysts try to fill the share with content, establishing links between the share, the company and various circumstances surrounding its operations. Thus associations are forged between the share and industry trends, developments on specific national markets, amongst other factors. Based on this content, the analysts assess the value of the share. This allows the analysts to estimate and ascribe a value to the share that is only loosely connected to the price at which the share is currently trading. Their preoccupation with share content also affects the role ascribed to investors, who frequently play the part of a generalized other, an anonymous type rather than an individual actor. The investors are invited to the market as dinner guests to a set table: the analysts have already put the dishes in place.

To analysts the share is thus not a thing in itself but a representative of something else. This makes it 'full of life' and awards it a role in shaping its market. The share becomes an intermediary through which analysts contribute to shape the market for investments. Placing something new or different inside the share, or looking at its familiar insides from a

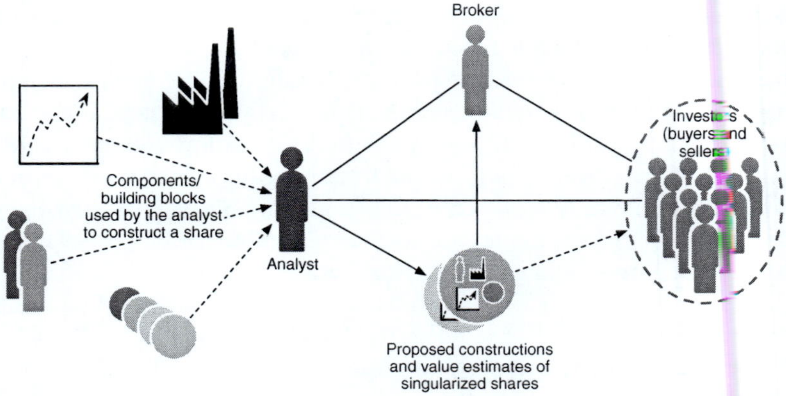

Figure 10.5 The market for singularized investment objects enacted by analysts

new perspective, provides the analyst with a topic for conversation with potential investors. Their written analyses are also circulated both internally within the investment bank and to external clients, potentially affecting how others view and value the share (Figure 10.5).

The time frame for this market is wider than for the market enacted by traders. Several activities contribute to this. First, potential investors remain in the market for some time and analysts establish personal relationships with their representatives through repeated contacts over time. Second, the objective of the transactions that analysts recommend is to gain returns over some period of time. Although this time frame varies, it always exceeds that of the actual transaction. Third, the content of the share changes over time; its trajectory is punctuated by the quarterly reports which may give rise to flurries of activity.

The markets enacted by brokers

The stock market versions that stockbrokers contribute to enacting consist primarily of actual and potential customers (investors). Their market versions thus resemble those of other types of sales people, and also the description of markets as 'collections of actual and potential buyers' that can be found in the marketing literature (Araujo and Kjellberg, 2009:195). As we have come to expect, given the embedded character of economic actions, most exchanges in these markets can be described as exchange episodes within long-term exchange relationships, although some may approach the classic arm's length transaction (Håkansson, 1982; Granovetter, 1985; Uzzi, 1997). Brokers insert themselves as middlemen in stock markets but, while they historically assisted in connecting buyers and sellers, their role in contemporary stock markets is much more that of the advisor, although they still transmit orders to traders.

Due to the brokers' advisory role, the share identity plays a less significant part in their enactment of markets than it does for the analysts. For the brokers, individual clients with specific needs and characteristics and with whom they have direct personal relations replace the generalized investor. The share plays a part in their enactment of the market, but becomes one of many means to maintain these relations and serve their clients. The brokers can be said to choose among the dishes on the table, seeking to offer something that they believe fits the client's palate. Of course the brokers are assisted by the analysts when composing their menu and also receive assistance from the traders with the actual serving (Figure 10.6).

Whereas the analyst's market can be said to be highly epistemic – grounded in knowledge about the investment object – the trader's market can instead be said to be highly instrumental – enacted by the very execution of trade. The broker's market has some of both, but also its very own character as being discursive and rhetorical – grounded in conversation and persuasion. The brokers are the rhetoricians of finance, where ethos and pathos is as least as important as logos. Thus, the markets enacted are closely related to the customers. In the broker's markets, the maintenance of relations to individual customers is a top priority, the enactment of shares is secondary.

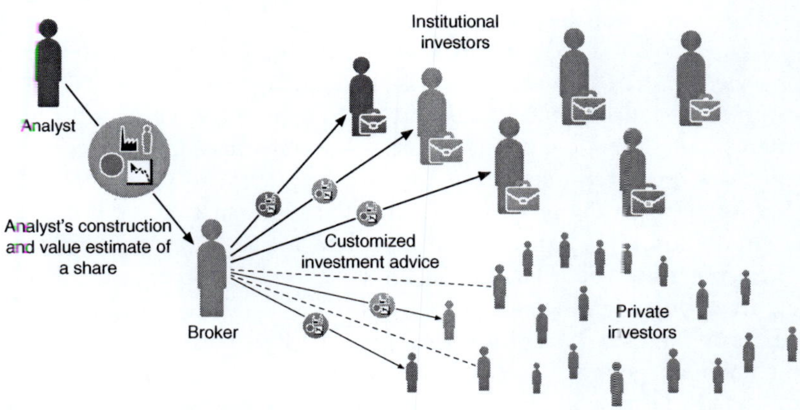

Figure 10.6 The market for customized investment advice enacted by brokers

Corporate banking enacts markets for singularities and commodities-to-be

What kinds of markets do corporate banking practices contribute to enacting? A first observation is that bankers engage with financial markets as sources of funding. In this capacity, the financial markets are seen as the ultimate arbitrators of the bankers' efforts. A good corporate banking project is one that achieves positive market response: it brings a good pay-off to the owners. But the bankers do not simply leave whatever they have built to its own devices and wait for the market to respond. Instead, they actively elicit market responses, making good use of the market constructing abilities of the other expert groups, triggering activities on behalf of analysts, brokers and traders alike.

In Chapters 6 and 7 we noted that bankers do not always accept the established boundaries of shares. By disqualifying the current identity of an exchange object in this manner, bankers also disqualify the work currently being performed by analysts, brokers and traders since this work is based on, and contributes to maintaining, the established identity of the share. This has important consequences for the market versions that bankers enact. When the boundaries of the current identity of a share are disqualified, an arm's length approach to the market becomes difficult to maintain. In fact, one could argue that the activities performed by analysts, brokers and traders on the basis of such boundaries are necessary in order to assume an arm's length relation when engaging in market exchange. So, what do bankers do instead?

As should be clear from our account, bankers typically work in close cooperation with a specific buyer and/or seller. A first step in this process is to have the counterpart(s) accept the proposed disqualification of a specific share and the new qualification proposed in its stead. This can require considerable efforts and typically involves close and thick interactions over some period of time. A second step in this process is to consummate economic exchanges of one or several *singular* objects that follow from the proposed new qualification, such as a division of a corporation. This typically involves engaging in an arduous process to establish the characteristics of the entity being exchanged, including involving due diligence procedures. These exchanges are thus very far from the ones typically taking place in the markets described in the previous sections. They concern unique objects that have not been subjected to the qualifying procedures involved in creating new shares (Karpik, 2010). This work remains, so to speak.

The procedures for qualifying shares can be seen most clearly when bankers enact primary markets for shares, such as when they participate

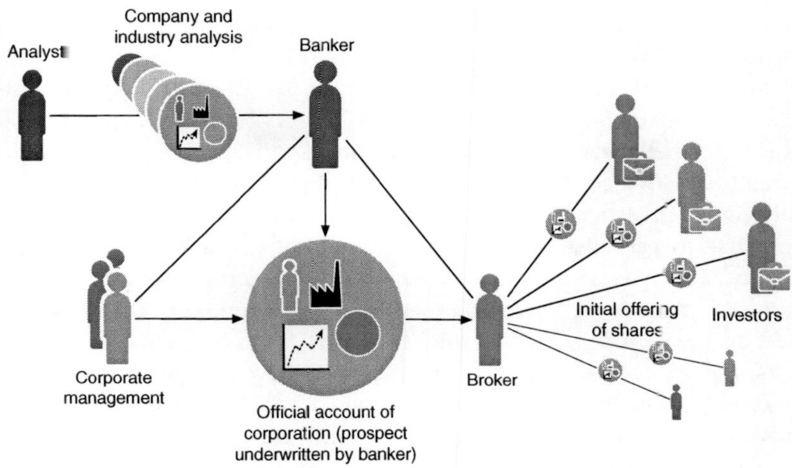

Figure 10.7 The primary market for shares enacted by bankers

in an IPO. The purpose of such a project is to publicly offer a particular share for sale for the first time (see Figure 10.7). In many instances, corporate banking departments are instrumental in setting up this primary market by publishing prospects and engaging brokers to attract investors to invest in the corporation. In addition, inhouse traders may be engaged in market making prior to the actual listing of the share on the stock exchange. As was the case in project Dolly (Chapter 7), this type of market making is often preceded by inhouse analysts offering a first assessment of the value of the share. Thus, the activities of analysts, brokers and traders are initially performed inhouse (or in a syndicate). Through these activities, the new share is introduced into the world of trading. One could say that a new force-field market is proposed. This market is then further solidified through a formal listing on the stock exchange, which places additional requirements on the share and on the corporation it represents. The listing allows other traders to engage in buying and selling the share, which, in turn, makes it interesting for analysts to perform value assessments and issue recommendations concerning the share.

Multiple overlapping versions of stock markets

While the expert groups enact qualitatively different market versions, these versions are not isolated from each other. The force-field trading markets enacted by traders are regularly included as part of the markets for investments enacted by analysts and brokers. However, they do not themselves constitute markets, as they do for the traders. The consummation of economic exchanges in these markets involves such activities as analyses, advice and investment policies. Decisions to invest/divest are then channelled through brokers to traders to trigger orders. Thus the 'force-field trading markets' constitute one mechanism through which investors can acquire investment objects. Since there are many alternative investment objects, many such trading markets are regularly included as part of the market for investments. In addition, investors and brokers may also enact alternative mechanisms, such as negotiating deals directly with buyers or sellers. This is common, for instance, when large volumes of shares are being considered for exchange. Under such circumstances, the exchange parties jointly engage in stabilizing both the object and the terms of exchange. In doing so, they realize dramatically different market exchanges than those taking place in trading markets. This type of exchanges is also common as part of corporate banking projects.

The outcome of our analysis is that what is regularly referred to as 'the Market' consists of a number of markets. In addition, it consists of qualitatively different market versions creating multiple frames for executing, understanding and evaluating transactions (Figure 10.8). Even though terms such as 'flow markets' may be useful for describing certain characteristics of financial markets, the use of such idealized notions

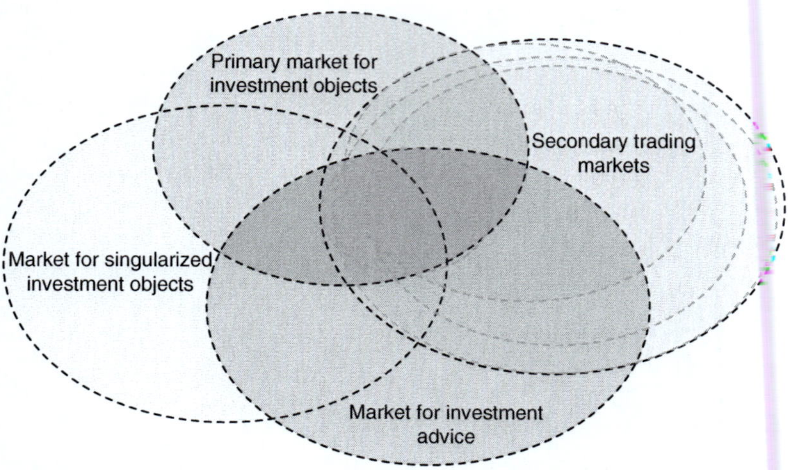

Figure 10.8 Markets for shares are constituted by overlapping market versions enacted by analysts, brokers, traders and bankers

does not capture, indeed hides, an important heterogeneity within each individual financial product market. Our analysis suggests that the borders between these various markets become blurred and their characteristics dependent on the perspectives and practices of the actors engaging with them. Analysing how different groups of actors construct their exchange objects offers one way of approaching the multiplicity of financial markets being enacted.

From multiple overlapping market versions to 'the Market'

The observed heterogeneity and multiplicity of market versions enacted by the investment banking experts stands in stark contrast to the rhetoric of 'the Market' which dominates public discourse on financial markets. This transformation from something multiple and varied to something singular and uniform is our concern in this final section. How do the investment banking experts contribute to producing this reductionist image of a uniform market and what do they stand to gain from doing so? Our starting point is the idea that representational practices are constitutive of markets (Kjellberg and Helgesson, 2007); markets are not 'out there' to be depicted but come into being by being depicted (Knorr Cetina and Bruegger, 2002b). At the very least, speaking of a market requires that a number of transactions be brought together (by aggregation or connection) based on an argument that they have taken, take, or will take place within one market.

When compared with other markets, a noticeable feature of stock and other securities markets is the frequency at which market images are generated. In contemporary securities markets, there is an incessant production of market images. Indeed, every single transaction results in a new market image being broadcast via stock tickers, bulletin boards, electronic trading systems, and so on (see Knorr Cetina and Bruegger, 2002b; Preda, 2006). These more or less mechanical and algorithm-based representations, supplied by stock exchanges and financial market intelligence firms and spread by business media, constitute one important distinguishing trait of the financial markets. In addition, or as a complement, investment banking experts are routinely invited, given room, or at least take upon themselves, to offer commentaries on the produced images, on developments taking place on specific product markets, on major events in the world, amongst other things. The specific representational practices employed to generate the widespread images of the stock markets provide a partial, yet important, explanation of the transformation of markets from multiple and heterogeneous to singular and uniform.

First, the representational practices give priority to one category of transactions out of the many that take place on the financial markets. Primarily it is the transactions of securities on the stock exchanges that are represented. In the extreme version, an entire world is compacted into one tidy figure: 'The S&P 500 closed 0.2 percent lower yesterday after a slump in commodity producers overshadowed investor optimism from the death of Osama bin Laden.' (Bloomberg News, 3 May 2011). More detailed images are of course available, such as the prices of individual stocks at the closing of each trading day at a particular stock exchange. Transactions of other types also enter into the produced images, such as when a major deal has been concluded involving a substantial share of the stocks in a corporation. This type of market information, however, is assumed to be reflected in the regular images that are being produced and is thus typically offered as an extension of, or commentary on, those images.

Second, only a very limited number of dimensions of the depicted transactions are represented. Specifically, the exchanges are reduced to information about which share (or other security) is being exchanged, what quantity of it and, above all, at what price it is exchanged. The shares that were so elaborately qualified by the experts are thus reduced to a label and the relevant information about them to price and quantity (confer Preda, 2008). Indeed, the growing importance of structured products introduces yet another layer of opacity to these markets, further de-emphasizing the individual securities. Third, and related, information about the transacting parties is minimal, unless there has been a major deal of the type mentioned above. The buyers and sellers are not claimed to be unimportant – indeed, quite the opposite, as Muniesa (2008) shows – they simply are not represented. The resulting image is one of discrete transactions of homogenous goods between anonymous buyers and sellers. The investors disappear from view, as do the qualitative differences between shares, and in some cases, even the shares themselves. They are replaced by a technical, numbers/index-focused market image that is commented upon and interpreted by investment banking experts.

Based on the above, it should be clear that these representational practices constitute an oligoptic rather than panoptic scoping system: they capture certain things very well, while hiding or obfuscating others (Latour, 2005). In particular, it seems that the representational practices that shape stock markets routinely disregard what we have argued to be necessary work in order for discrete and distal transactions to be possible. The resulting markets appear 'beast-like', seemingly beyond the control of any one actor (group). The representational practices thus produce an image of Smith's (in)famous metaphor of the invisible hand; what we have shown to be the result of expert practices in investment banking is transformed into an almost natural phenomenon. This leaves us with a final question: What do the investment banking experts stand to gain from perpetuating this natural(ized) market image, which clearly does not do a good job of representing their complex worlds? We offer three complementary answers, suggesting that there is little reason for investment banking to alter this market image. Under the cloak of acting as an information intermediary and reducer of market frictions, catering on the one hand to the need of corporations for capital, and, on the other, the needs of investors for risk reduction, investment banking experts gain considerable latitude in terms of increased revenues, reduced responsibilities and increased power.

First, portraying stock markets as subject to anonymous market forces affords a role for expert commentary. Seemingly impenetrable, or at least inaccessible to outsiders, navigating the financial markets requires guidance as suggested by, for example, corporate bankers providing second opinions on proposed projects. Assuming the role of interpreters and advisors behind the scenes, investment banking experts are able to access new revenue streams by perpetuating investment banking practices; performing a world under constant restructuring (Folkman et al., 2007). In this capacity, they are not only specialists but truly experts, to whom one is well advised to turn in order to get an initiated interpretation of the forces at play in these natural(ized) markets. Moreover, their own role in generating and fuelling these forces (for instance, the share of securities transactions in which they are involved) is obscured by the image of a market made up of impersonal exchanges.

Second, the impersonal character of a natural(ized) market provides a convenient way of dodging responsibility. As commentators, investment banking experts only interpret available signals and cannot be blamed if the basically unpredictable forces of 'the market' end up producing another output. Don't shoot the messenger. Our account has shown that the investment banking experts are co-producers of these market forces; the image of an anonymous market routinely reproduced through the oligoptic scoping system discussed above, does not. Consequently, it allows a dissipation of responsibility.

Third, the images of a natural(ized) market awards power to the experts. Employing Lukes' (2005 [1974]) classic three-dimensional classification of power, we can note that the experts: (1) gain influence over other actors' decisions by acting as advisors (as do analysts, brokers and bankers); (2) gain power over the agenda by routinely destabilizing the context, thus generating new decision-making situations, and offering worthy solutions to be employed in such situations (confer our discussion above on the repeated qualification of shares); and (3) gain power over interpretation by transforming the market from the admittedly complex, yet mundane, world described in our account, to a highly technical field of anonymous and uncontrollable forces, and by teaching others how to understand it.

Marketing shares, sharing markets

Investment banking experts jointly contribute to market shares, in the sense that they engage in a number of loosely coordinated practices that make transactions on the stock markets possible (Araujo et al., 2010). Rather than being passive lubricants in some global financial machinery, however, the experts actively contribute to shaping the character of these markets. Stock markets would not be the same without them. The experts perform their practices within heterarchical organizations that allow them to engage in distinctly different practices, yet enable them to coordinate their actions without (much) hierarchical control. In this final section of the book, we summarize the key points concerning how investment banking is organized and how it contributes to enact markets, and discuss implications of this image of investment banking for research and practice.

Organizing investment banking

The practices that investment banking experts engage in are specialized in ways reminiscent of a bureaucratic organizational logic, but are coordinated heterarchically. Both the specialization and coordination are made possible by boundary objects, notably shares, travelling back and forth between the various expert communities. There are also managerial attempts at organizing via bonus systems and risk control systems. But rather than controlling how the experts work, the bonuses primarily make them do more of what it is they do. The risk control systems, on the other hand, do not really do what they explicitly purport to do. These more bureaucratic organizing devices could be seen as failed attempts by management and other stakeholders to control investment banking practices, but they could also be seen as ritual and symbolic artefacts, promoting a view of investment banking as well-kept and controlled in regards to excessive risk taking. From the latter perspective, the practical organizing of investment banking via the share as a boundary object, the bonus incentives, and the ritual organizing via risk control systems all help explain the growth of investment banking in both volume and influence. They all make investment banking possible.

This conclusion has practical as well as theoretical relevance. From a practical point of view, it suggests that the combination of heterarchical organizing of expert practices and symbolic bureaucratic control could enable creative and innovative investment banking while securing legitimacy as a responsible and well-controlled organization. In a way, it *is* well controlled: the different expert groups successfully coordinate their efforts in support of each other. But in terms of preventing the production of financial bubbles that eventually burst, investment banking is evidently not that well controlled.

From a societal perspective, the unsuccessful attempts at controlling investment banking via risk control systems point in another direction. Instead of trying to enforce more and more elaborate risk control systems in investment banking, it might be better to 'reduce speed'. This could be done by reducing the performance-related bonuses and increasing their time horizon. Risk control management is an attempt to control the experts in the presence of major incentives to do profitable (and risky) business. Instead, we suggest that it makes more sense to ease up on the gas. With lower bonus levels, the speed should go down, and it will be easier to keep investment banking experts on a designated track. Instead, the current efforts to control investment banking can be characterized as turning at full speed. As a result the experts disconnect. The key to a more responsible and safer investment banking practice is to lower the bonuses, not invest in new risk control technologies.

From a theoretical point of view, our account of investment banking suggests that boundary objects are the key organizational devices in flat, network-like, self-organized, fluid organizations, aka heterarchies. This idea harks back to classic organization theory, for instance to Weber's authority types, and his ideal typical social relations. It also connects to previous research on investment banking with its emphasis on the autonomy of expert work (Eccles and Crane, 1988) and provides added precision regarding organizing processes in such contexts. But our central argument concerning the organizing of investment banking also raises questions concerning the practical alignment of different organizing principles, which we have not addressed. Thus, the link between different types of coordinating devices, such as boundary objects, bonus systems and risk control systems, deserves further attention. In our view, approaching these issues by mapping action nets rather than studying organizations is a fruitful research strategy.

Enacting stock markets

In addition to being loosely coordinated within investment banking organizations, the expert practices involving shares have considerable external consequences. Specifically, we have argued that these expert practices highlight some of the work necessary to enable seemingly atomized transactions to take place on the stock markets. By systematically destabilizing shares through re-qualifications based on their respective share identities, the experts trigger other experts (as well as third parties) to engage in their share-related practices. The result is a partially autopoietic action net that regularly enacts the stock markets, and as such constitutes an important engine within the wider financial system. While the experts thus contribute jointly to producing stock markets, they also enact distinct, yet overlapping, versions of these markets. Whereas the discourse on global finance typically revolves around the singular and uniform 'Market', what we see is the performation of multiple and heteroform market versions. Still, even the experts themselves promote 'the Market', and we suggest that they do so by systematically disregarding certain facets of their own work when re-presenting stock markets.

From a policy perspective, this view of the stock markets suggests a need to consider alternative ways of representing markets. It is generally argued that the financial markets (including stock markets) differ from other markets. But as we have sought to show, the difference is not necessarily due to the exchange of homogenous goods between anonymous buyers and sellers. Indeed, most investment banking experts seek to differentiate shares and trigger exchanges between parties that are well known. Rather, the difference is linked to how these markets are represented. Few if any markets are so vigorously monitored as the financial markets. But in our view, monitoring the financial markets requires not only ever more sharp-eyed meterological systems, like the ones currently being developed, but also more cursory and broad-minded approaches capable of capturing other facets of these markets (see also Helgesson and Kjellberg, 2009).

From a theoretical point of view, our account of stock marketing suggests a very different conception of the financial markets than that of anonymous natural forces which still dominates public discourse. Stock markets come across as ongoing, materially heterogeneous accomplishments to which investment banking experts make important, but not exclusive, contributions. These experts engage with markets not as neutral intermediaries reducing frictions, but as political actors seeking to produce particular kinds of markets. This provides support for a view of markets as one of many results of economic organizing processes, which are characterized by multiplicity and heterogeneity. Even the financial markets take on multiple forms.

As a closing comment, it seems appropriate to emphasize that the expert activities at the heart of the stock markets are full of nuances. Investment banking practice is part of a larger financial machinery, but it also contains an engine of its own that allows it to affect significantly the overall economy. Efforts to support and control the financial markets via technical fixes and regulations are likely to continue, but their efficacy will hinge on understanding the character of these markets. Simplistic market models decked out in elaborate mathematical algorithms will only take us so far in reaching such an understanding. In particular, they typically do a poor job in bringing out the expert work of stock marketing that we have sought to describe in this book. What do *you* see when you look at the stock markets?

Appendix: Notes on Method

The empirical material

Our account of investment banking practices is based on empirical material generated through extensive fieldwork. We have combined in-depth qualitative interviews, on-site non-participant observations and document analyses. The aim has been to generate thick descriptions of investment banking practices (Geertz, 1973). Over the course of five years, we have conducted more than 100 interviews with investment banking experts and managers, spent approximately 250 hours at four Swedish investment banks in Stockholm, and visited and conducted interviews at three foreign offices in Europe and the United States. The observations include reoccurring events such as morning meetings, corporate presentations on seminars and investor lunches, as well as evening events such as celebrations of the opening of new premises. The study also includes document analyses of annual reports, analysts' previews, cases and sector reports, IPO prospects, company presentations and regulatory texts. The investment banking experts under study are all working in firms with headquarters located in Stockholm, and with their main part of trading conducted on the Stockholm Stock Exchange. Both the firms and the experts under study are primarily active on the Scandinavian market, even though several of our respondents have worked in other financial centres at some point in their careers. More 'formal' interviews have been conducted with the following:

No. of interviews	Category of respondents
8	Traders
41	Brokers
25	Analysts
10	Corporate bankers
8	Risk & compliance officers
12	Managers investment banking
11	Managers client corporations

The case study presented in Chapter 7 is based on interviews, company internal documents, company presentations, reports, minutes of meetings and various external reports. Full access was given to the company internal archive of Dolly Ltd. In all, 48 semi-structured interviews were conducted with persons involved in the process, covering the two founding corporations, bankers and analysts at the two involved investment banks, as well as employees, managers and board members of Dolly Ltd.

Short note on interpretative methods

Based on this material, we have sought to construct faithful 'first-degree' accounts of investment banking practices (Schutz, 1962:58–60). These constructs are actor-oriented, in the sense that they are largely cast in terms of the language used by our informants (Geertz, 1973). As part of this work, we have been inspired by a narrative approach (Czarniawska, 1997, 1998) with respect to our interview data, attending to the respondents' accounts and explanations of their own work. The analyses of the actor-oriented first-degree accounts have been fuelled by our two main research questions (see Chapter 1), as well as by theory. Our major theoretical influence can be labelled micro-sociological organizational analysis (Alexander et al., 1987; Czarniawska, 2008), with an import from STS/actor-network theory (Law, 1986b; Star and Griesemer, 1989; Law, 1994; Callon, 1998b; Bowker and Star, 1999; Law and Hassard, 1999; Latour, 2005) and social studies of finance (Knorr Cetina and Preda, 2005b; Callon et al., 2007; MacKenzie et al., 2007).

We have used partly different interpretative strategies in different parts of our work. Major parts of the interview material with traders, brokers and analysts have been interpreted with a phenomenographic approach (Blomberg, 2004, 2006), while the study of bankers has followed an actor-network logic (Latour, 1996), with a distinct interpretative stance. Common to all our interpretative work has been the ambition to use our theoretical tools to create 'second-degree' constructs comprising both explanation and understanding (Schutz, 1962:59).

Notes

2 A Brief History of Investment Banking

1. 'Discretionary deposits' were used to circumvent the catholic probation on usury and rent. Investors could deposit money without having their names revealed, and received a gift (in the form of money) as remuneration for the use of their funds.
2. The large institutional investor became an integrated part of the Anglo-Saxon corporate governance model, characterized by a large number of shareholders at arm's length distance from corporate management, and an active control market (Koen, 2004). This 'outsider' model can be contrasted with the European 'insider' model of corporate control, characterized by relatively few large block-owners, owner spheres, or families with a major commercial bank at the centre and close relations to corporate management. Ownership control is executed via social interaction rather than through a control market. The merits of the two governance models have been debated. The 'outsider' model has been criticized for being short-sighted and too focused on shareholder value; the 'insider' model for being unjust, allowing block-owners to benefit from minority owners' relative lack of knowledge and influence over the investment object. Regardless of these debates, the outsider model has grown in importance since the late 1970s and is today viewed as part of the increasingly integrated global financial system (Bordo et al., 2003; Kay, 2004; Koen, 2004; Michie, 2006).
3. www.bis.org/bcbs/basel3.htm.
4. http://www.iosco.org/about/
5. According to the World Federation of Exchanges, the number of shares traded grew by 10.4 per cent/year on average from 1995 to 2007, from 7,260,569 million to 23,757,857 million (WFE, 2009a). The total value of shares traded grew by 18.5 per cent/year from 1990 to 2007, from $5,681,788 million to $101,189,135 million (WFE, 2009b).

3 Traders Activating the Stock Markets

1. In connection with the implementation of the European Markets in Financial Instruments Directive (MiFID) framework, the Swedish Financial Supervisory Authority has advocated a separation of customer and proprietary trading functions similar to that found in other countries, such as the United States.
2. Examples include the *Wall Street* movies directed by Oliver Stone and the novel *Liar's Poker* (1989) by Michael Lewis.
3. Nick Leeson gave his own version of this in his book *Rogue Trader* (1996), also filmed in 1999 by director James Dearden.
4. Partly on the basis of a statement given at Stockholm Tingsrätt, case no. B 2026–09.

4 Analysts Doing Stock Market Science – Sort of

1. We focus on fundamental analysis, that is we are concerned with analysts who seek to identify causes behind firm performance and relate this to the prices of shares. We do not cover analysts working with 'technical analysis', that is those who seek to detect patterns in market movements as shorthand indicators of future prices (Preda, 2007).
2. Although there were no corresponding cases in Scandinavia, the Swedish association of stockbrokers did introduce new stricter rules for analysts, requiring them to report their holdings, placing a two-day quarantine on trading in connection with publication of analyses, and prohibiting analysts from trading against their own recommendations.
3. The majority of the world's stock exchanges, professional investors, brokers, banks, ranking institutes and others use similar sector categories. The two major classification standards are the Industry Classification Benchmark (ICB), maintained by Dow Jones and FTSE Group, and the Global Industry Classification Standard (GICS), developed by Morgan Stanley and Standard & Poor's. The ICB use a system of 10 industries, partitioned into 20 supersectors, which are further divided into 41 sectors, which then contain 114 sub-sectors. The ten industries are Oil & Gas; Basic Materials; Industrials; Consumer Goods; Health Care; Consumer Services; Telecommunications; Utilities; Financials; Technology. The GICS consists of 10 sectors, 24 industry groups, 68 industries and 154 sub-industries, into which S&P has categorized all major public companies. The ten sectors are Energy; Materials; Industrials; Consumer Discretionary; Consumer Staples; Health Care; Financials; Information Technology; Telecommunication Services; Utilities.
4. This is an important observation since it questions the basic rationale of the principal–agent theory and how it is used in much of the debate on corporate governance and shareholder value (Koen, 2004).

6 Bankers – Matchmaking and Midwifery

1. There is also considerable variation in terms of the total values of IPOs, in the United States the dot-com boom of 1999–2000 meant a peak, which was followed by four years of steady decline (http://www.ipovitalsigns.com).
2. See, for example, http://www.careers-in-finance.com/ibsal.htm and http://www.payscale.com/ (accessed September 2010).
3. The situation that the bankers describe has much in common with Simmel's (1955) classic competitive situation with two parties striving for the exchange opportunities, love, or recognition of a third party. Whether the courted top managers really are to be regarded as *tertius gaudens*, however, is perhaps less obvious.

7 The Birth of a Share

1. Of course, several claimants at times engage in contests concerning specific ownership associations, thus making the forging of such associations less straightforward.

8 Behind the Scenes – Management, Risk and Compliance

1. For example, the Swedish business magazine 'Affärsvärlden'. Similar European rankings are published in magazines such as 'Euromoney' and 'Institutional Investor'.
2. See www.prospera.se. Prospera is also commissioned by the Swedish Central Bank to undertake quarterly and monthly surveys focusing among other things on the players in the money market.
3. See www.greenwich.com.
4. Within the sector, risk is commonly defined as the standard deviation of the return on total investment and the degree of uncertainty of return on an asset.
5. *Credit risk* concerns whether or not the issuer of a bond (the debtor or borrower) can pay back at the settled date of maturity. This probability affects the price of the bond. *Market risk* concerns the value of a specific security and how it is affected by changes in a number of risk factors, including stock prices, interest rates, foreign exchange rates and commodity prices. *Operational risk* relates to the conduct of business within an investment bank and includes legal risks (e.g. of fraud, lack of compliance with routines), the probability for human errors and IT system risks.
6. Some of the more important European directives concerning investment banking are the 'Markets in Financial Instruments Directive' (MiFID), the Third Money Laundering Directive (2005/60/EC), the Capital Requirements Directive (2006/48/EC), the Transparency Directive (2004/109/EC), the Market Abuse Directive (2004/72/EC) and the Consolidated Banking Directive (2000/12/EC).

9 Organizing Investment Banking

1. The share is not the only kind of security that investment banking experts work with, and thus not the only potential boundary object. But as argued in Chapter 1, the share is a fundamental financial instrument that is enacted by all expert groups within investment banking. Thus, we have simplified our empirical study and the analysis of investment banking by focusing on this one very important financial instrument.
2. This difference between our accounts might be due to differences in empirical focus. We seek to understand the organizing of investment banking, whether successful, stable or in the midst of a setback, while Engelen et al. (2010) seek to make sense of financial innovations and setbacks. As a result, our account has a more organizational and systemic character, while the account of Engelen et al. (2010) is more unstable and temporal.
3. The term 'heterarchy' was first used in organizational analysis by Sjöstrand (1985) as a contrast to hierarchy. Hedlund (1986) developed a conceptual view of a heterarchic multinational corporation characterized by flexibility and limited hierarchic control. Later, Hedlund applied the concept to knowledge management, highlighting lateral communication, temporal combinations of people and dynamic capabilities (Hedlund, 1995). Following Hedlund's conceptual development, Stark (1999) subsequently employed the term in his analysis of economic coordination and organizational innovation.

4. See Note 5 in Chapter 8 for a more detailed description of the different types of risks.
5. Star and Griesemer (1989:410) also make an analytical distinction between different types of boundary objects (carefully pointing out that the reality of boundary objects is that they are not easily defined and categorized). One of these types is the 'standardized form'. As we see it, there is considerable overlap between the notions of 'standardized forms' and 'standardized methods'. An important difference seems to be the materiality of the standardized form. Standardized forms are objects that can travel and hence work as boundary objects, e.g. a form to fill out. By being standardized, they approach what Latour has called 'immutable mobiles', objects that remain the same as they travel (Latour, 1987). Our analysis suggests that the risk models fail to work as boundary objects precisely on account of the standardization of methods implied in them, that is on how they seek to intervene in how the experts do things.

Bibliography

Abbott, A. (1991) 'The future of professions: Occupation and expertise in the age of organization', in P.S. Tolbert and S.R. Barley (eds) *Research in the Sociology of Organizations*, vol 8, pp. 17–42. Greenwich, CT: JAI Press.

Abolafia, M.Y. (1996) *Making Markets – Opportunism and Restraint on Wall Street*. Cambridge, MA: Harvard University Press.

Alderson, W. and Cox, R. (1948) 'Towards a theory of marketing', *Journal of Marketing* XIII(2): 137–152.

Alexander, J.C., Giesen, B., Münch, R. and Smelser, N.J. (eds) (1987) *The Micro-Macro Link*. Berkeley: University of California Press.

Appadurai, A. (ed.) (1986) *The Social Life of Things: Commodities in Cultural Perspective*. Cambridge: Cambridge University Press.

Araujo, L., Finch, J.H. and Kjellberg, H. (eds) (2010) *Reconnecting Marketing to Markets*. Oxford: Oxford University Press.

Araujo, L. and Kjellberg, H. (2009) 'Shaping exchanges, performing markets: The study of marketing practices', in P. Maclaran, M. Saren, B. Stern and M. Tadajewski (eds) *Handbook of Marketing Theory*, pp. 195–218. London: Sage Publications.

Ashmore, M. (2005) 'Review: The life inside/The left-hand side', *Social Studies of Science* 35(5): 827–830.

Azimont, F. and Araujo, L. (2007) 'Category reviews as market-shaping events', *Industrial Marketing Management* 36(7): 849–860.

Baker, W.E. (1984) 'The social structure of a national securities market', *American Journal of Sociology* 89(4): 775–811.

Barrey, S., Cochoy, F. and Dubuisson-Quellier, S. (2000) 'Designer, packager et merchandiser: Trois professionnels pour une même scéne marchande', *Sociologie du Travail* 42(3): 457–482.

Basking, J.B. and Miranti, P.J.J. (1997) *A History of Corporate Finance*. Cambridge: Cambridge University Press.

Bernanke, B. (1983) 'Nonmonetary effects of the financial crisis in the propagation of the Great Depression', *American Economic Review* 73: 257–276.

Bernanke, B. (2000) *Essays on the Great Depression*. Princeton, NJ: Princeton University Press.

Beunza, D. and Garud, R. (2007) 'Calculators, lemmings, or frame-makers? The intermediary role of securities analysts', in M. Callon, Y. Millo and F. Muniesa (eds) *Market Devices*, pp. 13–39. Oxford: Blackwell Publishers.

Beunza, D. and Stark, D. (2005) 'How to recognize opportunities: Heterarchical search in a trading room', in K. Knorr Cetina and A. Preda (eds) *The Sociology of Financial Markets*, pp. 84–101. Oxford: Oxford University Press.

Blomberg, J. (2004) 'Appreciating stockbroking: Constructing conceptions to make sense of performance', *Journal of Management Studies* 41(1): 155–180.

Blomberg, J. (2006) 'Making sense of stockbrokers' performance: Reflections about the phenomenographic approach', in J. Löwstedt and T. Stjernberg (eds)

Producing Management Knowledge – Research as Practice, pp. 53–71. Oxford: Routledge.

Blomberg, J., Kjellberg, H. and Winroth, K. (2011) 'Trading opportunities and risks: Conflicting methods of coordination in investment banks', in S. Long and B. Sievers (eds) *Towards a Socioanalysis of Money, Finance and Capitalism*, pp. 163–177. Oxford: Routledge.

Blum, J., Cameron, R. and Barnes, T.G. (1970) *The European World Since 1815: Triumph and Transition*, 2 edn. Boston, MA: Little, Brown and Company.

Bordo, M.D., Taylor, A.M. and Williamson, J.G. (eds) (2003) *Globalization in Historical Perspective (National Bureau of Economic Research Conference Report)*. Chicago, IL: The University of Chicago Press.

Boston Globe (16 September 2008) 'Stocks Plunge After Crisis in Investment Firms'.

Bowker, G.C. and Star, S.L. (1999) *Sorting Things Out: Classification and Its Consequences*. Cambridge, MA: MIT Press.

Brint, S. (1994) *In an Age of Experts – The Changing Role of Professionals in Politics and Public Life*. Princeton, NJ: Princeton University Press.

Brown, J.S. and Duguid, P. (2001) 'Knowledge and organization: A social-practice perspective', *Organization Science* 12(2): 198–213.

Bruegger, U. (1999) *Wie handeln Devisenhandler? Eine ethnmographische Studie uber Akteure in einem globalen Markt (How do Traders Trade? An ethnography of the Actors on a Global Market)*. Bamberg: Difo-Druck OHG.

Bruner, R.F. and Carr, S.D. (2007) *The Panic of 1907: Lessons Learned from the Market's Perfect Storm*. Hoboken, NJ: John Wiley & Sons.

Callon, M. (1986) 'Some elements of a sociology of translation: Domestication of the scallops and the fishermen of St-Brieuc Bay', in J. Law (ed.) *Power, Action and Belief: A New Sociology of Knowledge*, pp. 196–233. London: Routledge & Kegan Paul.

Callon, M. (1998a) 'Introduction: The embeddedness of economic markets in economics', in M. Callon (ed.) *The Laws of the Markets*, pp. 1–57. Oxford: Blackwell Publishers/The Sociological Review.

Callon, M. (ed.) (1998b) *The Laws of the Markets*. Oxford: Blackwell Publishers/The Sociological Review.

Callon, M. (2007) 'What does it mean to say that economics is performative?', in D. MacKenzie, F. Muniesa and L. Siu (eds) *Do Economists Make Markets? On the Performativity of Economics*, pp. 311–357. Princeton: Princeton University Press.

Callon, M., Méadel, C. and Rabeharisoa, V. (2002) 'The economy of qualities', *Economy and Society* 31(2): 194–217.

Callon, M., Millo, Y. and Muniesa, F. (eds) (2007) *Market Devices*. Oxford: Blackwell Publishing/The Sociological Review.

Calomiris, C.W. and Ramirez, C.D. (1996) 'The role of financial relationships in the history of American corporate finance', *Journal of Applied Corporate Finance* 9(2): 52–73.

Carosso, V.P. (1970) *Investment Banking in America: A History*. Cambridge, MA: Harvard University Press.

Carosso, V.P. (1987) *The Morgans: Private International Bankers, 1854–1913*. Cambridge, MA: Harvard University Press.

Carswell, J. (1960) *The South Sea Bubble*. Palo Alto, CA: Stanford University Press.

Clark, G.L. and Thrift, N. (2005) 'The return of bureaucracy: Managing dispersed knowledge in global finance', in K. Knorr Cetina and A. Preda (eds) *The Sociology of Financial Markets*, pp. 229–249. Oxford: Oxford University Press.

Czarniawska, B. (1997) *Narrating the Organization: Dramas of Institutional Identity.* Chicago: The University of Chicago Press.

Czarniawska, B. (1998) *A Narrative Approach to Organization Studies.* Thousand Oaks, CA: Sage Publications.

Czarniawska, B. (2004) 'On time, space and action nets', *Organization* 11(6): 773–791.

Czarniawska, B. (2008) *A Theory of Organizing.* Cheltenham: Edward Elgar.

Czarniawska, B. and Hernes, T. (eds) (2005) *Actor Network Theory and Organizing.* Malmö: Liber & Copenhagen Business School press.

D'Agostino, R., Hellgren, P. and Fröderberg, V. (2007) Processen vid nyintroduktioner och emissioner. *Finansinspektionens rapporter.* Stockholm: The Swedish Financial Supervisory Authority.

de Certeau, M. (1984) *The Practice of Everyday Life.* Berkeley: University of California Press.

Dubuisson-Quellier, S. (2010) 'Product tastes, consumer tastes: The plurality of qualifications in product development and marketing activities', in L. Araujo, J.H. Finch and H. Kjellberg (eds) *Reconnecting Marketing to Markets*, pp. 74–93. Oxford: Oxford University Press.

Eccles, R. and Crane, A. (1988) *Doing Deals: Investment Banks at Work.* Boston, MA: Harvard Business School Press.

Engelen, E., Erturk, I., Froud, J., Leaver, A. and Williams, K. (2010) 'Reconceptualizing financial innovation: Frame, conjuncture and bricolage', *Economy and Society* 39(1): 33–63.

European, U. (2004) Markets in financial instruments directive (MiFID). IN T.E.P.A. Council (ed.) *39/EC.* Official Journal of the European Union.

Fenton-O'Creevy, M., Nicholson, N., Soane, E. and Willman, P. (2004) *Traders: Risks, Decisions, and Management in Financial Markets.* Oxford: Oxford University Press.

Financial Times (09 December 2010) Chinese IPO success comes with a warning.

Finansinspektionen (2004) Finansinspektionen's (the Swedish Financial Supervisory Authority) regulations and general guidelines regarding financial advice to consumers. *FFFS 2004:04.* Stockholm: Finansinspektionen.

Finch, J.H. and Acha, V.L. (2008) 'Making and exchanging a second-hand oil field, considered in an industrial marketing setting', *Marketing Theory* 8(1): 45–66.

Fleuriet, M. (2008) *Investment Banking Explained: An Insiders's Guide to the Industry.* New York: McGraw-Hill.

Fogarty, T.J. and Rogers, R.K. (2005) 'Financial analysts' reports: An extended institutional theory evaluation', *Accounting, Organizations and Society* 30(4): 331–356.

Folkman, P., Froud, J., Johal, S. and Williams, K. (2007) 'Working for themselves? Capital market intermediaries and present day capitalism', *Business History* 49(4): 552–572.

Foucault, M. (1991) *Discipline and Punish: The Birth of the Prison.* London: Penguin books.

Fratianni, M. and Spinelli, F. (2006) 'Italian city-states and financial evolution', *European Review of Economic History* 10(3): 257–278.

Freeman & Co (1 October 2002) Investment Banking – 2002 and beyond. *White Paper.* New York: Freeman & Co.

Freixas, X. and Rochet, J.-C. (2008) *Microeconomics of Banking,* 2 edn. Cambridge, MA: MIT Press.

Friedson, E. (1973) 'Professions and the occupational principle', in E. Freidson (ed.) *The Professions and Their Prospects,* pp. 19–38. Beverly Hills, CA: Sage Publications.

Fujimura, J.H. (1992) 'Crafting science: Standardized packages, boundary objects, and "Translation" ', in A. Pickering (ed.) *Science as Practice and Culture,* pp. 168–211. Chicago, IL: The University of Chicago Press.

Gandel, S. (5 February 2010) 'Is Proprietary Trading Too Wild for Wall Street?' *Time.*

Gärtner, D.L. and Halbheer, D. (2009) 'Are there waves in merger activity after all?', *International Journal of Industrial Organization* 27(6): 708–718.

Gasparino, C. (2005) *Blood on the Street: The Sensational Inside Story of How Wall Street Analysts Duped a Generation of Investors.* New York: Free Press.

Geertz, C. (1973) *The Interpretation of Cultures.* New York, NY: Basic Books.

Geiger, S. and Finch, J.H. (2009) 'Industrial sales people as market actors', *Industrial Marketing Management* 38(6): 608–617.

Granovetter, M. (1985) 'Economic action and social structure: The problem of embeddedness', *American Journal of Sociology* 91(3): 481–510.

Grant, J. (30 November 2010) 'Super-fast traders pose risk to clearers', *The Financial Times.*

Green, S. (1996) *Serving God? Serving Mammon?* London: Marshall Pickering.

Grünberg, J. (2007) 'Subcontractors, lone rangers, and agents for hire: Empirical examples of intermediaries in the corporate governance process', unpublished manuscript, Uppsala: Uppsala University, Department of business studies.

Hägglund, P. (2000) 'The value of facts: How analysts' recommendations focus on facts instead of value', in H. Kalthoff, R. Rottenburg and H.-J. Wagener (eds) *Facts and Figures: Economic Representations and Practices.* Marburg: Metropolis.

Hägglund, P. (2001) Företaget som investeringsobjekt: hur placerare och analytiker arbetar med att ta fram ett investeringsobjekt. Stockholm: Stockholm School of Economics/The Economic Research Institute.

Håkansson, H. (ed.) (1982) *International Marketing and Purchasing of Industrial Goods: An Interaction Approach.* Chichester: Wiley.

Haldane, A., Brennan, S. and Madouros, V. (2010) 'What is the contribution of the financial sector: Miracle or mirage?', *The Future of Finance: The LSE Report,* pp. 87–120.

Hancock, R.J. (1995) *Citizens of the World: London Merchants and the Integration of the British Atlantic Community, 1735–1785.* Cambridge: Cambridge University Press.

Hasselström, A. (2003) 'On and off the trading floor: An inquiry into the everyday fashioning of financial market knowledge'. Department of Social Anthropology, Stockholm: Stockholm University.

Hasselström, A. (2004) 'Modes of knowing: The fashioning of financial market knowledge', in C. Garsten and M. Lindh de Montoya (eds) *Market Matters: Exploring Cultural Processes in the Global Marketplace,* pp. 137–157. Basingstoke: Palgrave Macmillan.

Hayward, M.L.A. and Boeker, W. (1998) 'Power and conflicts of interest in professional firms: Evidence from investment banking', *Administrative Science Quarterly* 43(1): 1–22.

Hedlund, G. (1986) 'The hypermodern MNC – A heterarchy?', *Human Resource Management* 25(1): 9–35.

Hedlund, G. (1995) 'A model of knowledge management and the N-form corporation', *Strategic Management Journal* 15(Special Issue: Strategy: Search for New Paradigms): 73–90.

Helgesson, C.-F. and Kjellberg, H. (2009) 'What care do healthcare markets need?', in H. Winberg, J. Rognes and C.-F. Helgesson (eds) *Leading Health Care – Organizing Healthcare for Greater Value*, pp. 135–148. Stockholm: EFI.

Helgesson, C.-F., Kjellberg, H. and Liljenberg, A. (eds) (2004) *Den där marknaden*. Lund: Studentlitteratur.

Hirst, P. and Thompson, G. (1999) *Globalization in Question*. Cambridge: Polity Press.

Ho, K. (2009) *Liquidated: An Ethnography of Wall Street*. Durham: Duke University Press.

Jalas, M. (2009) 'Making time: Reciprocal object relations and the self-legitimizing time of wooden-boating', in E. Shove, F. Trentmann and R. Wilk (eds) *Time, Consumption and Everyday life: Practice, Materiality and Culture*, pp. 203–216. Oxford: Berg.

Jaworski, B., Kohli, A.K. and Sahay, A. (2000) 'Market-driven versus driving markets', *Journal of the Academy of Marketing Science* 28(1): 45–54.

Jonathan, I. (2003) *The Anglo-Dutch Moment: Essays on the Glorious Revolution and Its World Impact*. Cambridge: Cambridge University Press.

Karpik, L. (2010) *Valuing the Unique: The Economics of Singularities*. Princeton: Princeton University Press.

Kay, J. (2004) *The Truth about Markets: Why Some Nations Are Rich but Most Remain Poor*. London: Penguin.

Kjellberg, H. and Helgesson, C.-F. (2006) 'Multiple versions of markets: Multiplicity and performativity in market practice', *Industrial Marketing Management* 35(7): 839–855.

Kjellberg, H. and Helgesson, C.-F. (2007) 'On the nature of markets and their practices', *Marketing Theory* 7(2): 137–162.

Knorr Cetina, K. (2005) 'How are global markets global?', in K. Knorr Cetina and A. Preda (eds) *The Sociology of Financial Markets*, pp. 38–61. Oxford: Oxford University Press.

Knorr Cetina, K. (2006) 'The Market', *Theory, Culture and Society* 23(2–3): 551–556.

Knorr Cetina, K. and Bruegger, U. (2000) 'The market as an object of attachment: Exploring postsocial relations in financial markets', *Canadian Journal of Sociology* 25(2): 141–168.

Knorr Cetina, K. and Bruegger, U. (2002a) 'Global microstructures: The virtual societies of financial markets', *The American Journal of Sociology* 107(4): 905–950.

Knorr Cetina, K. and Bruegger, U. (2002b) 'Traders' engagement with markets: A postsocial relationship', *Theory, Culture and Society* 19(5–6): 161–185.

Knorr Cetina, K. and Preda, A. (2005a) 'Introduction', in K. Knorr Cetina and A. Preda (eds) *The Sociology of Financial Markets*, pp. 1–14. Oxford: Oxford University Press.

Knorr Cetina, K. and Preda, A. (eds) (2005b) *The Sociology of the Financial Markets*. Oxford: Oxford University Press.

Koen, C.I. (2004) 'The dialectics of globalization: What are the effects for management and organization in Germany and Japan', *Research in International Business and Finance* 18(2): 173–197.

Kopytoff, I. (1986) 'The cultural biography of things: Commoditization as process', in A. Appadurai (ed.) *The Social Life of Things: Commodities in Cultural Perspective*, pp. 64–91. Cambridge: Cambridge University Press.

Kotter J.P. (1996) *Leading Change*. Boston: Harvard Business School Press.

Latour, B. (1987) *Science in Action: How to Follow Scientists and Engineers Through Society*. Cambridge, MA: Harvard University Press.

Latour, B. (1992) 'Where are the missing masses? The sociology of a few mundane artefacts', in W.E. Bijker and J. Law (eds) *Shaping Technology/Building Society: Studies in Sociotechnical Change*, pp. 225–258. Cambridge, MA: MIT Press.

Latour, B. (1994) 'On technical mediation – Philosophy, sociology, genealogy', *Common Knowledge* 3(2): 29–64.

Latour, B. (1996) *Aramis, or the Love of Technology*. Cambridge, MA: Harvard University Press.

Latour, B. (2005) *Reassembling the Social: An Introduction to Actor-Network-Theory*. Oxford: Oxford University Press.

Law, J. (1986a) 'On the methods of long-distance control: Vessels, navigation and the Portugese route to India', in J. Law (ed.) *Power, Action and Belief: A New Sociology of Knowledge*, pp. 234–263. London: Routledge & Kegan Paul.

Law, J. (ed.) (1986b) *Power, Action and Belief: A New Sociology of Knowledge*. London: Routledge & Kegan Paul.

Law, J. (1994) *Organizing Modernity*. Oxford: Blackwell Publishers.

Law, J. (2004) *After Method, Mess in Social Science Research*. Oxon: Routledge.

Law, J. and Hassard, J. (eds) (1999) *Actor Network Theory and after*. Oxford: Blackwell Publishers.

Law, J. and Urry, J. (2004) 'Enacting the social', *Economy and Society* 33(3): 39[illegible]–410.

Lawrence, P. and Lorsch, J. (1967) *Organization and Environment*. Boston: Harvard University Press.

Lopez, R.S. (1964) 'Market expansion: The case of Genoa', *The Journal of Economic History* 24(4): 445–464.

Lukes, S. (2005 [1974]) *Power: A radical view*, 2 edn. Basingstoke: Palgrave Macmillan.

MacKenzie, D. (2006) *An Engine, Not a Camera: How Financial Models Shape Markets*. Cambridge: MIT Press.

MacKenzie, D. and Millo, Y. (2003) 'Constructing a market, performing theory: The historical sociology of a financial derivatives exchange', *American Journal of Sociology* 109(1): 107–145.

MacKenzie, D., Muniesa, F. and Siu, L. (eds) (2007) *Do Economists Make Markets? On the Performativity of Economics*. Princeton, NJ: Princeton University Press.

Markowitz, H.M. (1952) 'Portfolio selection', *The Journal of Finance* 7(1): 77–91.

Maturana, H.R. and Varela, F.J. (1980) *Autopoiesis and Cognition: The Realization of the Living*. Dordrecht: D. Reidel Publishing Company.

Meyer, J. and Rowan, B. (1977) 'Institutionalized organizations: Formal structure as myth and ceremony', *American Journal of Sociology* 83(2): 340–363.

Michie, R.C. (2006) *The Global Securities Market – A History.* Oxford: Oxford University Press.

Miller, P. (2001) 'Governing by numbers: Why calculative practices matter', *Social Research* 68(2): 379–396.

Miller, D. (2010) *Stuff*. Cambridge: Polity press.

Millo, Y. and MacKenzie, D. (2007) Building a boundary object: The evolution of financial risk management, *Discussion paper.* London: Centre for analysis of risk and regulation, London School of Economics and Political Science.

Millo, Y. and MacKenzie, D. (2009) 'The usefulness of inaccurate models: Towards an understanding of the emergence of financial risk management', *Accounting, Organizations and Society* 34(5): 638–653.

Mintzberg, H. (1973) *The Nature of Managerial Work*. New York: Harper & Row.

Mol, A. (2002) *The Body Multiple: Ontology in Medical Practice*. Durham: Duke University Press.

Morrison, A.D. and Wilhelm, W.J. (2007a) *Investment Banking: Institutions, Politics, and Law*. Oxford: Oxford University Press.

Morrison, A.D. and Wilhelm, W.J. (2007b) 'Investment banking: Past, present, and future', *Journal of Applied Corporate Finance* 19(1): 42–54.

Mörth, U. (ed.) (2004) *Soft Law in Governance and Regulation*. Cheltenham: Edward Elgar.

Mouritsen, J. (2003) 'Intellectual capital and the capital market: The circulability of intellectual capital', *Accounting, Auditing & Accountability Journal* 16(1): 18–30.

Muniesa, F. (2004) 'Assemblage of a market mechanism', *Journal of The Center for Information Studies* 5(3): 11–19.

Muniesa, F. (2008) 'Trading-Room telephones and the identification of counterparts', in T.J. Pinch and R. Swedberg (eds) *Living in a Material World*, pp. 291–316. Cambridge, MA: MIT Press.

Noord, P.v.d. (2009) Economic crisis in Europe: Causes, consequences and responses. *The European Economy.* Luxembourg: European Commission, Directorate-General for Economic and Financial Affairs.

Oudshoorn, N. and Pinch, T. (eds) (2003) *How Users Matter: The Co-construction of Users and Technology.* Cambridge, MA: MIT Press.

Panic, M. (1995) 'The Bretton Woods system: Concept and practice', in J. Michie and J. Grieve Smith (eds) *Managing the Global Economy*, pp. 37–54. Oxford: Oxford University Press.

Patnaik, P. (1999) 'The real face of financial liberalisation', *Frontline: India's National Magazine* 16(4): 13–26.

Pickering, A. (1993) 'The mangle of practice: Agency and emergence in the sociology of science', *The American Journal of Sociology* 99(3): 559–589.

Pinch, T.J. and Clark, C. (1995) *The Hard Sell: The Language and Lessons of Street-Wise Marketing*. London: HarperCollins.

Pinch, T.J. and Swedberg, R. (eds) (2008) *Living in a Material World.* Cambridge, MA: MIT Press.

Pincus, S. (2009) *1688: The First Modern Revolution.* New Haven: Yale University Press.

Podolny, J.M. (1993) 'A status-based model of market competition', *The American Journal of Sociology* 98(4): 829–872.

Podolny, J.M. (1994) 'Market uncertainty and the social character of economic exchange', *Administrative Science Quarterly* 39(3): 458–483.

Power, M. (1997) *The Audit Society: Rituals of Verification.* Oxford: Oxford University Press.

Power, M. (2004) 'The risk management of everything', *The Journal of Risk Finance* 5(3): 58–65.

Power, M. (2005) 'Enterprise risk management and the organization of uncertainty in financial institutions', in K. Knorr Cetina and A. Preda (eds) *The Sociology of Financial Markets*, pp. 250–268. Oxford: Oxford University Press.

Power, M. (2007) *Organized Uncertainty: Designing a World of Risk Management.* Oxford: Oxford University Press.

Preda, A. (2006) 'Socio-technical agency in financial markets: The case of the stock ticker', *Social Studies of Science* 36(5): 753–782.

Preda, A. (2007) 'Where do analysts come from? The case of financial chartism', in M. Callon, Y. Millo and F. Muniesa (eds) *Market Devices*, pp. 40–64. Oxford: Blackwell Publishing/The Sociological Review.

Preda, A. (2008) 'Technology, agency, and financial price data', in T.J. Pinch and R. Swedberg (eds) *Living in a Material World*, pp. 217–232. Cambridge, MA: MIT Press.

Prus, R.C. (1989) *Making Sales: Influence as Interpersonal Accomplishment.* Newbury Park: Sage Publications.

Pryke, M. (2008) 'Making finance, making worlds', in N. Clark, D. Massey and P. Sarre (eds) *Material Geographies – A World in the Making*, pp. 58–103. London: Sage Publications.

Pryke, M. and Allen, J. (2000) 'Monetized time-space: Derivatives – money's "new imaginary"?', *Economy and Society* 29(2): 264–284.

Rao, H., Greve, H.R. and Davis, G.F. (2001) 'Fool's gold: Social proof in the initiation and abandonment of coverage by wall street analysts', *Administrative Science Quarterly* 46(3): 502–526.

Reed, M.I. (1996) 'Expert power and control in late modernity: An empirical review and theoretical synthesis', *Organization Studies* 17(4): 573–597.

Sassen, S. (2005) 'The embeddedness of electronic markets: The case of global capital markets', in K. Knorr Cetina and A. Preda (eds) *The Sociology of Financial Markets*, pp. 17–37. Oxford: Oxford University Press.

Schutz, A. (1962) *Collected Papers I: The Problem of Social Reality.* The Hague: Martinus Nijhoff.

Schutz, A. (1964) *Collected Papers II – Studies in Social Theory.* The Hague: Martinus Nijhoff.

Schutz, A. (1967) *The Phenomenology of the Social World (Der sinnhafte Aufbau der sozialen Welt: Eine Einleitung in die verstehende Soziologie).* Evanston, IL: North Western University Press.

Sevenius, R. (2007) *Bolagsstyrning.* Lund: Studentlitteratur.

Shankar, A., Whittaker, J. and Fitchett, J. (2006) 'Heaven knows I'm miserable now', *Marketing Theory* 6(4): 485–505.

Shove, E. and Araujo, L. (2010) 'Practices, products and trajectories of co-evolution', in L. Araujo, J.H. Finch and H. Kjellberg (eds) *Reconnecting Marketing to Markets*, pp. 13–28. Oxford: Oxford University Press.

Shove, E. and Pantzar, M. (2005) 'Consumers, producers and practices: Understanding the invention and reinvention of Nordic walking', *Journal of Consumer Culture* 5(1): 43–64.

Simmel, G. (1955 [1908]) *Conflict & The Web of Group Affiliations*. Translated by K. H. Wolff and R. Bendix. New York: The Free Press.

Sjöstrand, S.-E. (1985) *Samhällsorgansation*. Stockholm: Doxa.

Smith, C.W. (1981) *The Mind of the Market – A Study of Stock Market Philosophies, Their Uses, and Their Implications*. Totowa, NJ: Rowman and Littlefield.

Star, S.L. (2007) 'The history and boundaries of boundary objects'. Paper presented at the workshop *Boundary Object, Boundary work*, Grenoble University, 13 September 2007.

Star, S.L. and Griesemer, J.R. (1989) 'Institutional ecology, "Translations" and boundary objects: Amateurs and professionals in Berkeley's museum of vertebrate zoology, 1907–1939', *Social Studies of Science* 19(3): 387–420.

Stark, D. (1999) 'From bureaucracy and mass communication to heterarchy and interactive media: Organizational innovation in Silicon Alley', *Annual Meetings of the American Sociological Association*. Chicago.

Stark, D. (2001) 'Ambiguous assets for uncertain environments: Heterarchy in postsocialist firms', in P. DiMaggio (ed.) *The Twenty-First-Century Firm: Changing Economic Organization in International Perspective*, pp. 69–104. Princeton: Princeton University Press.

Stark, D. (2009) *The Sense of Dissonance. Accounts of Worth in Economic Life*. Princeton: Princeton University Press.

Stichele, M.v.d. (2008) 'Financial regulation in the European Union. Mapping EU decision making structures on financial regulation and supervision'. Eurodad.

Strange, S. (1994) 'From Bretton Woods to the casino economy', in S. Corbridge, N. Thrift and R. Martin (eds) *Money, Power and Space*. Oxford: Blackwell Publishers.

Svedberg Helgesson, K. (2011) Governance, surveillance and the limits of corporate accountability', *Surveillance and Society* 8(4): 471–484.

Svedberg Nilsson, K. and Winroth, K. (2005) 'Properties of expertise', in S. Furusten and A. Werr (eds) *Dealing with Confidence: The Construction of Need and Trust in Management Advisory Services*, pp. 75–91. Copenhagen: CBS Press.

Swedberg, R. (2005) 'Conflicts of interest in the US brokerage industry', in K. Knorr Cetina and A. Preda (eds) *The Sociology of Financial Markets*, pp. 187–203. Oxford: Oxford University Press.

Tallman, E.W. and Moen, J. (1990) 'Lessons from the Panic 1907', *Federal Reserve Bank of Atlanta Economic Review* 75: 2–13.

Temin, P. (1990) *Lessons from the Great Depression*. Cambridge, MA: MIT Press.

Trompette, P. and Vinck, D. (2009) 'Revisiting the notion of boundary object', *Revue d'anthroplogie des connaissances* 3(1): 3–25.

TT Nyhetsbanken (20 September 2008) 'Börsras gör dålig PPM-affär sämre'.

Turner, A., Haldane, A., Woolley, P., Wadhwani, S., Goodhart, C., Smithers, A., Large, A., Kay, J., Wolf, M., Boone, P. and Johnson, S. (2010) *The Future of Finance: The LSE Report*. London: London School of Economics and Political Science.

Uzzi, B. (1997) 'Social structure and competition in interfirm networks: The paradox of embeddedness', *Administrative Science Quarterly* 42(1 (March)): 35–67.

Weber, M. (1947 [1922]) *The Theory of Social and Economic Organization*. New York: The Free Press.

Weick, K.E. (1979) *The Social Psychology of Organizing*, 2 edn. New York: Random House.

Wenger, E. (1998) *Communities of Practice: Learning, Meaning and Identity.* Cambridge: Cambridge University Press.

Wenger, E. (2000) 'Communities of practice and social learning systems', *Organization* 7(2): 225–246.

WFE (2009a) Annual statistics: Total number of trades and shares traded. World Federation of Exchanges.

WFE (2009b) Value of share trading. World Federation of Exchanges.

Wilhelm, W.J. (1999) 'Internet investment banking: The impact of information technology on relationship banking', *Journal of Applied Corporate Finance* 12(1): 21–27.

Willman, P., Fenton-O'Creevy, M., Nicholson, N. and Soane, E. (2001) 'Knowing the risks: Theory and practice in financial market trading', *Human Relations* 54(7): 887–910.

Winroth, K. (2004) 'Från antikropp till aktie. Hur en produkt konstrueras genom text och grafer', in C.-F. Helgesson, H. Kjellberg and A. Liljenberg (eds) *Den där marknaden*, pp. 149–175. Lund: Studentlitteratur.

Winroth, K., Blomberg, J. and Kjellberg, H. (2010) 'Enacting overlapping markets', *Journal of Cultural Economy* 3(1): 3–18.

Woolgar, S. (1991) 'Configuring the user: The case of usability trials', in J. Law (ed.) *A Sociology of Monsters: Essays on Power, Technology and Domination*, pp. 58–99. London: Routledge.

Zaloom, C. (2006) *Out of the Pits – Traders and Technology from Chicago to London.* Chicago: University of Chicago Press.

Zeiss, R. and Groenewegen, P. (2009) 'Engaging boundary objects in OMS and STS? Exploring the subtleties of layered engagement', *Organization* 16(1): 81–100.

Zuckerman, E.W. (1999) 'The categorical imperative: Securities analysts and the illegitimacy discount', *The American Journal of Sociology* 104(5): 1398–1438.

Zuckerman, E.W. (2000) 'Focusing the corporate product: Securities analysts and de-Diversification', *Administrative Science Quarterly* 45(3): 591–619.

Index